BD444 .W97

Wyschogrod

Spirit in

SPIRIT IN ASHES

Spirit in Ashes: Hegel, Heidegger, and Man-Made Mass Death

EDITH WYSCHOGROD

YALE UNIVERSITY PRESS
NEW HAVEN AND LONDON

Designed by Sally Harris
and set in Galliard type by Graphic Composi-
tion, Inc.
Printed in the United States of America by
BookCrafters, Chelsea, Michigan.

The epigraph on p. 106 is from "Burnt Norton"
in *Four Quartets* by T.S. Eliot, copyright 1943 by
T.S. Eliot; renewed 1971 by Esme Valerie Eliot.
Reprinted by permission of Harcourt Brace Jovanovich, Inc.

Library of Congress Cataloging in Publication
Data

Wyschogrod, Edith.
  Spirit in ashes.

  Includes index.
  1. Death. 2. Hegel, Georg Wilhelm Friedrich,
1770–1831. 3. Heidegger, Martin, 1889–1976.
I. Title.
BD444.W974 1985   128'.5   84–26932
ISBN 0–300–03322–2 (alk. paper)

The paper in this book meets the guidelines for
permanence and durability of the Committee on
Production Guidelines for Book Longevity
of the Council on Library Resources.

10 9 8 7 6 5 4 3 2 1

I once said, perhaps rightly: The earlier culture will become a heap of rubble and finally a heap of ashes, but spirits will hover over the ashes.

Ludwig Wittgenstein

Contents

Preface

*A*MONG THE ACCUMULATED HOR-
rors of the twentieth century none
has left so deep a wound as nuclear annihilation and the creation of
the concentration camp as an institutional form. These phenomena
are epitomized in the names "Hiroshima" and "Auschwitz." They
have received wide public attention, as well as specialized analysis.
But, in the course of time, this scrutiny has domesticated what was
at first freshly encountered and has blunted their radically new, radically apocalyptic character. Yet whether cordoned off, ignored, or
turned into private obsession they cannot be avoided: present-day
life is related to them as figure to ground.

Though these events permeate personal and social experience, philosophers have been strangely silent in regard to their meaning. This
is not to say that philosophers have remained aloof from public de-
bate over such specific issues as disarmament, biological and chemical weapons, torture, and the like. To the contrary, they have joined
the fray by sorting out relevant considerations and refining arguments in regard to specific questions. Yet they have abandoned, to
historians on the one hand and to painters, poets, and filmmakers on
the other, questions about the meaning of these phenomena. Despite
philosophers' sensitivity to specific ethical issues, the impact of man-
made mass death upon larger themes of philosophical concern has
gone largely unnoticed. I hope to show, however, that the meaning
of self, time, and language are all affected by mass death: from now
on the development of these themes and the meaning of man-made
mass death wax and wane together. We are in the grip of immense
experiential changes which both create and reflect new philosophical
perspectives. These must be brought into the open if we are not to
drift, metaphysically blind, from one concrete issue to another. Yet
the map we still carry shows the world as flat even if we know otherwise.

No doubt, it could be argued, mass death has occurred in the past.
Has humankind not always been the victim of earthquakes, volcanic
eruptions, and epidemic disease? How is our experience substantially

different from that of plague victims in the fourteenth century? Is our world unique if a survivor of the Black Death can write:

> And in many places . . . great pits were dug and piled deep with the multitude of dead. And they died by hundreds, both day and night, and all were thrown in these ditches and covered with earth. And as soon as these ditches were filled, more were dug. And I . . . buried my five children with my own hands. . . . And so many died that all believed it was the end of the world.[1]

Could not these words, deprived of ascription, easily be mistaken for the memoir of a witness of the Nazi massacres at Babi Yar? Did not the Black Death eventually destroy more people than the number of combatants killed in World War II?[2]

Even though this is true, scale is not measured by head count alone. What is unprecedented in the new phenomenon is that the *means* of annihilation are the result of systematic rational calculation, and scale is reckoned in terms of the compression of time in which destruction is delivered (for example, an anticipated one hundred million dead in the United States alone in the first half hour of a nuclear attack). Short of nuclear war, other new and efficient strategies for bringing death to vast numbers of people have appeared: mass deportation, planned starvation, biological and chemical weapons, and gas chambers in death and concentration camps. What is more commonplace by now than photographic records of the implementation of these strategies? Yet the "true" scale is vaster still: the ever-present danger of the irreversible null point, the destruction of all human life probably emptying the immense cosmic spaces forever of that "thinking reed" who alone, Pascal claimed, apprehends them.

Even if we concede the novelty of man-made mass death, philosophical interest in death is hardly new. Classical philosophers declared death their muse and shaped their systems in accordance with these conceptions. Why not simply tinker with the tradition, bring it up to date? For how can a factor like scale alter the hard fact that each and every one of us must face death individually? How can we hope to outstrip classical philosophy in its grasp of our mortality?

But it is just this understanding of our finitude which is at issue: death in Western thought, despite varied articulations, has been dominated by a single pattern which depends upon interpreting the self as a cognition monad and the process of dying as requiring behavior appropriate to a rational subject. To be sure, this perspective has fallen into disrepute in both Continental and recent Anglo-American analytic philosophy. But only now, in the light of multiple forms of mass death, do the limitations of the model make themselves existentially felt. For when we hold the classical paradigm of both the self and the demeanor appropriate to its dying before the light of atomic conflagration and death camps the paradigm can only appear as a tour de force.

Must it then be concluded that we lack useful philosophical precedents? In fact, we have not been left altogether without sketches of the new terrain. In the present context Hegel's reflections on death in the nineteenth century and Heidegger's in the twentieth are indispensable if we are to make some headway in understanding the present sea change. Not only have these thinkers shown the importance of death for the emergence of meaning, but each—albeit in different, indeed opposed, fashion—has shaken off the allergy to concrete history which has plagued modern philosophy since Descartes. Thus each has legitimized a back-and-forth movement from specific historical matters to speculative concerns, Hegel by showing what is rational in concrete history and thus in the end sublating history; Heidegger by showing that the root of history lies in the historicity of human being, which he uncovers by turning to quotidian experience for clues leading to a deeper understanding of the meaning of existence. Rather than building a *cordon sanitaire* around "situation," around our particular historical circumstances, we are free to use concrete data as access routes to a transcendental framework. Although I do not hope to find such a framework if we mean by it something eternal and immutable, I hope to locate a new historically conditioned a priori by considering the logical and ontological structures exhibited by man-made mass death in our century. Hegel and Heidegger dip into concrete experiential and historical matters in quest of philosophical clues because they see such matters as intrinsic to philosophical speculation. I shall do the same. I do not use this strategy to justify my claims empirically but rather to bring into view a form of life, a region of being, whose manner of being is to exist as the obliteration of cultures and as the possible extinction of human life.

The reader will soon discover the radical character of my claims, but it may nevertheless be useful to state these at the outset so that he or she can see my presuppositions and where the argument is headed.

1. I maintain that despite its rich diversity the Western philosophical tradition is fairly well agreed upon its view of death and the meaning of self which determines and is determined by this understanding of mortality. Death is the coming to an end of a self conceived as a cognition monad. The virtues appropriate to dying are arranged in conformity with this view, which holds irrespective of whether a portion of the self is believed to live on or come to an end *tout court*. I call this view the *authenticity paradigm* and argue that it persists in the way death is grasped even now. But, by turning to the work of the poet Rilke, I show that, beginning with the events of World War I, there is a strong tendency toward recognizing the impact of man-made mass death.

2. During World War I a new process burst upon the historical horizon, a multifaceted state of affairs which later included such features as nuclear, biological, and chemical warfare and death camps. I call this social, political, and cultural complex the *death event*. Its logic is based on an implementation in society and history of a purely formal structure that has dominated Western mathematical imagination: Zeno's paradoxes. Zeno contends that these paradoxes arise when we deny the unity of being. I show that both the specific content of the paradoxes themselves and the ontological claim they support are relevant to grasping the meaning of the death event. Zeno argues for the infinite divisibility of finite quantities. I believe this claim is mirrored in the logic of the death event—when those exercising power interpret the finite number of persons they plan to destroy as if this finite number constituted an infinite reserve.

3. Hegel and Heidegger have also given us useful sketches for grasping the death event. Although these are different from my own mapping they must be included in any philosophical account of this event. By attending to Hegel's generally neglected philosophy of nature I hope to show how the forces of negation lead to implementation of the death event in time and history. In the *Phenomenology* and the *Philosophy of Mind* Hegel opens up for us a model of a transactional self of great use in the context of man-made mass death. He

gives us a brilliant, disturbing, and remarkably prescient critique of the "philosophy of reflection," a manner of understanding the meaning of reason opened up by Kant that dominates philosophical thinking in the present age. Without a grasp of this turn philosophy has taken, we can only flounder helplessly within the ambit of the philosophy of reflection as Hegel, I believe, persuasively shows.

4. Heidegger has, on the face of it, remained well within the domain of the traditional view of death based on the authenticity paradigm. But in his later work he opens up the meaning of the being of technology; without this understanding, the present state of affairs is incomprehensible. I argue that, in spite of these amazing insights, his account falls short because he has not grasped the root of human social relationships. Because of the primacy he gives in the history of thought to *things* over *persons* he falls victim to the tradition he criticizes. In this context I return to my earlier themes and bring him into conversation with Rilke, a poet very important to Heidegger's work.

5. I conclude by offering my own account of the self in this new age of devastation, a self which rests on the primacy of the interpersonal sphere. I show the view of language, thinking, self, and society which follows from these arguments, one which the reader may find pessimistic but not entirely without hope.

This study is not an effort to think through the meaning of death in the work of two seminal thinkers in systematic fashion from a historically oriented comparative point of view. Scholarly studies of the meaning of death in Hegel and Heidegger abound. Instead, I shall try to interrogate their work freshly and without inhibition from the perspective of the theme of man-made mass death in the present age. Thus I must pass over in silence issues relevant to the understanding of each thinker's work as a whole. For example, the meaning of Hegel's doctrines of Being and Essence from the standpoint of his logic, or Heidegger's ontological/hermeneutical approach to the meanings concealed in the transmitted texts of the philosophical tradition, must be shunted aside. To be sure, one breaks interpretive pathways whether one will or no. But to expose the grounds for my interpretive choices would take me too far afield if I am to make any inroads into the problem at hand. Thus I shall eschew questions which separate my analyses from the theme of man-made mass death. The phenomenon itself is not, however, merely incidental to philosophical thinking: it is not a historical matter that can be held to one side, but one which we must make thematic if we hope to understand the meaning of self, language, and time.

Because English is likely to be the first language of most of my readers, I have used standard English translations of the German works cited. The translators of Rilke, for metrical and other reasons connected with the unique difficulties encountered in translating poetry, take considerable liberties with the text. I have allowed these free readings to stand but have also included the original texts for longer citations.

Acknowledgments

I AM GRATEFUL TO THE NATIONAL Humanities Center in Research Triangle Park, North Carolina, where I was a Fellow in spring of 1981, for making possible the completion of several chapters of the present study, and to the City University of New York Research Foundation, which awarded me a travel grant for 1982 and 1983 enabling me to pursue a line of inquiry the results of which are reflected in the final chapters of this work. I also want to thank those colleagues in the Philosophy Department at Queens College of the City University of New York who shared both time and viewpoints with me during the years that this study was in the making. I am indebted to the many participants and audiences at various conferences where I have read drafts of chapters. Their remarks have helped me reshape several portions of this book. I am also grateful to Professor Thomas J. J. Altizer for reading the manuscript and for his many helpful suggestions. I owe a special debt to Professor Emmanuel Levinas of the University of Paris at Nanterre, whose work I seldom cite only because its perspectives have been decisive for my work as a whole.

Portions of chapters 1 and 2 have appeared in *Centerpoint: A Journal of Interdisciplinary Studies*, The Graduate School and University Center of the City University of New York, vol. 4, no. 1, Fall 1980, a special issue on the Holocaust, ed. Ellen Fine, Jane Gerber, Rosette Lamont, et al. Portions of chapter 7 appeared in *The Union Seminary Quarterly Review*, vol. 38, no. 1, 1983.

Abbreviations

I / Kingdoms of Death

> . . . *I fled, and cri'd out* Death;
> *Hell trembl'd at the hideous Name, and Sigh'd*
> *From all her Coves, and back resounded* Death.
> —*John Milton*

*W*HAT IS THE MEANING OF DEATH in the twentieth century, when millions of lives have been extinguished and the possibility of annihilating human life altogether remains open? Is there an art of dying which is useful in this time and circumstance? Or does quantitative change, the emergence of the numberless dead, so alter our perspective on death that no interpretation is adequate to the apocalyptic character of the phenomenon except perhaps the gasp of horror, the scream, that in Greek tragedy accompanies the revelation of things unspeakable? For meaning can only be created when what is radically new appears in the context of what is most familiar, the taken-for-granted continuities of interpretation that stand fast for us as a horizon for further experience and its integration into the already accepted significations that guide the life of a society. The present situation emerges from a new horizon, one so vastly different from what we have historically inherited that the phenomena which appear against it seem to make no sense.

It is tempting in these circumstances to revert to familiar paradigms, the *artes moriendi* which have tamed death in the past, and to import these strategies into the new context on the hope that what serves the dying individual can be stretched to accommodate vast numbers, as if numbers did not alter the significance of death and the process of dying. But the question "What conception of world, experience, and self is required in order for these numbers to become possible?" is covered over when a sheerly additive procedure is brought to bear upon the problem of scale and the masses of the dead are conceived as a sum total of the deaths of monadic individuals. The purpose of this chapter will be threefold: to explore the difference in meaning between individual and mass death; to cast phenomenological light upon mass death by disclosing its distinctive aspects—the mass annihilation of untold numbers of persons and the creation of a new social form, a death-world made up of mini-cosmoi of the living dead embedded in larger societies; and to lay open the metaphysical perspective and linguistic structure which prepared the way for the phenomenon of man-made mass death and of which this phenomenon is the expression.

The Authenticity Paradigm   **B**EFORE MASS DEATH CASTS ITS shadow over contemporary existence, the most significant meaning structure which governs individual dying and attains consensus in Western culture is the assumption that a good death, even if not free of pain, is the measure of a good life. If we can face our own eventual non-existence, if not affirmatively at least without fear that our lives have been moral failures, we have come to terms with "last things." And this coming to terms is a necessary though not sufficient condition for assuring ourselves that our exit is free from that worry which casts a blemish not only on our final hours but on all of life: fear of pain, anxiety over the loss of self, and terror before the unknown. The view of some Buddhists that he who cries out in his last hour, who does not die without flinching, will be reborn in some debased animal form is only an extreme version of the attitude that the manner in which we make death our own is a determinant of character. On this interpretation the actions of our final days are a touchstone for determining our value as moral beings.

Dying acceptably is only possible if death has become ingredient in life itself long before life is extinguished. Life in turn can be lived with integrity only if death is already accepted as inseparable from it. Death is the wound life bears in itself: to know and accept this frees us for the pursuit of rational contemplation, integration into the cosmic whole, or more intense participation in the here-and-now, depending upon the pattern that organizes experience. The assumption that there is a necessary relation between dying and the good life persists into the present with suitable emendations as to what counts as the final hour; that is, we are not held responsible for ourselves in the comatose state of a medically or naturally prolonged existence, but we are responsible for the way we conduct ourselves in the penultimate time of a final illness when we are still present to our own dying. Let us call this durable point of view, which posits a reciprocal relation between the manner in which death is appropriated and a person's moral situation, the *authenticity paradigm*. Its compatibility with a range of philosophical perspectives attests its power to integrate death into a heuristic structure through which wider experience is organized. Still, we may be compelled to seek fresh insights if the authenticity paradigm fails to make sense of the phenomenon of mass death or to provide the axis around which other meanings of death can turn.

It may be worthwhile to take a first sighting by setting side by side two contrasting views of death which have only the authenticity paradigm in common, in order to gauge our distance from it and as a preliminary to further inquiry. We may then discover that the phenomenon of mass death leaves us equally removed from both ancient and contemporary articulations of the paradigm. Ancient views hinge upon a historically frayed but still exemplary instance—the death of Socrates. Contemporary thought also offers numerous examples. Let us, however, restrict our choice of a recent paradigm to its postmodern, intensely personal casting in the work of the twentieth-century poet Rainer Maria Rilke, for in this form the authenticity paradigm is unencumbered by the attempt to render it consistent with an embedding metaphysic.[1]

Consider the ancient example. Nothing so palpably illustrates the refinement and self-control of a person as the fearless and noble management of his dying. In a tableau of Socrates' last hours drawn from the *Phaedo—The Death of Socrates*, by the nineteenth-century painter Jacques Louis David—a Socrates of heroic stature, still shackled but supremely confident, holds forth in his cell to his sorrowing admirers. He has risen from his pallet; the others are at his feet.[2] In his left hand he holds the hemlock; the right is raised in a teaching gesture. The painter is attentive to the affective tone of the dialogue. Socrates is calm, in contrast to the mixed emotions of his friends. Of course, pity and grief are unnecessary since all would be well with Socrates: "Divine providence was with that man as he passed from this world to the next and on coming there also it would be well with him, if ever with anyone that ever was."[3] No doubt. The requirements for the good life had been met—the philosopher's *arête*, the examination of life; the soldier's courage in the face of death; and the plain man's repeated self-deprecatory proclamations of ignorance. In the soul of Socrates is writ small the class virtues of the well-ordered state. His last hours are *pars pro toto* a dramatic condensation of the total life of mind and polity.

It is not impossible from the Socratic standpoint that the dead sink into non-existence. In the *Apology* Socrates considers this alternative together with that of the soul's postmortem existence. Death is one of two things: either the dead man is nothing, and lacks all consciousness, or the soul upon death migrates from this place to another. Either death is nothing or, if it is something, it is a winnowing from what decays of what does not decay, an intellectual and moral kernel that perdures. Both death as nothingness and death as separation of the soul from the body offer similar psychological and moral gains: first, the assurance that suffering comes to an end—for even if the process of dying is painful, it too shall pass—and, second, that dying is not an evil thing. It is consistent with both views of death to hold that evils occur only when the norms of conduct are violated—but do not occur fortuitously or as the result of natural events. Thus no harm in the true sense may befall the good man in this life or in any other, if there is another. Death has become tamed death, the subject of moral reflection. As thought content, death has its *nomos* and, thus transformed, loses its sting.[4]

The notion of a subject that is the bearer of moral properties is carried forward, at first mediated by Stoic philosophy, Neo-Platonism, and Christian doctrine. Later Cartesian and Kantian rationalism deviate little from the essence of this tradition. Both abstract from the concrete particularity of the person by continuing to identify persons as rational cores which persist after biological death, although for Descartes the afterlife is the scene of reward and punishment while for Kant it is a sphere for realizing further moral perfection. Of course, Kant's notion of infinite moral progress continuing into the afterlife diminishes the drama of dying, but death still marks the completion of one phase of the rational agent's moral life. If we are to find a truly postmodern rendering of the authenticity paradigm, one which breaks decisively with the classical model, we must turn to a version of it which identifies neither personal reality with a rational core nor moral conduct with conformity to rational principles, but at the same time makes personal appreciation of death the touchstone for assessing moral stature. We shall discover these qualities—the rejection of the primacy of reason together with an affirmation of the existing individual freed for the presence of phenomena—in the work of Rilke. In its freedom from traditional philosophical concerns, Rilke's poetry, together with his voluminous correspondence, treats death not by investigating the properties of the cogito but by fastening upon the penumbra of the thinking subject and finding there passions unable to recognize themselves because man as cogito is in headlong flight from death.

Let us bear in mind the intellectual climate in which Rilke's poetry first appears. It is generated by a type of philosophical thinking which emerges not organically but as a bitter reaction to the rationalism and subordination of the individual attributed to the speculative metaphysics of Hegel. In the two generations succeeding Hegel, the perceived limitations of Hegel's system were seen to derive from what was believed to be his conception of an all-inclusive and fatally bloated Absolute.[5]

Individual death could become a theme for philosophical reflection and go proxy for other issues only when the radical contingency of thought itself was brought to the fore, when thinking was seen to depend upon something more primordial than itself: the existence of the thinker.[6] Speculative thought thus became the mask which had to be torn away from existence, not in order to understand existence, but in order to expose its fragility. For there was in fact nothing to understand, no original rational core which reason could image. Reason would merely mirror a mask. We could only take on existence, live it, in full awareness of our radical finitude. In this new context the authenticity paradigm was expressed as the reciprocal relation between the profundity of the thinker and the degree to which death was ingredient in the thinker's personal experience.

It is only in the context of this post-Hegelian response to the Ab-

solute of an Idealist metaphysics that a meaningful version of the
authenticity paradigm could arise. For we must assess the paradigm
from our own acquaintance with mass death, not from its locus classicus but from its most compelling postmodern expression. If the
paradigm proves inadequate to the contemporary phenomenon of
mass death, it is no straw man which will have fallen short of our
experience but the paradigm's presence in the work of a poet who
says of last things:

> That within the Christian church ways to God of most blissful
> ascent and of deepest achievement can be trodden, we have the
> prodigious evidence of the saint's lives. . . . But this conviction
> . . . does not exclude in me the certainty that the most powerful
> relationships to God, where there is need and urge for them,
> can develop in the extra-Christian spirit too, in any struggling
> human being, as all Nature, after all, where it is allowed to have
> its way, passes over inexhaustibly to God.[7]

Once and No More   *I*T IS IMPORTANT NOT TO CONFUSE
these last things with the "last
things" of Christian eschatology. For Rilke's post-Christian sensibility, last things are not to be found in a beyond. We are redeemed in
the here-and-now or not at all. The moment is unique, unrepeatable,
its own final opportunity. "Just once, everything, only for once.
Once and no more," Rilke sings in the ninth of the *Duino Elegies*.
Every instant belongs equally to life and death: "Lovers do not live
out of the detached here-and-now . . . *for being full of life, they are full
of death,*" Rilke writes in 1915 (2:149). And in 1925, in the well-
known letter to his Polish translator, he adds: "*Death* is the *side of life*
averted from us, unshone upon by us." We must make it our task to
hold life and death together and to live within this wider orbit "a
purely earthly, deeply earthly, blissfully earthly" expanded awareness
of the whole. To understand life, to know "its true figure," we must
accept its extension through "both spheres," for "the blood of the
mightiest circulation flows through *both*" (2:373). Death is no
longer—as it had been for the young Rilke—Duhrer's knight riding

forth "into the stirring world" but part of that world, the dark side of the stirring.[8]

This wider orbit is not a new more fundamental grounding of thought with death as its foundation. Like Yeats's widening gyre ("things fall apart, the center cannot hold") or Nietzsche's tightrope walker, existence for Rilke is suspended over that which has no ground, the bottomless, the *Abgrund*. Only on this premise does the affirmation of life becomes possible (2:372). To be sure, the terror of death paralyzes us—how could it not?—so that we become numb to this side of our experience and extrude it from ourselves: "Death . . . is probably so near us that we cannot determine the distance between it and the life center within us without its becoming something external, daily held further back from us, lurking somewhere in the void in order to attack this one and that according to its evil choice" (2:148). We make death the enemy without realizing that in turning away from death we turn also from life. The loss is immense, Rilke claims, for in our alienation from death we cannot live as beings turned towards "the Open," the "nowhere without no," the world in which the tension of opposites is resolved. Animals and children can catch a glimpse of "the Open." "But your eyes, as though reversed, / encircle it on every side, like traps / set round its unobstructed path to freedom."[9] Only by taking death into ourselves and no longer confronting it as the great negation can we affirm the whole. We cannot force affirmation by frontal assault, for then we only lock ourselves more firmly into the opposite of "the Open"— the "world," that which is set against us as a field of discrete objects. If we try to force affirmation we only turn our backs upon that "never nowhere without no: that pure, unsuperintended element one breathes, / endlessly knows and never craves."[10] The problem is to turn ourselves round so that we look out of, rather than at, things in the world, to take up the standpoint of the things themselves.[11]

Rilke's way of seeing the difference between "world" and "the Open" is that of the painter.[12] Limited by the density of things, ordinary experience can only see them from the spectator's point of view as multifaceted, but the painter can treat this density so that it yields a wider inclusion.[13] We may consider the problem of "the Open" as one of bypassing density by knowing where to station ourselves:

> Who knows . . . whether we do not always approach the gods
> so to speak from behind, separated from their sublimely radiant
> face through nothing but themselves, quite near to the expres-
> sion we yearn for, only just standing behind it—but what does
> that mean save that our countenance and the divine face are
> looking out in the same direction, are at one; and this being so,
> how are we to approach the god from the space that lies in front
> of him? (2:147)

What is important is to make the canvas show the painter looking in
the same direction as the gods he paints, seeing with their eyes what
they see while at the same time, *per impossibile*, turned round, his gaze
fixed on their faces. But our limitations can, to an extent, be overcome. Something of the depth and richness of the whole is attained
if we do not shun death as something alien, but regard it (as we
regard the gods) as close to us; if we fail in this the here-and-now is
thinner because of what has been extruded from it. Rilke also imagines this diminution dynamically as the spin of a smaller orbit. We
revolve faster and faster and the increased spin appears to us as progress. In contrast to the ersatz and frenetic quality of this progress,
those who take death into themselves—lovers and preeminently
poets—revolve in a wider orbit.

   For Rilke, we are not unique in the fleeting and provisional character of our existence. Nature and "the familiar things of our intercourse and use" are in the process of vanishing forever. Upon us falls
the burden of wresting meaning from their transiency by inwardizing them before they are gone. But this new relationship between
two dwindling streams, self and world, makes us the necessary instruments for their (and our) redemption:

> Earth, isn't this what you want: an invisible
> re-arising in us? Is it not your dream
> to be one day invisible? Earth! Invisible!
> What is your urgent command, if not transformation? [14]

We must become "bees of the invisible," curators of the co-present
world of Nature and familiar objects of daily use which are rapidly
passing into nonexistence.[15]

Still, the immutable law of becoming does not permit the flux of things to cease, as if we—if we could complete the task of inwardization—could bring the process to a halt. Instead, becoming grinds on endlessly, only now the things of familiar use are being replaced by different objects: "Now from America empty indifferent things are pouring across, sham things, dummy life" (2:374). They are "sham" because it is for the things as it is for us: When the death in things—not the death produced by them, but the death that is *in* them—is shut out, they can only be meaningless mechanical objects. By contrast, speaking of the cherished possessions of childhood, Rilke writes: "This Something, worthless as it was, prepared your relationships with the world, it guided you into happening and among people, and further: you experienced through it, through its existence, through its anyhow-appearance, through its final smashing or its enigmatic departure, all that is human, right into the depths of death."[16] He thought of his generation as the last that could still achieve the transformation, still name things that, so to speak, have their deaths in them: "Are we, perhaps, here just for saying: House, Bridge, Fountain, Gate, Jug, Olive tree, Window?"[17]

Rilke's vision of life and death as a unity, of a world that permits a yea-saying to this wholeness, comes to dominate one strand of postmodern sensibility: the tendency toward a nostalgia for pretechnological culture (in which this wholeness was still thought to be present) together with a hope for its recovery as one measure of authenticity. For Rilke the renewal of the world will come about through poetry, though the naming of the fleeting beings, since language, unlike things, offers fresh possibilities for revitalization. For Heidegger, who follows Rilke on this path (see chapter 5), the world's ills are traced to the progressive obscuring of the meaning of Being by the Western metaphysical tradition. For Rilke wholeness is no longer possible because, he reminds us: "The terrifying thing is that we possess no religion in which . . .[erotic] experiences, being so literal and palpable as they are, . . . may be lifted up into the god, into the protection of a phallic deity who will perhaps have to be the *first* with which a troop of gods will again invade humanity, after so long an absence" (2:302). Heidegger also laments: "Only a god can save us now."[18]

Although we cannot restore the gods to the world, we can at least refrain from living as if life consisted of grasping finished patterns already built into existence, patterns which we apprehend at the price of closing off whole orders of experience because we align ourselves with what is most abstract in it. If we open ourselves fully to life, to hitherto unexplored experiences in which death is supremely present, a metaphysical as well as a psychological end is served: the familiar distinctions which organize experience, subject-object, inside-outside, are broken. This break is not the outcome of mystical union—the merging of I and Other—but something altogether different. The putative subject becomes an antenna, as it were, a forward point for a single unbroken stream of experience, one demanded by the stream itself. Rilke writes, "This Here and Now . . . seems to require us,"[19] and in a transcript from his Notebook, he says: "[In Capri] a bird-call was there, both in the outside and in his inner being, concordantly, so to say, since it did not break at the boundary of his body, but formed of the two together an uninterrupted space in which . . . only one single spot of purest, deepest consciousness remained" (2:369). The "bees of the invisible" in this context are no longer modeled after the *Schöpfer*, the creator and shaper of things—like Rilke's mentor, the sculptor Rodin, casting the hand of God—but rather they are nodal points of most intense consciousness intersecting the wider stream of experience.[20] But whether Rilke speaks of the self as the experiencing subject in the more usual sense or as the forward point, a point of intensity in a single stream, the authenticity paradigm as the reciprocal relation between the acceptance of death and the profundity of the person holds: we redeem experience, render ourselves worthy of it, and it of us, by living up to the death in it.

To see this Rilke compels us to focus on experiences of such subtlety or to view things from vantage points so far outside the usual that we bypass the ordinary while at the same time extending its frontiers. It is as if we were asked to see the unicorn tapestry from the standpoint of one of its flowers. From this point of view we must bring life and death into visibility. If we are to ambush life we are forced to take up an odd position in regard to it. We must station ourselves outside it—where the dead are—and see ourselves with their eyes:

> True it is strange to inhabit the earth no longer,
> to use no longer customs scarcely acquired,
> not to interpret roses, and other things
> that promise so much, in terms of a human future;
> . . . and to lay aside
>
> even one's proper name like a broken toy.
> . . . —Yes, but all of the living
> make the mistake of drawing too sharp distinctions.
> Angels, (they say) are often unable to tell
> whether they move among living or dead.[21]

If we imagine this verse from a painterly perspective, life is the subject of the canvas but the painter's feet are planted in a different terrain, in death. Creaturely existence is depicted from the standpoint of the dead. But this is not all. Rilke shows us *how* we are to think the respective modes of temporalization of life and death. The boundary between life and death has too often been shown as a sharp line of demarcation, whereas for Rilke there is a mode of being— that of the angels—which, unlike our own, renders all worlds, life and death alike, co-present. Still there is something which cannot be canceled in creaturely existence, the temporal *mode* of our having been, of having ever existed. This means we cannot be apprehended even by the dead (following Rilke's figure) in the mode of a lifeless tableau, for if life is to be grasped it must be apprehended in all its fullness *with the future ingredient in it.* The everyday structures of our lives are promissory notes: their coming due constitutes the horizon of our "blissfully earthly" expectations. If the dead (even they) mean to grasp the meaning of the here-and-now, they must include the anticipation that belongs to life or they will achieve only a depleted version of the present. This ineradicable notion of the future, as we shall see, is challenged by the phenomenon of mass death.

This last point brings us back to the main strand of our inquiry, the relevance of the authenticity paradigm to contemporary manmade mass death. Within the ambit of Rilke's verse, it is impossible to break with the dimension of the future, for even the dead from their point of view must admit that this mode of temporalization is inherent in life. Anticipation, the promise in things, constitutes the organic tie between life and death. For this reason the fundamental assumption, the hidden premise, which undergirds this verse is the indestructability of an accustomed field of reference—"the things that promise so much," "customs scarcely acquired," "roses," "the name laid aside"—since these are the stuff through which any meaningful grasp of the future comes about. The possibility of aesthetic ordering central to Rilke's version of authenticity depends upon this anticipated continuity.[22]

To an extent the vast annihilatory capacity of the twentieth century had been foredisclosed to Rilke. The first shrinking of things beyond the possibility of redemption actually came about during World War I when his personal history intersected the larger catastrophe.[23] The Great War was a watershed in his life which, until then, he had spent readying himself for the work of aesthetic transformation. For Rilke the horror of the war was its incomprehensibility: "Not to understand, not to understand, not to understand," he moans (2:214). How was the poet to "transform into the invisible" the nearly ten million people who died, six thousand each day for fifteen hundred days?[24] The authenticity paradigm could only seem hopelessly inadequate in this context. Here was a new *prose du monde* that defied aesthetic reordering. Indeed, Rilke had fully grasped this point. Reflecting on the Great War, he writes in 1920:

> There may indeed have been such periods before, full of destructions, but were they equally formless? With no figure to draw all this around itself and expand it away from itself—*this* way tensions and counter-tensions are set up without a central point that first makes them into constellations, into orders, at least orders of destruction. My part in this is only suffering. . . . Suffering with and suffering beforehand and suffering after (2:214–15).

But having nothing else Rilke could only fall back upon what had been true bread: the authenticity paradigm. During the intense agony of his final illness, leukemia, he refused any drugs that might dull his awareness, yet he was still able to write to Nanny Wunderly-Volkart, "Never forget, dear friend, life is a glory (2:449).

It is ironic that Rilke's postmodern version of the authenticity paradigm clashes with twentieth-century experience at just those points where its appeal to modern sensibility might be expected to be greatest. We have seen that for Rilke the integrity of experience is measured by the intensity it generates, which, in turn, is determined by the extent to which death is integral to it. The assessment of quality in terms of intensity is fully in accord with the contemporary stress upon peak experience as a measure of value in life.[25] At best, however, a death-derived depth can be a useful criterion for evaluating the authenticity of experience only if death does not overwhelm the vital pole of experience. But the phenomenon of mass death makes vividly present the possibility of the foreclosure of all experience by destroying countless living beings together with the structures which make human existence possible. Thus if the appropriation of death is to be true to twentieth-century experience, if "being full of life" we are also "full of death" as it is present in our time, the authenticity paradigm is reduced to self-parody. If instead we choose to renounce the experience peculiar to the present age— that of mass death—and assess authenticity by integrating only one's own death into one's life, then life is lived in monadic isolation in which the deaths of others have lost significance. To be sure, this criticism holds even in the absence of contemporary man-made mass death. Nevertheless, scale is all-important: mass death "lights up" the horizon from which death can be interpreted so that the death of the individual due to the natural hazards of existence seems insignificant when contrasted with ending one's life in an event of mass extermination. Indeed, a simple death which occurs fortuitously through disease or accident might prove to survivors of the new world of mass death a consummation devoutly to be wished. One such survivor writes: "Be happy, you who torture yourself over metaphysical problems, and . . . you the sick who are being cared for, and you who care for them, and be happy, oh, how happy, you who die a death as normal as life."[26] Thus, according to this new counter-poetry of survivors, it would no longer seem heroic to accept personal death in one of its expected forms given the possible terms on which we might be forced to encounter it.

We should also not be surprised to find the authenticity paradigm jeopardized in relation to the question of the death in things. It may be recalled that for Rilke authentic things (*Dinge*)—those in which death and life are maintained in balance—together with Nature are to be inwardized by us as "bees of the invisible." The appeal of Nature lightly tamed and its corollary, objects crafted to human scale, has been an accepted theme of a Romantic tradition culminating in the ecological concerns of the present.[27] But an irony appears in this understanding of things when it is applied to the depleted environments which make up the newly cordoned-off centers of mass death. Deprived of the minimal technologies required for sustaining life, living conditions in the death-world make a mockery of the idea of Dinge: implements in the death-world, if they can be fashioned at all, are of the simplest sort, replete with human input but hopelessly inadequate for their destined use. Moreover, the belongings of the victims of man-made mass death which derive from their old lives (most frequently objects of human use least marked by advanced technology) constitute instantly recognizable symbols of death. Instead of the thing holding life and death in equipoise to create a microcosm of human meaning, death streams forth from these piled-up ownerless possessions. They become the symbols of displacement and alienation, tropes for the pure annihilation of the death-world.

The change thus effected in the meaning of Dinge, altering the manner in which the world is experienced at the most fundamental levels of awareness, has also changed our consciousness of the mode in which temporality is experienced. To think temporally is to think the now so that the future is ingredient in it. But we live the future through the accustomed series of references constituted by things. When these change noncatastrophically in day-to-day life, the symbol systems of ordinary existence are maintained, but when their significance is radically altered, meaningful structure in terms of which we interpret the future to ourselves collapses. By destroying the system of meanings which rendered death-accepting behavior possible, the effect of man-made mass death has undercut the power of the authenticity paradigm which permitted mastery over death.

The End of the Life-World   THE INCONGRUITIES AND PARA-
doxes generated by the phenomenon of contemporary extermination challenge our understanding of finitude as set forth in the authenticity paradigm. A contingent phe-

nomenon, a historical event, rebounded upon the structure of the dominant paradigm without at the same time fully revealing itself as a radically new meaning constellation with its own structures and laws. We have yet to draw a boundary around this phenomenon so that we may define, analyze, and reconstruct our object of inquiry. At what point can it properly be said to have begun? What are the characteristic patterns which by virtue of "family resemblance" enable us to determine what is to be included in its scope? Since the object with which we are concerned has a temporal character, I shall call it "an event." But temporality is not the only characteristic of events. I shall interpret the term *event* to mean: actions "running off" in a temporal sequence dialectically related to reflective analysis so that the historical sequence attains its full meaning when taken up by thought.[28] "Event" designates the nexus of dynamic, but ephemeral occurrences, "the pieces of flotsam combed from the historical ocean,"[29] that, taken together, form the segments of a single meaning constellation. This pattern becomes generative for the self-understanding of its time (even if this understanding is only partially glimpsed by contemporaries). Colliding with antecedent systems of meaning, the event henceforth dominates cognitive, ethical, and aesthetic signification. In the case of contemporary man-made mass death we are in the eye of the storm and so cannot hope to constitute it both retrospectively and as a whole. Our reading must remain archeological to the extent that we can only lift out shards from their embedding strata in the interest of attaining insight into the larger structure.[30]

I shall define the scope of the event to include three characteristic expressions: recent wars which deploy weapons in the interest of maximum destruction of persons; annihilation of persons, through techniques designed for this purpose (for example famine, scorched earth, deportation), *after* the aims of war have been achieved or without reference to war;[31] and the creation of death-worlds, a new and unique form of social existence in which vast populations are subjected to conditions of life simulating imagined conditions of death, conferring upon their inhabitants the status of the living dead.[32] It is difficult to pinpoint the beginning of this event but I shall (arbitrarily) designate its inception as World War I without of course specifying a concluding point. My analysis of the death event will, in this chapter, attend particularly to the laws and structures of one of its segments, the death-world, since in its full-blown form the death-world is without antecedents. We may gain access to this world by consulting the accounts of its survivors, which fix for us the concrete day-to-day organization of existence in the death-world and highlight its difference from our taken-for-granted world of everyday life.

The world of concentration and slave labor camps as concrete actualities emerges from a systematic effort to deconstruct the life-world—the sphere of micropractices which make human existence possible—to dismantle it and not merely to compress its range. Here a space is created in which is changed not merely this or that component of experience—work, sexuality, habitation or the even more fundamental modes of eating and sleeping—but the scaffolding of experience itself. Thus Nadezhda Mandelstam, widow of the Soviet poet Osip Mandelstam, writes in her memoirs of their first exile to the town of Cherdyn, "The collapse of all familiar notions is, after all, the end of the world."[33] The full conceptual force of the idea of background praxes becomes manifest only in the context of the relation of everyday experience to the emergence of meaning. By life-world we may understand the horizon of experience from which human meanings originate.[34] Since the life-world is prior to any theoretical or reflective attitude that we may hold and in fact makes such attitudes possible, it is particularly difficult to grasp conceptually.[35] For once it is subjected to theoretical scrutiny, it ceases to be what it is: the whole of our prereflective experiential field, the point of intersection between what is constructed through our manner of being in the world and what is given. Edmund Husserl says of it:

> The life-world, for us who wakingly live in it, is always already there, existing in advance for us, the "ground" of all praxis. . . .
> The world is pre-given to us, the waking, always somehow practically interested subjects, not occasionally but always and necessarily the universal field of all actual and possible praxis, as horizon. To live is always to live-in-certainty of the world, being constantly and directly "conscious" of the world and of oneself as living *in* the world.[36]

Historical self-understanding is truncated when it fails to take account of the life-world. Thus Fernand Braudel reads the history of dramatic occurrences, "the headlines of the past,"[37] as playing contrapuntally against their background: "those thousands of acts that flower, reach fruition without anyone's having made a decision, acts of which we are not even fully aware . . . countless inherited acts . . . incentives, pulsions, patterns, ways of acting and reacting," that characterize daily practice.[38]

This view of the life-world does not leave our understanding of the human person unaffected. Human existence can no longer be interpreted as being inserted into the world in the manner of an isolated subject, a consciousness which surveys the world from a privileged position of subjectivity, nor is the world itself a system of physical objects whose existence can be described as *partes extra partes*, with the individual as only another entity in the world. In the latter case the individual is reduced to an object of physics, in the former the individual becomes an isolated monad for whom the phenomenal world is the content of consciousness. Instead, persons are nodes of activity which constitute and are constituted by the phenomenal field in which they live. The world toward which we are directed offers itself as an existing or possible task. We may express this intersection of person and world as the "lived body."[39] The lived body inhabits a world of indeterminate horizons from which phenomena arise.

The life-world can be envisioned as a three-tiered field of experience. The first tier, the inanimate world, is given in primary sensation and in practical, goal-determined transactions. A second level, the vital world, consists of living beings characterized by self-motion, self-differentiation, and self-boundedness. Such beings may be understood as the objects of human projects or, in the case of higher life forms, as having independent goals. The third level is the social sphere in which other persons are apprehended as interacting with varying degrees of impact upon the self. These worlds are interconnected like concentric circles: the interpersonal world cannot emerge without the existence of anterior levels, that is, of the vital and the inanimate, as its ontological ground. All sociocultural forms of existence "live on" or express this fundament although no *specific* pattern of culture is endemic to the life-world as such. The structure of experience is perceived by way of cultural forms; it is clothed in some cultural expression, but at the same time this foundation allows these forms to emerge. Prior to the appearance of slave labor and concentration camps it was possible to imagine the destruction of the life-world, but it was not possible to imagine the paradox which arises when human life perdures but the life-world as we have described it ceases to exist.

Consider the way each of these levels functions in the life-world. At the stratum of the vital, we experience ourselves in our spatiotemporal orientation. Prior to a theoretical grasp of geometrical space, we encounter the world as oriented beings. The motility of our bodies is directional; movement is experienced as up or down, backward or forward, left or right, while distance is apprehended as near, farther away, or remote. As temporal beings we live the past as the sediment of our completed acts, the future as the field of our possibilities. Generally as the past lengthens the future is foreshortened, but this process can, under special circumstances, be experienced quite differently. Thus, when some long-range project is undertaken the foreshortening of the future can be arrested whereas, on the other hand, its course can be accelerated by hedonic experience. We learn to depend upon this spatiotemporal order when we modify our activity in accordance with ongoing experience. Still we expect a thread of continuity to run through our various experiences. Each new experience will be taken to belong to the same body and the same memory stream.[40] There must be some uniformity in the ground of experience or we could not survive.[41]

We have already seen that the authenticity paradigm in its modern form depends on the continuity governing our lives as temporal beings, particularly in relation to the future. The potential fulfillment of things despite the possible foreclosure of their fruition is what we mean by "anticipation" in the temporal unfolding of the life-world. But in some cases for slave labor camps, and always for concentration camps, the ultimate aim is the death of every inmate even if the proximate aim is to permit their survival for an interim period during which they are forced to work until they die of disease or drop from exhaustion. In effect they are already reckoned as dead. Although the mode of temporalization in the death-world closes off the future of its inhabitants, its aims are often in the interest of another quite different future, that of the collectivity from which its inhabitants are excluded. This future can be calculated in terms of millennia. Indeed, all concerns of self-interest in the larger society—national, economic, and military—are discarded in the service of this vaguely defined, far-off new age.[42] In fact there are two futures. One is the end of ongoing existence for the inmate, the other the glorified time to come held up as the eschaton for the embedding society.

This new mode of temporalization is created and enforced at the vital level of existence by the system of compulsory enclosure which removes the individual from familiar surroundings and reduces mobility.[43] This spatial compression begins before arrival in the camp world itself when the process of deportation is initiated since it is here that the separation from ordinary life with its system of symbolic continuities begins. Historically, whole communities are uprooted before the actual construction of the camp system.[44] In fact it can already be found in the earliest episodes of the death event (as I have defined it). Thus, Robert Morganthau, American ambassador to Turkey, writes of the Armenian massacres of 1915 and 1916: "The Armenian massacre evidenced an entirely new mentality. This new conception was that of deportation. . . . [It meant moving the Armenians] bodily from their homes where they had lived for many thousands of years and [sending] them hundreds of miles away into the desert."[45] Once the camp system had been created as a new form of social existence, the conditions of transit, quite apart from the relocation itself, have been described by survivors as a separate episode in the history of this spatial compression. It is the experience of the boundary, of crossing over from free space to forced enclosure. The sealed-off transports with their human cargo, the vast hordes on the highways supervised by armed guards, constitute the first restriction of mobility. Intolerable levels of population density continue and are systematically enforced by the camp system itself.[46] The crowding which characterizes conditions of eating and sleeping is attenuated only by regimens of meaningless work. Summing up his prospects after arrival in Auschwitz, Primo Levi writes: "Every day according to the established rhythm, *Ausrücken und Einrücken*, go out and come in; work, sleep and eat; fall ill, get better or die."[47] Alexander Solzhenitsyn contrasts the Russian slave labor camps with prison or village life which slave labor camps might naively be thought to resemble:

My spirit was numb from the first two days in camp. Oh that was not a prison! Prison has wings! Prison is a treasure house

of thought. It was gray and easy to starve and argue in prison.
And just try that here—ten years of starvation, work and silence. . . . Over there beyond the barbed wire was . . . a little
village—ten houses. . . . So close to us and the very opposite of
a camp. . . . And if they should say to me . . . That's your freedom! Just live in that village until your death! Are you willing?
. . . Oh, not only willing, but good Lord, please send me a life
like that!⁴⁸

At the levels of vital existence the life-world suffered a severe condensation of meaning. But the same short-circuiting of significations
that occurred at the vital level is also present in the sphere of inter-
subjectivity, reflected in the attempt to change the basic structure of
one's apprehension of persons. In ordinary experience we make a
distinction between persons and anything else that may be encountered as phenomenon. This distinction is experienced when, in apprehending other persons, we are aware that we ourselves are possible objects of apprehension for others. To be sure, while both
things and persons may be seen as beautiful or ugly, sturdy or fragile,
only in the case of persons is reciprocal apprehension experienced.
This difference also bears upon the way in which qualities are ascribed to objects. We know that things are fragile, break, and get
used up, but the manner in which persons disintegrate is quite different; the person exists as corporeality, as a self-bounded vital being,
as a spontaneity which expresses itself in motility and language.
Moreover, included in our grasp of other persons as vital beings is
our apprehension of others as imposing a demand upon us: that we
recognize them as corporeal and, as such, vulnerable. The other *appears* expressing his vulnerability through his mere existence,⁴⁹ and
his self-presentation is always in the manner of soliciting his continued existence. This vulnerability given as a datum of experience is,
outside the death-world, socially confirmed: disregarding this principle of the other's right to existence violates the rules of most societies. The other's inviolability is considered forfeit only in the case
of punishment for the breaking of society's rules. In the concentration camps and, to a lesser extent, in slave labor camps (where a
minimum market value is placed upon its inmates) the camp inmate
is taught to experience the lives of other inmates as valueless and

expendable while the lives of guards and camp bureaucrats are to be apprehended as inviolable. Thus the inmate is systematically conditioned not only to see himself and other inmates as slated for destruction, but as somehow meriting this fate.

Some simply surrender to the pressures of this sytem and become living dead while others struggle to survive through purely self-serving behavior. The camp system even in its most effective form never fully succeeds in forcing inmates to accept officially sanctioned distinctions.[50] For as soon as survival is no longer an end in itself but a means, a sense of solidarity with the dead develops. The living speak for those who can no longer speak for themselves. Leon Wells, a survivor of a death brigade, a corps of workers forced to eradicate the traces of mass murder, expresses this solidarity after his liberation: "Today the anguish for those who had been killed flooded over me."[51] Nadezhda Mandelstam writes, "If nothing else is left, one must scream. Silence is the real crime against humanity."[52] Once the desire to represent the dead is conceived as the motive for survival, this hope begins to irradiate behavior in the present. If one survives, one retains a memory of one's stance in extremis. For this reason it becomes important to retain some area of spontaneity, however small. In the absence of the assured continuity of a symbolic system of meanings, this means stripping away sentiments that usually accompany ethical acts and leaving the acts to stand for themselves. Thus Alexander Donat, a Jewish journalist from Warsaw, writes: "Prisoners helped one another as best they could, but they shied away from sentiment. Help yes, compassion no."[53] Behavior that confirms the inviolability of other persons, affirms their sphere of rights however limited, guides the hope for survival. Richard Glazar, who worked in an extermination camp, remembers: "Of course there were people who survived who were loners. They will tell you now that they survived because they relied on no one but themselves. But the truth is probably—and they may either know it or not be willing to admit it to themselves or others—that they survived because they were carried by *someone*, someone who cared for them as much, or almost as much as for themselves."[54] In order to ascribe value to other persons, the newly constituted conditions of the death-world are bracketed, put out of play however briefly, in order to reinstate in fantasy the older symbolic continuities as if they alone prevailed.

Thus Primo Levi, a Jewish chemist from Italy, remembers carrying a vat of soup with a young French boy, a "pikolo" (a privileged adolescent who because of personal beauty or charm is excluded from the heaviest manual labor), and inserting a fragment of his own remembered world into the camp's system of significations:

> The canto of Ulysses. Who knows how or why it came into my mind. . . . Who is Dante? What is the Comedy? . . . Here, listen Pikolo, open your ears and your mind, you have to understand for my sake:
>
> > *"Think of your breed; for brutish ignorance*
> > *Your mettle was not made; you were made men,*
> > *To follow after knowledge and excellence."*
>
> As if I also were hearing it for the first time: like the blast of a trumpet, like the voice of God. For a moment I forget who I am and where I am.[55]

Although old meanings are destroyed at the vital level of existence, this collapse of meaning does not come about in the interpersonal sphere in the manner intended by the system. Once some value other than sheer survival—such as living for the destroyed sociocultural community—comes to the fore, "unauthorized" values can be attributed to persons in a manner proscribed by the system. In some cases a curious reversal of ordinary values takes place. Remaining alive under odious conditions is more difficult than suicide, thus rendering survival a self-sacrificial act. Even with the virtual destruction of the vital level, the apprehension of the other as a node of inviolability can sporadically be affirmed and can even generate a rough moral code. Thus Alexander Donat writes: "In camp slang 'to organize' meant to look after Number One. It was to steal soup from the kitchen, for example; but to steal bread from another inmate, however, was to *really* steal."[56] More often than not, strategies required for self-preservation force recognition of the corporeal vulnerability of others into the background. Still, unlike the vital level where the field of existence expands or shrinks as a whole, single acts recognizing other persons as centers of vulnerability "irradiate" the larger field of existence and take on paradigmatic quality. While the camp system extinguishes the interpersonal stratum of the life-world for many—for the system aims to destroy this level of existence—altruistic acts have a "ripple effect" in the death-world. Any break with the point of view of the camp bureaucracy is of considerable significance since the death-world is intended to disorient the victim so that none of his old stock of beliefs is left standing. The system is designed to create a new set of beliefs in place of the old, which are to be extirpated root and branch. But the practical importance of this rift with camp structure should not be overestimated, since such behavior has little impact on one's chances for survival or on the power structure of the camp itself. It does, however, represent a breach in the system of significations forged by that structure. The creation of psychic distance sometimes makes it possible to act in accordance with the insights gained. Unexpectedly, the act also puts the taken-for-granted structures of the remembered "ordinary" world into a new perspective. Seen through the grid of camp life, they seem somehow false and hypocritical. This perception of the difference between old and new places a parenthesis of irony around ordinary experience and calls its certainties into question. Thus Solzhenitsyn writes: "Pardon me, you . . . love life? You, you! You who exclaim and sing over and over and dance it too! I love you life! Oh, I love you life! Do you? Well, go on, love it! Camp life—love that too. It too is life."[57]

Technological Society and the Death-World

AN OUTLINE OF THE DEATH-world takes shape by way of contrast with the scarcely visible practices which constitute the life-world. But it is also important to distinguish the newly created death-world from the technological society, the interpersonal world founded on and ruled by technique, a "totality of methods rationally arrived at," having as its sole interest the criterion of efficiency in every domain of life.[58] It is embedded in the life-world with which it can nevertheless be contrasted, and it comes into existence through the concealment of this pregiven fundament as a result of the development of modern science on the one hand and of the philosophy of the Enlightenment on the other. More accurately, it exists as the expression of that concealment and of the world view of the Enlightenment.[59]

There are already hints of the manner in which the alienation characterizing technological society comes about in the development of the idea of the life-world itself. The life-world is, to be sure, the structure of micropractices constituting concrete everyday existence. But the life-world can also be contrasted with the conceptual structure of modern science. There is, of course, no idea comparable to that of technological society in Husserl's thought. But once the existence of technological society is posited, its meaning can be grasped only after we understand the relation of modern science to its embedding matrix, the life-world.[60]

Phenomenological analysis is concerned with the emergence of modern science from its origin in the life-world. From the beginning science depends upon mathematical reason and self-consciously sets itself apart from the intuitively given structures of existence. Yet geometrical thought, the first language of modern science, though abstract, is still informed by perceptual sensibility, for it is the discursive handling of shapes. Early modern science uses geometrical thinking, which overcomes the relativism of the perceptual world by positing necessary relations between ideal entities while at the same time remaining applicable to the world from which it originated.[61] Science treats physical phenomena as if they were ideal entities such as those of mathematics. It can then borrow from the mathematical language which expresses its laws the certainty that belongs to mathematical demonstration itself. At the same time, the world of immediate qualitative experience grounds the constructed idealities of science. Without it they would hang free of any meaningful context and would lose their spheres of origin and applicability.[62]

The philosophy of the Enlightenment, like science itself, loses sight of the immediacy of the life-world. It "forgets" the life-world as the locus of pretheoretical fullness and validates only the constructed, theoretical, and mediated aspect of sociocultural existence, which derives from it. Thus the philosophy of the Enlightenment reinforces the attitude of the natural sciences by interpreting social existence as if it were the sphere of an already alienated natural existence.[63] The matter is further complicated by the fact that the ideal constructs of science, together with its style of thought, its practices, and its institutions, fall back into the life-world since the life-world is the horizon or referential context of greatest inclusion.[64] Thus, in thinking of technological society we need not imagine the destruction of the life-world but, instead, the alienation of technological society from the larger whole which still continues to function as its matrix but which now lies in concealment.

It is not difficult to see the difference between the pregiven horizon of utility and meaning on the one hand and the world of science as a manifold of mathematized constructs together with the sociocultural institutions which borrow their criteria from it on the other. But what of the death-world? It is far less easy to see the difference between technological society and the death-world—for without the spiritual and material apparatus of technological society, how would the death-world have come into being? The procedures and instruments of death which depend upon the quantification of the qualitied world are innovations deriving from technological society and, to that extent, extend its point of view. But while the death-world trades on technological society, it would be a misunderstanding to consider it as part of that society or, conversely, to imagine technological society as a "universal concentration camp" from which all human freedom is absent.[65] Although alienated from the life-world, technological society depends on it for its continued existence, but the death-world is wrenched almost free of the life-world: its aim is simply death. At present technological society and the death-world exist side by side. If the death-world were the only world, the resulting monolith would spell the end of all life and so the end of technological society as well.

To identify technological society with the death-world obscures the uniqueness of the death-world. At the same time this veiling of its uniqueness leads us to think of it as a transitory stage in the evolution of technique. Thus we might imagine that, if its efficiency were increased, technological society could supplant the repressive mechanisms of the death-world with benign conditioning.[66] To be sure, in the death-world the language of technique is applied to persons. This faulty use of language creates a fatal "category mistake" which permits people to be fed into the maw of an efficient and impersonal productive process, a feature the death-world shares with technological society. But the death-world, for which technological society is the precondition, also develops a quite independent and unique system of meanings whose inner logic is expressed in a language which grows up in opposition to both the life-world and technological society itself. This language is designed to create terror which is not incidental to the process but its very essence.[67] The apparatus created by the technological society provides the means through which terror is achieved. But the point and purpose of technological society is the increase of technique, whereas the raison d'être of the death-world is the proximate or delayed death of its inhabitants. Thus Alexander Donat writes:

> We had arrived in the kingdom of death, in the Third Field of the Maidenek concentration camp.
>
> Maidenek was hell. Not the naive inferno of Dante, but a twentieth century hell where the art of cruelty was refined to perfection and every facility of modern technology and psychology was combined to destroy men physically and spiritually.[68]

The difference between technological society and the death-world is perhaps best grasped by attending to the manner in which meaning is achieved in the technological society. The language of technique rests upon two ways in which language signifies. The first of these functions belongs to the process of signification from the outset and reflects our ability to distinguish things immediately existing from the possible future efficacy of these things.[69] Things which merely *are* have properties available to us in their immediacy, but once their use is discovered—the link between the thing in its brute existence and its consequences—this use is apprehended as the *meaning* of the thing. The connection which persists in memory *is* a bit of language: the stick when perceived as useful for lifting becomes the lever.[70] But this shift from brute existence to language and memory is not innocuous, for it establishes the primacy of utility over immediate quality. The language of technique loses sight of the qualitied world in which this utility is embedded.

The second function of the language of technique belongs to a fully conceptual aspect of language which appears in scientific thinking. The objects of science are spatiotemporal nodes lending themselves to mathematical formulation, abstracted from the qualitative properties of the life-world and then given quantitative expression. These ideal entities represent the propertied objects. We can manipulate them conceptually: what they mean is now expressed by homogeneous units which can be exchanged for one another in a system of unlimited conceptual transposability. The advantage of this exchange is that entities of this sort can have unlimited relations with all other entities of the same sort.[71] In technological society the sphere of application of this second feature of language has been widened to include the sphere of social relations. Together with the first feature of language, the substitution of utility for immediate quality, the transformation of the propertied life-world into units of quantity results in one of the most widely noticed features of technological society: the reification of persons. The totality of language is exhausted by the two functions described: the expression of relations of utility and the interpretation of the given in quantitative terms. Language itself becomes rationalization, "the methodical attainment of a definitely given and practical end by means of a precise calculation of adequate means."[72]

What is unique to the language of technological society is its non-teleological character. Nothing in the scheme tells why a given technique is desirable other than that it promotes some aspect of technique itself.[73] Thus we may designate a stick as a lever, but in the framework of technique, *why* we should want to lift anything can only be answered in terms of further utility. Similarly, we may improve the efficiency of an organization, but the larger context never transcends the sphere of means (it is cheaper or production is faster, and so on). The language of technological society cannot "refer" beyond utility because it can provide no encompassing structure of meaning to organize its disparate processes. What is more, such a meaning system cannot be derived from techniques themselves because techniques are devised to be self-contained. Nietzsche's description of decadence might well be applied to technological society: "The whole no longer lives at all: it is composite, calculated, artificial and artifact."[74] Only mythical thought, "which seeks to reach by the shortest possible means a global understanding of the universe,"[75] could provide the relational structure for the unification of these diverse functions. A unique and paradoxical situation is generated by the technological society: a movement toward a single homogeneous culture, global in scale, whose functions are transparent to everyone has emerged along with technique, but no overarching system of meaning has accompanied it, because such meaning cannot derive from the language of utility and quantification.[76]

The death-world makes its appearance upon this already demy-thologized ground as an effort to sacralize a world of impoverished symbolic meanings by creating a totalizing structure to express what is irreducible even in technological society: the binary opposition of life and death. But this remythologization does not restore, nor can it restore, the mythological wholeness of pretechnological societies. It can only borrow from the material and spiritual culture available to it, treating the detritus of that culture as older mythic systems had treated natural existence.[77] Thus new modes of efficiency—the bu-reaucratic and material means of technological society—are now the "raw" stuff to be organized in the interest of resacralization. A world is created in which death breaches the broken totality, becomes its ultimate signification and the whole of its content. The new "sacred" space, the enclosures of the death-world, and the new "sacred" time, the future moment when the ultimate meaning of the death-world will be brought to closure, are the spheres for the realization of this meaning.[78] The death-world is thus the child of technological soci-ety; it is an attempt to give meaning to the alienation of that society from qualitative natural existence as well as from cultural experience. But the death-world is not the extreme expression of technological society itself, for what characterizes that society is its rationality, its divorce from mythic consciousness, its uprootedness from the life-world.[79] Instead the death-world is an attempt to make whole the broken cosmos by an imaginative act of radical negation, the destruc-tion of the embedding matrix for all social forms, the life-world, and by consigning to itself all that seems worthy of death.

We can gain additional perspective on this process by envisioning it in terms of power. In the context of technological society we can define power as the exercise of productive capacity. By contrast, power in the death-world is annihilating force. I shall examine the relationship of these concepts in succeeding chapters when I take up the logic of the death-world and Heidegger's view of technology. At present we need only notice that, in relation to the death-world, those who have the power to negate ascribe being and meaning to themselves and non-being to others. But when the meaning of being is parasitic upon annihilatory power, it is inherently unstable and thus fails to provide the basis for a unifying paradigm. More, self-affirmation requires accelerating the pace of annihilation since, as Nietzsche notes, power depends upon resistances to be overcome and preserves itself only by an increase in its exercise. Present-day myths which organize existence in terms of annihilation lack fixity on other grounds as well. As I hope to show in detail later, the categories of the myths are both abstract and fluid, so that, under their terms, now one, now another group can be selected for extinction, a process facilitated by technological society's tendency to transpose existing things and persons into quantifiable homogeneous parts.

Interpreting meaning in terms of annihilatory power holds not only for the world of the camps, but for the phenomenon of nuclear war as well, however dissimilar it may be in other respects. Although in full-scale nuclear war those who wield power will almost certainly die, they allot vast quantities of power to themselves by igniting nuclear conflagration. Power of this magnitude determines that *all* shall die, thus creating a pure void in existence and bringing the mythic discourse to closure by destroying life in its entirety. Just as the world of the camps is both distinct from and tied to technological society, so too the nuclear void is embedded in the matrix of technological society but not related to it in simple cause and effect fashion. In contrast to the camps, the nuclear void is connected to technological society temporally rather than spatially. While camps are enclaves *within* technological society, in total nuclear war technological society *precedes* the ensemble of phenomena that constitute the nuclear void (blast, radiation, nuclear winter). The all-encompassing character of total nuclear war, of course, erases all spatial distinctions so that the world that precedes it and the void which supervenes are spatially coextensive and technological society itself is eradicated. Still, because being and meaning depend on non-being as annihilatory power in all the disparate phenomena of the death event, the death-worlds of the camp system and nuclear war lie along the same gradient.

The Language of the Death-World

BUT HOW CAN THE LIFE-WORLD, which functions as a primordial system of significations for technological society even if this system is hidden from view be radically negated? How is it possible to undermine the context of all practice? Such a change cannot come about by trading old meanings for new. Indeed, new meanings in the prereflective sphere of everyday life can often be accommodated even when a change in individual and cultural conditions is profound because of the basic stability of the life-world.[80] In the death-world, change is not a sporadic process but one of massive intervention in a taken-for-granted system of meanings. Nietzsche has shown that what is fixed as ineliminable is that which is written by means of pain in the language of the body.[81] In the death-world, new meanings become affixed to the body through the systematic substitution of pain for the ordinary complex of meanings that constitutes our corporeal transactions.[82] This fixing of meaning through the language of pain lies outside any linguistic referential system. In fact it is first noticed as a gap in linguistic possibility: there seems to be no language which can make sense either of the death-world as a whole or of the particular experiences it generates. Thus Primo Levi writes: "Then we became aware . . . that our language lacked words to express this offense, the demolition of a man."[83] Still, because of his pressing need for such a language, he imagines its possibility: "If the Lagers had lasted longer a new harsh language would have been born; and only this language could express what it means to toil the whole day in the wind, with the temperature just below freezing, wearing only a shirt, underpants, cloth jacket and trousers, one's own body nothing but weakness, hunger and knowledge of the end drawing near."[84] But the very failure to develop a radically new language (even in the Soviet slave labor camps, which lasted for a much longer period) attests the unique linguistic situation of the death-world.[85] Since new syntactic and semiotic possibilities arise from the enrichment of the field of experience and not from its depletion, the linguistic process itself must reflect this shrinkage. In fact the older language remains. It is permitted to subsist while new and contradictory meanings are added. The existing system is made to go proxy for these additions which occur at the most primordial levels of experience. In effect, a systematic effort is made to create confusion in regard to accepted, taken-for-granted meanings by developing opposed meanings in order to produce the widest possible discrepancies between alleged and actual significations.[86] Thus a pattern of multiple and contradictory sense constitutes a "law" of experience in the death-world.

If we consider the life-world of ordinary experience in its everyday operations as a linguistic field, a nexus of meanings that are bound up with one another, its structure can be described in terms of the relationship between a signifier—the term of the relationship that intends something else—and a signified—that which is meant or intended.[87] Thus, if we consider the term "food" as a signifier, multiple concrete meanings can be attached to the signified: the dinner one eats, the shared conviviality of friends, the taste, warmth, and satiety that together constitute the event of eating. In the world of ordinary experience it is clear that the signified (the multiple meanings of food) surpasses the signifier "food."[88] But in the death-world, a new and complex relationship governs language behavior. On the one hand, all the patterns of the life-world as we understand them persist (in the case of food, its concrete physical character, satiety, warmth, and flavor that result from the act of eating). *But at the same time the signified is also and always death.* The signifier collapses into the signified, which is now no longer greater in range than the signifier. For each and every signifier the range of obsolete meanings is retained together with the new signified, death. Tadeusz Borowski, Polish writer, poet, and survivor of Auschwitz, illustrates the exercise of this technique in a story which shows how contradictory meanings coalesce. Borowski depicts hunger as the omnipresent background of concentration camp life; no one could evade the threat of its depradations. But for those few camp workers who unloaded the human cargo which was deposited at Auschwitz, food (often in quantity) was available. Relief from hunger depended upon unloading this human freight and hurrying the herded masses to their deaths. The continuing supply of food depended on the continuing destruction of human life. Thus, when the narrator in one of Borowski's stories expresses his fear of impending hunger, his friend, with the cynical wisdom engendered by camp life, replies, "Stop talking nonsense. They can't run out of people."[89]

While some anomalies occur fortuitously, most are systematically created. Thus Primo Levi writes:

A band begins to play, next to the entrance of the camp: it plays *Rosamunda*, the well-known sentimental song, and this seems so strange to us that we look sniggering at each other. . . . Suddenly the squads of our comrades appear returning from work.

They walk in columns of five with a strange unnatural hard gait, like stiff puppets made of jointless bones; but they walk scrupulously in time to the band.[90]

The anomaly is pronounced when prisoners accept the world as presented because they are unable to penetrate the disguised meaning. Thus Richard Glazar, a planner and executor of the revolt at extermination camp Treblinka, describes the unloading ramp at the camp as disguised in the form of a provincial railroad station festive with flowers: "I saw a green fence, barracks, and I heard what sounded like a farm tractor. I was delighted."[91]

It is of course fatal to lapse even for a moment into accepting the old significations at face value, for without the utmost vigilance death is assured. On the other hand, forgetting the old significance is equally fatal. In the Nazi camps those who succumb to the power of death become "*Musselmänner*," those who surrender the will to live. Primo Levi writes: "They crowd my memory with their faceless presences, and if I could enclose all the evil of our time in one image, I would choose this image which is familiar to me: an emaciated man, with head dropped and shoulders curved, on whose face and in whose eyes not a trace of thought is to be seen."[92] A new concept of language has to be learned by the camp inmate. Reading from each and every old signifier, the person learns to decipher the new meaning, death, as it applies in every situation at every instant. The inmate soon learns that death is always intended and that this intention can be fulfilled at any moment. A double layer of language has to be maintained: the old significations, and death. Alexander Donat, describing the ordeal of his introduction to the Maidenek camp, cites the advice of an old inmate:

> With brutal frankness he told us what it was like there. "This is a K.L.," he said. "Remember those two initials. . . . *Konzentrationslager*. This is a death camp, a *Vernichtungslager*. You've been brought here to be destroyed by hunger, beating, hard labor and sickness. You'll be eaten by lice, you'll rot in your own excrement. . . . Forget who and what you were. . . . Everyone here is the same. . . . All are going to die.[93]

The language of the death-world is never straightforward or "sincere" because it bears a phantasm, death, which rides on every sig-

3

nifier. This double reference accounts for the cynical wisdom of survivors to which I have already alluded. It also points up the false character of the presented world of the camps: things never bear the character ascribed to them by the camp system. This becomes particularly apparent in the slave labor camps where the life-world is less depleted than in the concentration camps so that the vestiges of ordinary life are present, but these only reveal their sham character. Thus Alexander Solzhenitsyn writes of the language of the Gulag:

> The Zek language dearly loves and makes stubborn use of . . . disparaging diminutive Russian suffixes. . . . By this insistent bias of the language the Zek demonstrates also that nothing in the Archipelago is genuine, everything is a forgery, everything is of the lowest grade. And that they themselves do not set any value on the things that ordinary people value. They show awareness of the fake nature of the medical treatment they get, the fake character of the petitions for pardon for which they wrote out of compulsion and without faith.[94]

This system of multiple and contradictory meanings is not merely a procedural matter, a technique used in the interest of some end extrinsic to the destruction of meaning itself. On the contrary, the destruction of meaning is the *telos* of the death-world.[95] It makes no sense to think that the raison d'être of the death-world could be achieved by the use of conditioning techniques which, without harsh and repressive measures, would remold individual behavior so that dissent from some prevailing ideology would never erupt. Such techniques might secure greater efficiency in the technological society. But the death-world *is* its own raison d'être, created as a new form of social existence, a remythologization of a world which has lost touch with natural existence and cultural particularity. It is materially and formally self-contained; it exists to provide the global system of meaning absent in the society of technique and actualizes this meaning in social existence. Thus there is no question of doing better, more expertly, what the death-world does poorly since its aim is the negation of life. What is required is a new myth to repair the broken totality, one for which death is not the ultimate signified. But such an integrative myth cannot return to antecedent structures of meaning, to still another version of the authenticity paradigm which has presided over the praxes of death for Western culture. Present experience is not comparable to life before the advent of the death event of which the death-world is a part. The life-world, such as it is, now and in the future, includes in collective experience and shared history the death event of our times, which is the death-world of the slave labor and concentration camps and the other means of man-made mass death. Once the death-world has existed, it continues to exist, for eternity as it were; it becomes part of the sediment of an irrevocable past, without which contemporary experience is incomprehensible.[96]

In this chapter I have tried to show how the death event has undermined the schema of interpretation governing the meaning of death in Western culture, particularly the authenticity paradigm. The Socratic version of the paradigm presumes that the style of one's dying will reflect the character of one's life: the good man dies well. If a satisfactory pattern of values is realized, in this case a life lived in conformity with rational norms, then it becomes possible to face death with courage either in anticipation of an afterlife or in recognizing death as the termination of all experiencing. The postmodern version of the authenticity paradigm, as exemplified in the poetry and letters of Rainer Maria Rilke, places a priority on the quality of experience, on the actualization of the present as an eternal now so that the miracle of consciousness, of sheer existence, is affirmed. But such affirmation requires taking death up into life as integral to it and as decisive for the manner in which future time is understood and experienced. Pain is not absent from such a life. Indeed, death is ingredient in Nature and in the world of things for death belongs to all existence. Only by integrating death into the texture of life is an authentic living and dying possible. But neither the older nor the newer version of the paradigm can any longer provide meaning for death in a world in which the death event, contemporary man-made mass death, has come into being, and in which a death-world, a sphere of life in which the living are forced to exist as if already dead, has been created. The death-world reflects the attempt of technological society, which is alienated from the life-world, the embedding matrix of all praxes, to repair the broken cosmos by an act of radically negative remythologizing: death becomes the ultimate meaning of the totality.

II / The Logic of
Mass Death

There is nothing more illogical than absolute logic:
It gives rise to unnatural phenomena, which finally collapse.
—Johann Wolfgang von Goethe

*T*HE DEATH EVENT INCLUDES A VA-
riety of phenomena, of which the
death-world is an important part. Its horrors remain visible because
the victims of the death-world are not all destroyed outright. But to
understand the magnitude of the death event we must also explore
those aspects of it in which the victims are eliminated altogether:
war, extermination camps, mass shootings, famine, and so on. Here
it will not do to examine the meaning of the phenomenon in terms
of the destroyed life-world, or to show that a new language has been
created for the inhabitants of an inner world surrounded by a larger
society in which there is relative mobility. Death in these cases is not
a phantasm borne by the given within an enclosed system of signifiers. Instead, vast numbers of persons are simply marked for annihilation as part of an impersonal process of destruction. By examining the larger event, a heuristic structure—the "logic" governing the
various segments of the death event—may become visible. This
structure should operate independently of other meanings and apply
to one or another of the death event's aspects alongside political,
economic, and social significations. Indeed, it may surpass and over-
ride these concerns and become the operative meaning structure of
the death event.

But why should it be supposed that there is a discernible logical
pattern at work in the death event simply because such patterns play
a strategic role in technology? The answer is implicit in my earlier
remarks that the death event reflects efforts to restore wholeness to a
fragmented spiritual and material cosmos by remythologizing the
broken totality. Like genuine cosmogonic myths, these myths of ne-

gation try to order and systematize relations and connections by articulating the particulars to be annihilated. Thus it should come as no surprise that a peculiar pattern of logical relations inheres in the death event. But this structure cannot impose coherence upon that which inherently cannot be thought, namely nonbeing. Thus the logic of the death event must be one of paradox. I hope to show that the particular paradoxes at work in the death event are those first articulated with extraordinary logical force by the pre-Socratic philosopher Zeno of Elea.

In the face of experienced multiplicity, Zeno devised a number of paradoxes to support the position that being is one. The idea of infinite divisibility which lies behind Zeno's paradoxes presupposes an infinite supply of parts. When this formal structure is unconsciously applied to human societies, they too can be imagined to contain infinite numbers. This logic expresses the bizarre deformations of the death event. When combined with the myths of totalitarian societies, which themselves are born from the ashes of technological society, this mode of reasoning provides a principle in terms of which those segregated for death can be eliminated. These mythical structures compatible with Zeno's paradox can be found both in post-Biblical apocalyptic thought, and in contemporary remythologizations which retain the essential features of apocalyptic thinking: a metaphysic of impurity. I hope to justify the conclusion that the logic and myth of the death event, together with the unique structures of the death-world, constitute a new historical a priori, the sine qua non of all further experience.

Zeno's Paradox

ACCORDING TO PLATO, ZENO'S paradoxes are designed to show the absurd conclusions reached if we accept the premise that many things rather than the One exist.[1] Zeno, arguing against the Pythagoreans, believes that the conclusions which follow from the idea that everything that is, is multiple, are even more absurd than those following from the idea of Zeno's Eleatic master, Parmenides, that being is one. In a series of brilliant strokes he develops imaginative arguments which, flying in the face of experience, demolish the possibility of multiplicity and motion by showing that neither of these two obvious features of experience could exist. The fragments we have are startling in their originality and power. Their impact upon ancient thought is attested by the attention, even if derisive, they receive from Plato and Aristotle.

But Zeno's paradoxes cannot be dismissed as mere tour de force because they reflect a concern with a deep and important problem: the relation of the infinite to the finite and the bearing of this relation upon the structure of continua.[2] Zeno's third fragment is of particular interest since it formulates his position in terms of the widest generality:

> If there is a multiplicity of things, it is necessary that these should be just as many as exist, and not more nor fewer. If there are just as many as there are, then the number would be finite. If there is a multiplicity at all the number is infinite, for there are always others between any two, and yet others between each pair of these. So the number of things is infinite.[3]

Let us suppose (with the Pythagoreans) that the real consists of many individual units. If there is a "many," then we ought to be able to say how many there are, for everything that exists can be counted. If not, how could we say that they exist? What is must be finite. But, on the other hand, the many cannot possibly be finite but must be infinite. Why? Because between any things that are, however small, it is always possible to insert some other thing. Thus the things that are, are infinite in number. But it is absurd to say that the many are both finite and infinite.

The paradox is generated by starting from two different points of view. Beginning with an analysis of the parts, all the parts taken together will make up the whole. All must be included or the enumeration will be incomplete, and if all are included, their number is finite. On the other hand, if the whole is our starting point and we look inward towards the parts, we can never count all of them, for the number of parts is infinite.[4] Zeno's argument hangs on the assumption that there exists no ultimate indivisible unit. There is no gradual transition from the very small to that which has no magnitude at all, the unextended. The process of divisibility can be imagined to continue indefinitely, which implies that one never runs out of units to be divided. But if this is the case, the issue shifts from divisibility to exhaustibility: how can this series of divisions, by definition inexhaustible, be exhausted? [5]

The premise that the whole—by analogy with a straight line—is infinitely divisible and the supply of parts to be subdivided inexhaustible provides the logical paradigm for the death event. This is not to say that the paradox contained in the gnome of Zeno functions *causally* as a totalitarian plan to create the death-world; rather, the logic of the paradox can be constituted *proleptically* by us as the formal structure exhibited by the various elements of the death event. The only imaginative leap required is that we picture a demographic unit, a people, as a spatial continuum. On analogy with Zeno's idea of the whole, such a unit, however reduced in size, will always provide an infinite supply of parts. The point is made in essence in the words of Tadeusz Borowski previously cited: "Stop talking nonsense, they cannot run out of people." What is "forgotten" in the death event is that a group of people is a *collection* which is exhaustible. Its individual members are not "parts" which can be subdivided over and over again. The existential application of Zeno's argument in the death event points up a category mistake that unconsciously dominates totalitarian discourse. A collection is interpreted as a spatial continuum which is conceptually divisible into an infinite number of parts but which in actuality can be exhausted.

To be sure, in the death-world, every individual destined for extermination is to be eliminated. The obsession with numerability—head counts, census taking, and the like—pervades the literature of authorities and victims alike. Yet the unconscious underlying assumption is that the null point—at which not a single individual in the group to be eliminated is left—functions as a *regulative ideal* which cannot be attained. Although these persons will be eliminated, still others will come who will continue to bear the symbolic significance of their predecessors.

Zeno's ultimate purpose was to establish the unity of being. The paradoxes are meant to show the futility of holding that the many exist or that motion is possible. For Zeno, such claims lapse into incoherence since to assert them is to think the unthinkable: that nonbeing is. Thus Zeno's paradoxes open up the abyss of nonbeing inherent in becoming and flux, a sheer void the Eleatic vision of being tries to breach. The death event, in recapitulating the structure of Zeno's paradoxes (which both affirm and deny finite magnitudes), also repeats their articulation of radical nullity. Numbering a collection of persons while assuming the inexhaustibility of this collection mirrors in existence the incoherent "logic" of nonbeing. For Zeno the paradoxes result when we reject the unity of being. There is no managing the infinite particulars, for they will continue to loom up so long as a specified magnitude is conceived as both *actually* divisible and *actually* traversable. Of course the Eleatic vision of being denies the nonbeing which threatens it. The death event also requires an ontological counterpoise, a myth which expresses the paradoxes but, at the same time, sublates and overcomes them.

Although Zeno's argument dictates division, nothing in the argument tells us how the whole is to be cut up. If we imagine a line to be divided it makes no difference on Zeno's premises at what point we place the cut. The logic of his argument holds for every part. But in the death event we are no longer in the presence of an abstraction.[6] A generative or sorting myth is required, a principle by means of which the whole is to be divided. Sorting myths rely on taxonomical structure: their meaning depends on names of classes which are arbitrarily ascribed.

The elements of the myth are derived not from observation but from available historical or quasi-historical content; they are then gathered up into narrative form so that the story functions as a global explanation for the present sociopolitical state of affairs.[7] This structure is of course independent of Zeno's arguments. Zeno's paradox attaches to the sorting myth as a phantasm, but the myth expresses logical relations of its own. The historical elements of the sorting myth are forced to do the work of logical concepts and are elevated to the status of necessary truths or laws of nature. Thus what originated in the historical world is frozen. Any attempted correction by means of facts destroys the myth, which allows for no exceptions derived from experience.[8]

Once the taxonomical system is in place, the sorting myth attempts to confine reason to its deductive functions. The all-embracing classification system "forgets" that the myth's claims are supposed to have originated in experience and pursues the logical conclusions dictated by its hard and fast premises. An exemplary instance of the extreme ideality of such system building and of the incorrigibility of premises can be found in this description of the work of Soviet psychologists among the peasants of Central Asia in 1931:

> [A formal syllogism is presented to some peasants of Uzbek.] "In the far North where there is snow, all bears are white. Nova Zemlya is in the far North, and there is always snow there. What color are the bears?" A peasant replies: "There are different sorts of bears. . . . I've seen a black bear. I've never seen any others. . . . We speak only of what we see; we don't talk of what we haven't seen. . . . Our czar isn't like yours. Your words can be answered only by someone who was there, and if a person wasn't there, he can't say anything on the basis of your words."[9]

The peasant does not question the formal validity of the psychologist's argument but simply makes the point that observation statements contain referring terms and the correct application of such terms can only be derived from experience. The words *bear* and *white* are not themselves bears or white. Sorting myths presume a leaching of meaning between words and world. The world is seen to ape the formal relations of language and language borrows the ontological status of what it purports to disclose.

In the case of the death event, various criteria have been used to divide up the world irrespective of its actual complexity. These criteria include the separation of a nation or nations along ideological lines and in accordance with racial distinctions. Contemporary sorting myths differ from their predecessors in that divisions are not only envisioned as global but are actualizable on a global scale. The bureaucratic and technological means for the existential application of the myth are available to technological societies. More, the aim is not the sublation of designated enemies but their annihilation, since only then is the myth's operation secure against the incursions of experience.[10] As we shall see, the annihilation of persons as an end in itself is the aim not only of the death-world but also of contemporary warfare, thus transforming war into a component of the death event.

The force of Zeno's paradox in this context lies in its compatibility with a wide variety of sorting myths. So long as the process of division continues, irrespective of the sorting principle, an inexhaustible supply of parts is expected to be available. The destruction of parts does not preclude an infusion of fresh parts. The criteria used for sorting—ideology, race, and so on—become the bearers of the logical paradigm which itself remains invisible. The myth when it first appears must be so powerful that all considerations of fact are swept aside. Sufficient power is generated through the propulsive force of a mass movement or a revolutionary elite to continue the process of division, to sort without end. Thus annihilation proceeds under cover of the myth. In his film *Aguirre Zorn Gottes*, the filmmaker Werner Herzog shows the operation of this logic combined with a sorting myth of an imperial type. Aguirre, the mad conquistador and follower of Pizarro, slaughters or loses his opponents until none is left. Destitute, he floats on his raft through the jungles of the Amazon babbling his fantasies of conquest to a band of monkeys, for they are the only remnant of his party, the last of an "inexhaustible" supply of parts.

Apocalypse, Gnosis, and the Death Event

THE RELIGIOUS ROOTS OF THE death event—the division of a cosmic whole based on a powerful sorting myth—can be traced to Jewish apocalypticism of the intertestamental period and to later Christian apocalyptic. In the literature of apocalypse the logic of infinite divisibility is applied to two disparate continua: time and mankind. These two continua are caught up in a new situation of crisis. People will be divided according to sin and righteousness, while time will be split into all that has gone before and the present age on the one hand and the present age and the time of redemption on the other. In Jewish apocalypticism time is twice divided: into historical time and the posthistorical Golden Age to follow, and, before all of this can come about, into the past and present age of woes. The present is the nadir of history, a necessary penultimate state prior to the consummation of history. Even the full significance of the present is unclear since everything is, even now, being divided up. For those who have eyes the signs of the times are full of hidden meaning.[11] Experience teaches that the present age is to be regarded with radical pessimism, but this vision is mitigated by remanding present evils to the realm of transiency destined to pass away:

God has established two kingdoms and has created two ages, and has decreed that the present cosmos which is unimportant and is quickly passing away shall be given to the evil; but he will give the coming age to the good, because it is great and eternal.[12]

The new age lies outside of time because time will be destroyed. More startling still, death will be slain, for if time has disappeared then its fruits must also perish.[13] The age to come is utterly and radically different from anything hitherto experienced, unique in every sense, a new creation.

The sorting myth of apocalyptic is structured around the adversary relations between God and Satan or Belial, depicted as a mythological dragon or a historical figure. Now Satan sets himself against the divine plan, but in the new age he will be powerless.[14] End-time will see a final cataclysmic encounter between God and cosmic demoniacal forces culminating in divine victory. God alone will rule the future while Satan has dominion over the present world which, corrupt in its foundations, is worthy of destruction. Adam is the agent responsible for this corruption; he is its propagator and he draws all of mankind in its train.[15] Although man remains responsible for personal righteousness, he is powerless before the tide of the history in which he has been caught up.

But the sorting myth of Jewish apocalyptic also derives from another source: the prophetic motifs which enter Jewish apocalyptic piety. Apocalyptic writing is pseudonymous, but its newly written oracles are attributed to ancient prophetic sources. These oracles are allegedly sealed up and only now have become available to the generation for which they are intended. Like its prophetic models, this writing includes both moral and predictive content: divine judgment is to be rendered upon the nations with the deliverance of a righteous remnant leading to an age of peace and justice. Still, apocalyptic writing is different from the prophetic sources it succeeds. It reflects a nostalgia for immediacy in an age in which the direct prophetic word is no longer spoken. The ideal of wholeness supplants the immediacy of divine-human intercourse. The broken cosmos is to be restored at the end of history, when man can anticipate a new creation.[16]

This aspect of apocalyptic thought is of particular significance. As we have seen, technological society in breaking with the life-world has been severed from a unifying horizon of meaning, and the death-world is an attempt to repair the broken totality through the existential application of a sorting myth. But this myth functions as a radical act of negation. The desiccation of spirit which follows the drying up of prophetic utterance presents the intertestamental period with a roughly similar crisis. A new negative eschatological discourse is fashioned in the hope that it will restore immediacy by creating a new wholeness.[17] But this is not all. When the day of reckoning passes without ushering in the end, the possibility is opened up for the addition of new quanta of time on the ground that the age is not yet ripe for the advent of end-time. Thus hope can be indefinitely prolonged. The New Age functions as a regulative ideal approached asymptotically but never reached. The categories of the sorting myth gain eternal status since the process of adding on units of time need never come to an end.

The related speculations of Jewish and Christian gnosis provide still another conceptual nucleus which, together with apocalypticism, forms the religious root for the sorting myths of the death event. Unlike apocalyptic thought, which envisions the drama of end-time within the sphere of historical existence, gnostic speculation conceives the opposition of its primal principles, light and darkness, as grounded in being itself. The demonic forces of gnostic myth either are primordially distinct or have broken away from a celestial matrix and have acquired their evil properties as a result of this alienation. But once evil has been acquired, the demonic forces are imagined in ontologically static terms.[18] Material existence, especially human corporeality, is a prison for the divine sparks thus breaking up the being of heavenly light. The heavenly element "forgets" its divine origin. This dualism is reflected in human existence as the war between flesh and spirit in the individual person. Demonic powers controlling the cosmos prevent the ascent of the soul to its place of origin, but a savior from the world of light initiates the process of redemption by disguising himself and entering the dark realm of earthly existence. He seeks to illumine the souls of those already belonging to the realm of light by imparting the saving gnosis, which will enable them to awaken from sleep or amnesia and return to their celestial home. The nullity of the created world will be fully revealed only when the saving gnosis has penetrated the entire cosmos.[19]

The difference between apocalyptic and gnostic speculation lies in the ontological status of their systems of oppositions. In gnostic speculation fundamental principles, for example, light and darkness, are for all practical purposes eternal. The truth concerning their existence has only been covered up. Based on the orphic conception of the preexistence of the soul, this truth is brought to consciousness for those in whom the potential for truth preexists. But for apocalyptic thought, anamnesis and truth emerge at the end of a process of historical development, although in conformity with Jewish prophetic eschatological norms, the end of history is providentially determined. Jewish and Christian gnosis envisions the cosmos as coming to an end when it has run its course and all the pneumatic souls are released.[20] Both apocalyptic and gnostic speculation concur in their evaluation of historical existence as requiring redemption. But in apocalyptic thought the world, such as it is, remains God's creation and is therefore never wholly evil, whereas in gnostic thought material existence as such is corrupt.

Contemporary sorting myths governing the death event mingle elements from gnostic and apocalyptic myths just as these elements are frequently run together in the sources themselves.[21] This conflation is hardly surprising. Both gnostic and apocalyptic forms are a response to the same crisis: the closing of the channel of divine-human communication. Contemporary sorting myths retain the sense of historical urgency found in apocalyptic thought, the experienced separation of past time and the present hour, while the division into the saved and the reprobate is interpreted along gnostic lines. Racial sorting myths depend upon static categories while ideological versions impute metastable categories of purity to individuals. However, in times of crisis even ideological distinctions take on the increasingly rigid character of gnostic classification. Thus the quest for the true proletariat may require not only class allegiance but elaborate procedures of self-scrutiny to determine the purity of revolutionary motives.

The cosmological and soteriological speculation of apocalyptic and gnostic myth is carried forward in the underground millenarian movements of the Middle Ages although it is, in large part, rejected by the authoritative teaching of the Church.[22] The early Christian thinker Origen derails millenarian expectation by transposing the drama of end-time to the individual soul so that the process of salvation is conceived as the perfection of self beginning in this world and continuing into the next. Similarly, Augustine deflects millenarian hope by suggesting that canonical Christian apocalyptic is to be interpreted allegorically: the millennium begins with the advent of Christianity and is "fully realized in the Church."[23]

Despite the absence of official sanction, the apocalyptic vision of Antichrist as a destructive and anarchic power persists. Medieval apocalyptic speculation reaches its apogee in the thought of Joachim of Fiore. Accepting the apocalyptic mode of temporalization, Joachim integrates its eschatological hope into a trinitarian frame. History is an ascent toward end-time taking place in three successive stages: the Age of the Father or the Law; the Age of the Son or the Gospel, and finally the Age of the Spirit. Gnostic antinomian elements are also present in Joachite eschatology. The final age is to be one of light and fulfillment, of joy, love, and freedom in contrast to earlier stages of fear and submissiveness. The knowledge of God will be perceived in the hearts of men without mediation; the New Age is to be a Sabbath of the Spirit.[24] Joachite eschatology retains the historicity of apocalyptic thought but extends historical time to include his own: the first age spans the time from Adam to Abraham, the second from Elijah to Christ, the third from St. Benedict to Joachim's day. Each age has its period of gestation: his own time was only now coming to fruition.[25] In the interim between his age and the end, a new order of monks, a saving remnant, is to emerge which will preach the new gospel, and from among them will come a still more select group of twelve patriarchs who are to convert the Jews. At the end, a teacher of mankind will appear who will spiritualize humanity.[26] The criterion of the sorting myth in Joachim's thought retains the categories set in motion by Jewish and Christian apocalypticism, but these are applied mutatis mutandis to a lengthened temporal continuum.

The modern sorting myth takes for granted the apocalyptic division of time into the Present Age and the World to Come. But the latter is an altered time in which the elements of impurity, the alleged evils of modern society, are to be purged. The New Age is envisaged as a this-worldly, posthistorical time of redemption. In the absence of a transcendent dimension, the new creation is not remanded to an atemporal future having no connection with antecedent time. Instead, purity is to be achieved in the here-and-now as the result of a wholly temporal cleansing process. The radical historization of time renders impossible the cessation of the process; such a terminus cannot even be imagined as an ideal. Theological transcendence is supplanted by a freshly created totality: the whole of mankind in its biological, sociopolitical, and cultural relations. The New Age is to be ushered in by seizing the sources of power and altering the structure of state, culture, and economy to bring a new order into being. The absence of transcendence forecloses the possibility of bringing the process to an end not only in fact but on principle. Thus a society, once caught up in the myth, is impelled to sort a seemingly inexhaustible supply of parts until the null point is reached. This is why, for example, the ideal of permanent revolution is not an aberration but the logical outcome of revolutionary sorting myths as they reflect the logic of Zeno's paradox. Although derived from earlier gnostic and apocalyptic myths of purity, the myths of the death event are ontologically self-contained. Unlike earlier myths organized around a God who brings history to an end, these myths can only restart themselves. They reflect not so much an assault upon transcendence as the creation of a new wholly immanent totality.[27]

The Metaphysic of Impurity I HAVE DESIGNATED THE POSTMOD-
ern sorting myths by means of which Zeno's paradox is given existential application a *metaphysic*, since an attempt is made in totalitarian discourse to create a totalizing vision of the world and to give speculative coherence to its basic categories. The myths themselves are quasi-narrative structures borrowing the historical detritus of the embedding culture in order to give a comprensive account of the culture's most compelling questions: its origins, its now radically immanent division into the sacred and the profane, its classificatory hierarchies. The elements of the myth are themselves mediated by elaborate interpretive theories. Their appeal to postmodern consciousness lies in this complexity. Thus such no-

tions as race and class reflect antecedent conceptual histories which give the mythic use of these elements their force. By appealing to rational modes of verification (a congeries of disparate techniques of observation borrowed from the physical and social sciences), a note of factuality is struck which lends credence to the structure as a whole.

In the postmodern sorting myth in which race is the operative criterion, it is easy to see the support the sorting myth receives from this conceptual reinforcement. In the locus classicus of racial myth, Adolph Hitler's *Mein Kampf*, a partly speculative, partly mythological system for breaching the broken totality is developed. Three points are of interest. First, Hitler designates the ideological content of National Socialism a "philosophy of life." Thus this content is not a political doctrine but a scheme in which political, economic, and cultural factors are subordinated to an encompassing vision of the whole. For a philosophy of life attempts to provide unified meaning for all spheres of existence. Second, all manifestations of social structure are interpreted as epiphenomena, the expressions of a more primordial "natural" base: "race" or "blood." This ideology is elaborated in terms of a distinction between culture-founding and culture-bearing races. The culture-founding Aryan is destined to conquer and rule the multitude of races who are seen as necessary but dispensable channels through which the stream of Aryan life may pass but which, in the end, are fated to become extinct. This racial doctrine demands a demonic double, the counterpart for the term Aryan. This double is not to be found in the "slave" races but in the Jew, who is interpreted as a perpetual anomaly, neither true nomad nor settled inhabitant.[28] The Jew is seen to propagate an antinatural pacifism and thus to thwart the design of a nature red in tooth and claw—one which favors Aryan aspirations. Third, the principle of "humanitarianism and aesthetics" must be sacrificed in the interest of a putative elite. Citing Moltke, Hitler asserts: "As for humanitarianism . . . in war it lies in the brevity of the operation, and that means that the most aggressive fighting technique is the most humane."[29] The world of the Other—the non-Aryan—is a de jure world of death. It cannot be mediated by symbolic structures but must be transformed into an actual sphere of death. In *Mein Kampf* the means for bringing this about are not yet made explicit, but the core of the argument for bringing the death-world into existence is already present: a "true" world is assumed to exist, a world of being, from which the non-Aryan world is to be excluded. Lacking significance, the being of inanimate nature is attributed to this non-Aryan sphere: "When [Aryan man] departs from the world, these concepts [humanitarianism and aesthetics] are again dissolved into nothingness, for Nature does not know them."[30] The non-Aryan world is feared as the sinister obverse of the true world and as a threat to the true world's existence; at the same time, it is interpreted as a nullity. This vacillation in meaning is significant. It portends an attempt to bring the world of fact into conformity with one of these meanings, whatever the cost. Proceeding by degrees, the sorting myth will be used to sublate the "sinister" existence of the non-Aryan world by extirpating it from the world of being and confirming its lack of value, its nullity. Once this world-picture displaces all others, the dynamics of Zeno's paradox together with the division of peoples into "pure" and "impure" races can be seen to constitute the context for socially validated knowledge.

The theistic vitalism of the nineteenth century already presages this conceptual structure.[31] In the philosophy of Paul Lagarde, the mythical structures of apocalyptic and gnostic thought are retained while many elements of the modern racial sorting myths are also present. Like his more magisterial intellectual contemporaries, Kierkegaard and Nietzsche, Lagarde proclaims the vacuousness of contemporary Christian practice. But for Lagarde the individual acquires his special characteristics only through the still healthy larger whole, the *Volk*. The *Volkisch* approach despite its apparent incompatibility with New Testament teachings, is applied to Christianity: the apostolic community is itself a Volk.[32] Christianity is to become teutonized by purging itself of its Judaic roots. The emphasis upon unique historical events against the universal message of the gospel is an instance of this Judaizing tendency in Christianity and is to be rejected.[33] The old religion must be supplanted by an ecumenical religion of the future which will draw from the essence of all religions but will exclude Judaic elements. Since the German Volk is seen to be endowed with a particularly vital spiritual character, the new religion is to restore this spirit. But since this vitality is preserved only in the lower classes, it is unlikely that a transformation can be achieved without the intervention of the "pure, strong will of a Single Man."[34] This new religion will then dominate the world, for it is the mission of Germany to colonize non-German lands of the Austrian empire, who will then acknowledge German cultural and spiritual leadership.

To be sure there is much that is new in Lagarde's vision: the teutonization of Christianity, the mystical conception of the German nation, a new psychology of the will as the foundation for national unity. But, like older apocalyptic speculation, the metaphysic of purity rests upon the idea of a totality with specific criteria for determining the saving remnant and bringing about a new order: "Contrary to the fashionable philosophy of the day, we are convinced that the world is a totality, ordered towards a goal, and that its disorder is only a means to our education. We are also convinced that every man . . . has a definite place in the world . . . assigned . . . only to him."[35] Lagarde's Christianity rests on a protomyth of the type required for the creation of the death-world. Still clinging to transcendence, its laws are not yet mandated as society's praxis.[36] But once the break with transcendence is achieved, the apocalyptic elements of the myth belong to historical existence and are taken up both as *raison d'état* and as an ontological vision of the whole.

I have already alluded to the possibility of a quite different metaphysic of purity, one which does not, at least initially, ontologize its sorting criteria. Ideological purity as exemplified in revolutionary consciousness divides the continua of time and persons by using a metastable system of classification: membership in a given social class as well as individual ideological commitment. In the latter case states of mind as well as acts constitute sufficient grounds for declaring the individual impure. Once given such a status, he may be remanded to a penal segment of the death-world or annihilated.[37] It is always possible to proclaim new enemies of the state, since on the one hand ideological criteria and their applications are so fluid that they can never be properly grasped, and on the other individual conscience can be forced into paroxysms of ever greater scrupulosity leading to the confession of idiosyncratically interpreted or imaginary transgressions. Thus it is the task of the "true" revolutionary to seek out enemies wherever they may be found, even within the recesses of personal consciousness. Stalin declared in 1936: "The inalienable quality of every revolutionary under present conditions should be the ability to recognize an enemy of the party no matter how well disguised he may be."[38] Ideological purity becomes the pretext for terror, and the sorting myth is relentlessly applied even after all opposition to the ideology borne by the myth has ceased.[39]

Individuals as well as classes may be enemies of the state. If an individual identifies with the broad masses of workers and peasants, his existence manifests being and value, the positivity of the class of which he is a member. But according to a dictum of Mao Tse-tung: "If tomorrow he ceases to do so . . . he becomes a non-revolutionary or a counter-revolutionary."[40] Since ideological content is in constant flux, revolutionary consciousness can only be counterfeit, since it is almost impossible to close the gap between the ideology held by a given individual and that currently maintained by the state. Reeducation is thus a necessary and permanent part of maintaining ideological purity. Moreover no fact counts to vindicate the purity of an erring revolutionary conscience. Thus an account of a red guard remanded to a rural part of Jiangsu province in central China in the early 1970s describes the creation of fresh facts in the retraining of his refractory consciousness:

"They were never satisfied," he said. "They wanted to squeeze things out of me that never happened. But you couldn't deny things, they insisted."

When he balked at furnishing their version of events the guards would take him before a struggle session. . . . "They made you memorize a text they had written out for you. They would say 'Read this sentence sadly.' In some places they added the word 'pause.' That was so the masses could yell at you."

Once I couldn't remember what came next. They said I was trying to cover up. Actually, I just forgot."[41]

The point and purpose of revolutionary consciousness is to approach asymptotically the ideal subjectivity of one's class, to achieve total solidarity with its members: peasants, workers, the masses.[42] To fail in this endeavor is to fall into the class that has no being; counter-revolutionary, enemy of the people, saboteur. Thus Mao writes,

"Revolutionary war is an anti-toxin which not only eliminates the enemy's poison but also purges us of our own filth."[43]

The creation of a subhuman class has no end outside itself. Indeed, the liquidation of classes is often destructive to the fragile economic life of newly established revolutionary societies since the classes having technical knowledge are often the first to be eliminated.[44] Thus Solzhenitsyn writes about the building of the White Sea Baltic Canal in which a quarter of a million men were lost:

> In 1934 . . . there was already a project for reconstructing it. Because of that *time limit* [Stalin] imposed upon its completion, because of those norms [of production], they not only cheated on the depth but reduced the tonnage capacity. . . . And what had they to haul on it anyway—and where? They had cut down all the nearby timber. . . . For half the year the canal is frozen anyhow, maybe more. So what was it needed for anyway?[45]

Similarly, Primo Levi, speaking of the Buna factory which was to have produced synthetic rubber for the German war effort and which was manned by forty thousand slave laborers, comments: "The Buna factory upon which the Germans were busy for four years and for which countless of us suffered and died, never produced a pound of synthetic rubber."[46]

One reason for the lack of productivity is the refusal in many cases to use technologically efficient production procedures. This is partly the result of the penal aims of the system, either to correct or to liquidate the slave population. But, more important, the death-world is a remythologizing response to the technological society and, as such, resists the use of means derived from the alienated world from which it arises. I have already alluded to the archaic technologies of the death-world as a mockery of the authenticity of handmade things. But this retrograde technology (which is essentially self-destructive) is, nevertheless, intended to create up-to-date results. The death-world resists technological society and at the same time derives its alleged raison d'être, economic productivity, from it. Thus, speaking once more of the building of the White Sea Baltic Canal with wheelbarrow and pick, Solzhenitsyn writes: "The very grandeur of this construction project consisted in the fact that it was carried out without contemporary technology and equipment and without any supplies from the nation as a whole! 'These are not the tempos of noxious European-American capitalism these are Socialist tempos! . . . Our own industry at the canal' [a Soviet account boasts]." Similarly, a Chinese Protestant minister sentenced in 1957 to *laodang gaizao*, "reform through labor," reports: "In a labor camp near the city of Datong in Shanxi province in Northern China . . . he had worked in a coal mine, along with ten thousand other prisoners scraping up chunks of black rock with his bare hands for 23 years."[48] The immediate aim of slave labor has little to do with efforts at modernization or economic growth. Instead, an apparatus of terror is created to achieve unconditional and unswerving loyalty to the state. The hidden force of Zeno's paradox as the operative logic borne as a phantasm by the sorting myth must, in the end, divert all other purposes to one single purpose: ideological purity. Ideological enemies must be relegated to the penal colonies of the death-world.

War and the Death Event   *T*HE DEATH EVENT IS FAR WIDER than the death-world. In the definition of the death event are included modern war together with such ancillary phenomena as expatriation of populations, man-made famine, the effects of chemical defoliation, and so on. Since war is one of man's oldest activities it is important to distinguish the phenomenon of contemporary warfare as it is expressed in the death event from preceding kinds of wars.

In Western political philosophy, war—whether or not it is seen as inevitable or ultimately eliminable—has these defining characteristics: First, it has a temporal structure and is thus a limited phenomenon, marked by the start and conclusion of hostilities. Although wars may have roots that antedate the first skirmishes marking their beginnings and we cannot always locate the first and last battles of wars, the duration of wars is generally well defined. Second, the end of any given war is peace. Third, wars have invariably aimed at the death of the enemy. But the phenomenon of war has traditionally been circumscribed in time, purpose, and lethal result.

Both the epic and philosophical traditions of ancient Greece maintain the point of view that war is limited. But war is also seen as natural. The gods themselves engage in warfare, both inciting the warring forces and participating in the battle. Thus Homer: "So the blessed gods rallied the opposing forces, forced them together, and opened up strong strife among themselves."[49] For the human adversaries, an honorable death in battle assures immortality, the preservation in cultural memory of one's heroic deeds. While war provides the opportunity for the exhibition of heroic virtues, valor and cunning, its depredations are also lamented, thus maintaining its limited character. A more unambiguously martial standpoint is exhibited in the fragments of Heraclitus, in which war belongs to the order of nature itself; it is "the father of all and the king of all." Without war nothing would exist, for it is through strife that things come into being and pass away. The present order can be explained only as the result of eternal strife. Even Plato, who rejects the Heraclitean philosophy of becoming, understands the necessity for war in the arena of politics. Moreover, if wars can be expected to occur the state should anticipate them and—like Sparta—prepare itself for attack. Of course foreign aggression is less likely if no economic motive exists which would make conquest attractive. Thus it is necessary to avoid the growth of the luxurious state which nurtures injustice internally while inviting attack from the outside.[50] But the heroic virtues extolled in the epic tradition are retained in the Platonic state, for death in battle is to be honored if it helps to preserve a polity in which virtue can be cultivated.[51] For Plato courage is to be praised— this is the source of the authenticity paradigm—but death is not loved for its own sake.

The Israelite tradition of warfare reflects elements common to the Greek epic tradition, but aspects of the Israelite view are unique and have become part of the controlling framework in which war has been conceived in later Western thought. This difference stems from the covenant relation of the Israelites to Yahweh. Yahweh is the God of Israel; the Israelites are his people. Victory in battle depends upon the support of Yahweh. To be sure, the Lord is a warrior. The Ark brought to the field of battle attests the presence of God in the midst of the fighting (Samuel 4:1–11). But victory is the result not only of the Israelites' prowess in arms but also of their obedience to the word of God. Since God demands moral as well as heroic acts, victory in battle is linked to ethical as well as heroic virtues.[52] Thus war itself is

both valued and decried. God prevents David from "building a rest-
ing place for the ark of the covenant of the Lord" because David is
a man of war. An even stronger revulsion against the martial tradition
manifests itself in the writings of the prophets. Firm advocacy of
peace together with the depiction of the god who will put an end to
war dominates the visions of Isaiah, Hosea, and Micah. Thus in an
oracle contained in *Hosea* 2:18, the Lord promises: "I will break bow
and sword and weapon of war and sweep them off the earth, so that
all living creatures may lie down without fear." Peace, not the mere
cessation of hostilities but a new condition of human wholeness, is
envisioned as the end of war.[53]

This later Israelite view plays an important role in the formation
of the Christian understanding of war. The Gospels indicate that
Jesus rejects political power as a temptation of Satan: "All those who
take the sword shall perish by the sword." This conception never
ceases to play a role in the Christian understanding of war, although
it is modified in the early Christian apologetic tradition to allow for
the just war.[54] Three elements must be present if a war is to be just:
It must be taken up for a just cause, a formal declaration of war by a
constituted authority is required, and the war must be justly conducted.[55] In early use, the doctrine is applied to non-Christians and
to the pre-Christian period but, once the fortunes of the Church are
linked to those of Empire, it is applied to Christians. Life is com-
partmentalized: the laity can remain Christian while engaging in just
wars but the clergy are to adhere strictly to original Christian teaching.[56] This position, taken up by Ambrose and fully elaborated by
Augustine, is definitive for later conceptions of the just war. For
Augustine, war is a part of life in the earthly city: "There is one war
after another, havoc everywhere, tremendous slaughterings of
men."[57] But if war is seen as at least potentially global, its temporal
duration is finite, and the end for which it is fought is peace. Since
peace is a natural human desire, "it is not that they [the violators of
peace] love peace less, but that they love their kind of peace more."[58]
For Augustine, order constitutes the fundamental ground of existence. Without order organic life would cease to be. Peace is the
natural, "true" condition of society, war its disruption: "This does
not mean that war as war involves peace; but war insofar as those
who waged it or have it waged upon them are beings with organic

natures, involves peace—for the simple reason that to be organic means to be ordered and therefore to be, in some sense, at peace."[59] War may be a chronic aspect of the human condition, because human desires cannot all be sated, but peace is always its terminus ad quem. This perspective is clearly formulated in Aquinas: the pacifist message of the New Testament does not apply to those in public authority who undertake war in a just cause for a just end. Still, the notion that peace is the natural end of man is crucial to Aquinas' argument.[60] Although kings have the duty of defending the state, war is an unnatural condition and must end in peace. Vital to the just war arguments of the Middle Ages is the notion that war is an evil to be undertaken as a last resort if all other methods of resolving disputes fail, and that peace is to be incorporated in the conditions of war as its only possible end.

Enlightenment thought about war retains this point of view. Although Hobbes sees the human condition in the state of nature as the war of every man against every man, as soon as we reflect upon the jeopardy in which this places life, reason declares as a general rule, "Every man ought to endeavor peace, as far as he has hope of obtaining it" and may resort to war only when he "cannot obtain it."[61] Similarly for Locke, "peace and tranquillity [are] the business of government and the end of Humane Society."[62] In the political philosophy of Kant the realization that peace is difficult to achieve and that it is urgently required is brought to a head. For Kant, war is a global phenomenon, not only because the potential for violence exists everywhere, but because the violation of rights in any given place has a ripple effect. Thus peace must be established everywhere if it is to prevail anywhere.[63] Although for Kant the state of peace is not natural to man but must be established, the idea of perpetual peace is a necessary concept whose actualization is guaranteed by Providence.[64] Nature allies itself with human passions so that peace will be the result. This consummation is the end of a long process the temporal duration of which cannot be predicted with certainty, but it is enough to apprehend the concept in order to see that working for perpetual peace is a duty.

The main strand of this long tradition shows war to be understandable in terms of conflicting interests. These are resolved by means of violent confrontation whose aim is to alter the balance of power by eliminating threats to, or by transforming, existing power structures. In either case, war is seen—theoretically at least—to aim at the cessation of hostilities.

But World War I and wars conducted thereafter have operated under a quite different set of assumptions.[65] To be sure, the alleged purpose of war remains the resolution of a dispute, a resolution which may result in such changes as the alteration of territorial lines, the conquest of a people, or a change in the structure of government within an already existing state. But the character of warfare itself overwhelms these alleged aims: the line between the old conception of war and the new reality—full-scale modern warfare—is blurred, if not obliterated. The aim of World War I was for each side to deprive the enemy of its army. There is only imagined leadership since the aim of battle is almost exclusively the mass destruction of persons rather than the development either of tactical genius on the field of battle or of traditional military relationships. The creation of sophisticated weapon systems and their efficient deployment determine results.[66] To be sure, the aims of modern war have been expressed in the language of traditional war: to procure the enemy's surrender in order to make peace on the victor's terms. But the full deployment of contemporary weapons creates a situation in which the semblance of conventional war, one that might render its aims viable, can no longer be maintained. The actual strategies of modern war express the logic of Zeno's paradox: the assumption that there exists an infinite and inexhaustible reservoir of persons to be consumed without end. The concentration and slave labor camps of the death-world do not exist in isolation but are related to the phenomenon of war, which is still under the aegis of the old understanding of the purposes of war. These older purposes may then be used to legitimize the unlimited destruction of persons by these new means. It could be argued that traditional wars too permitted violence to leach into adjacent territories. Thus Augustine comments, "Massacres frequent and sweeping, hardships too dire to endure are but part of the ravages of war."[67] But these ravages are ancillary phenomena, not primary manifestations of the conflict. In addition, premodern wars provide paradigms deriving from a more or less unitary heroic tradition which enables human beings at least to imagine a measure of responsibility for their own deaths: acts of heroism, the display of tactical intelligence, martyrdom. These values are reflected in the authenticity paradigm. But in contemporary war, as well as in the death-world, adversary lines are drawn between complex bureaucratic structures which control the technologies of man-made mass death and those who lack effective counterforce. Many who died in recent wars and almost all who died in the death-world never participated in the events which resulted in their own deaths. Victims, divested of personal identity, they enter the ranks of the numberless dead.[68] The heroic ideal rests on the concept of the worthy adversary, whereas the pragmatic view of war supports economic, political, and military advantage or the defense of existing structures as the legitimate aims of war. But in the death event victims take on a mythic negative identity that conforms exclusively to the ideological needs of the death machine.[69]

History and the A Priori HOW DOES THE EMERGENCE OF the death event, including war and related phenomena, as well as the death-world, affect present historical existence? Does the knowledge of the death event enter into experience as day-to-day information, in the shape of facts, or does the existence of the death event overflow individual occurrences and impinge upon the structures of intelligibility in a manner which has hitherto gone unnoticed? Is it possible that the existence of the death event constitutes a new historical a priori, a new grid that determines further experience? If so, how can we account for the emergence of an a priori that is temporally determined, and is a temporally determined a priori not a contradiction in terms? I have already suggested that once the death event comes into existence it becomes a residue of an irrevocable past without which the present is incomprehensible. Perhaps this is merely a property of all historical facts. But if not, the death event must be more than a collocation of facts; it must be a specifiably unique meaning constellation which, once grasped, casts light on otherwise incomprehensible aspects of existence. In the context of these questions it is of no small interest to consider Kant's view of the a priori and how it is modified in subsequent philosophical discourse.

The distinction between a priori knowledge—knowledge derived independently of sense experience—and a posteriori knowledge—knowledge which abstracts and generalizes from the particulars of sense—is well fixed before it becomes the focal point for the epistemological problematic in Kant's thought. Indeed, it would seem that these two types of knowledge exhaustively cover the totality of what can be known.

But Kant focuses on this distinction in order to consider a central question for his thought: how can we know that the conceptual order of our minds, an order independent of experience, is applicable to reality? [70] To be sure, we can distinguish between sense objects, which are apprehended through perception, and concepts, which are objects of thought and grasped through the understanding. But if we are to claim certainty for our empirical knowledge, the mind must be shown to impose its concepts upon matters of fact, that there are grounds for the peculiar fit between the conceptual order and the order of the world. To gain a conceptual hold on the world it must be established that, although a priori concepts are not derived from experience, they are nevertheless applicable to it.

The distinction between the conceptual order and the order of the world is incorporated in the language in which our concepts are framed. This language is made up of propositions which are uttered by someone or, as Kant calls them, "judgments." These propositions are of two types: first, analytic propositions, the truth or falsity of which depends upon the relations of the concepts of the judgment or proposition as determined by the laws of contradiction; and second, synthetic judgments or propositions, in which the predicate adds something new to the meaning of the subject rather than merely elucidating it. The content of analytic propositions is a priori, whereas that of synthetic propositions is derived from experience and is a posteriori. But Kant tries to show that there are still other sorts of propositions, the truth or falsity of which does not depend upon the logical relations of their constitutive concepts: synthetic a priori propositions. These are known without recourse to experience, although they make objective experience possible. A proposition such as "every event has a cause" is an example. [71]

There are a priori elements not only in thinking but also' at the most primitive levels of experience, in perception itself. These elements are in fact the organizing forms of perception. Thus time and space are the forms of sense, the grid through which our percepts are as they are. At the other end of the spectrum are the ideas, whose generality neither derives from nor is applicable to sense. The use of the ideas is governed by the faculty of reason, which has a theoretical aspect that establishes the foundations of science, and a practical side, which applies to the realm of morals.

Those of Kant's intellectual heirs who continue to insist on the a priori features of thought (roughly) as I have described them, think that these features provide the key to placing the possibility of the knowledge of phenomena on a secure foundation. This point of view leads to the elevation of mathematics and the physical sciences as paradigmatic cognitive structures.[72] Any conceptual entity which fails to meet the stringent criteria of these disciplines is seen as something less than knowledge. Eventually not only metaphysics but all nonscientific thought is assigned less than cognitive status.[73]

Yet Kant's own thinking offers clues which lead to a departure from this rigid interpretation of the a priori. Once it is recognized that this concept of the a priori, seemingly so fruitful for grounding physical science, is inapplicable to beauty and natural form, the way is prepared to develop a quite different conception of experiencing. In the *Critique of Judgment*, Kant stresses that the free play of the imagination is necessary for a grasp of natural and aesthetic objects. They, unlike the phenomena apprehended by natural science, should be interpreted as purposive wholes, opening the way for a philosophy of forms. The cultural world—languages, myth, religion, art— must be grasped in terms of teleological structure. It is a short step from this new understanding of aesthetic and natural wholes to a quite different type of analysis of experience in which the a priori can itself become some element of form.[74]

Such a transformation can only be fully realized through the radical historization of reason by means of an analysis of its relation to cultural products. This is the achievement of Hegel. Once the structure of reason is radically altered by its "fall" into temporal process, the break with a strictly formal conception of reason makes possible the development of a phenomenology of cultural forms. This is the direction taken in the neo-Kantian philosophy of Ernst Cassirer.

Like Kant, Cassirer departs from the Platonic conception of form as an independent ideal entity and from Aristotle's interpretation of form as pattern abstracted from the given. Instead, form is applicable to and constitutive of sensuous content: the form realizes itself in phenomena and becomes a concrete constituent of the appearances. But now the images of perception are transformed into symbols which mediate sensuous content and concept. Symbols are not merely a mark of something given, but a transformation of some sensuous element. Each cultural form is a function of the symbol-making power of consciousness. A hierarchy of forms embraces the richly nuanced expressions of cultural life in which mathematics and science, though privileged expressions of form, become part of an irreducible diversity, a multiplicity of forms.

It would seem that the historical actualization of forms, their expression as cultural life, would be particularly useful for an inter-pretation of the death event as a new historical a priori. To be sure, nothing rules out on principle an analysis of the death event as a new cultural form. But Cassirer's position is insufficiently radical for a genuine understanding of the death event, for he fails to see the significance of the power of the negative in culture which Hegel is able to grasp. (Heidegger picks up this thread in Hegel's thought while shifting its locus to the existential analytic of Dasein, the tem-poral manner in which existence unfolds for a being who is com-pletely historical.) Although death functions as the trigger for myth-ological consciousness in Cassirer's thought, myth is seen as a construct used in the denial of death.[75] Thus culture becomes the vehicle for man's immortality. Of course Cassirer could see that cul-ture might come to an end, but that death could become the prius for the foundation of culture, as well as culture's final achievement is unimaginable in the context of his philosophy of forms. The neo-Kantian vision of the world loses sight of the apocalyptic root of culture.

There is still a significant advantage in the philosophy of form from our point of view. The a priori no longer belongs exclusively to the subject but is now a cultural achievement to be given concrete expression in the world. The a priori can be seen not merely as the grid through which the world is apprehended but as belonging to objective meaning constellations as their constant features.[76] Science and mathematics too are seen as open-ended, part of the fluid world of cultural forms, rather than as closed systems reflecting fixed a priori structures of thought. We can now imagine a system of forms as nexuses of meaning coming into existence and passing away, the dynamic interplay of possibilities potentially present in the subject and actualized in culture. The subject is no longer a cognition monad. Instead, the subject can be imagined as a corporeal and cultural existent, a node of activity engaged in a field of primordial bodily, as well as cultural, meanings.

The understanding of the a priori as a system of historically conditioned significations is also an essential insight of modern pragmatism. Pragmatists acknowledge that our world-apprehending acts depend upon basic patterns of thought, deep-seated attitudes which we hold as the constancies in our total cultural experience. Yet new experiences continually modify these attitudes: pragmatism is committed to the dynamic character of experience.[77] To this extent, the distinction between the fluid but still a priori elements of experience and empirical generalizations is particularly significant. According to C. I. Lewis, a priori patterns of experience, unlike empirical generalizations, do not determine the content of experience and no experience can render them invalid. But on the other hand they can and do change when they no longer articulate the *context* of our total experience.[78] It could be argued that this point of view represents a covert rejection of permanent structures in experience. But C. I. Lewis points out that the real difference between a priori concepts and empirical generalizations is that we can show empirical generalizations to be false while a priori concepts can never be disproved by experience. They are a priori because, as conditions of subjectivity, they impose no restrictions upon experience. Yet they are subject to change when they can no longer serve to explicate the context of experience.

Philosophies of language also recognize that there are relatively permanent features of experience which are reflected in the structure of language. Ludwig Wittgenstein reaches for a new grammar of experience which will reflect these constancies without openly reverting to the Kantian notion of the a priori. Turning to propositional structure for a grasp of these constants, Wittgenstein claims that there are propositions which lie halfway between empirical and logical propositions. Unlike standard empirical propositions, their truth is not open to doubt. We can imagine any empirical proposition as false, but these special propositions cannot be thought false, since to do so would be to demolish the framework within which truth and falsity can emerge. Their contradictories cannot be imagined as making sense. Consider for instance the odd consequences entailed in denying the statement that the earth existed for many years.[79] Such propositions stand fast for us; they function as "hinges" upon which our actions depend. To deny them is madness of a sort; to affirm them enhances our confidence in the order of things.

If we turn to the death event with this structure in mind we can imagine some one of its aspects framed as a proposition that stands fast for us. "Nuclear weapons can destroy all living things." More than an empirical generalization, it establishes a frame of reference: the possible destruction of the world. But far from providing a stable context, its implications are profoundly unsettling. Unlike other propositions that stand fast for us, it precludes the possibility of any secure framework for experience.

Analysis of the changing conceptions of the a priori reveals that a viable conception of the a priori as permanent mental structure has come to mean the actual contextual grid shaping our experiences. This contextual totality is itself subject to change if historical forces radically undermine it.[80] Whether interpreted as generating new propositions that stand fast for us or as a new mode of articulating the background of experience, the death event must be viewed in this light.

The death-world poses a challenge to the authenticity paradigm by altering the character of the life-world and attaching death as a phantasm to all signification. Now we turn from an aspect of the death event, the death-world, to a far wider collocation of forms that constitute it as well as to the logical structure it expresses. The logic of the death event follows a type of reason developed in Zeno's paradoxes. Zeno holds that if Being is multiple, we can imagine it, on analogy with a line, as divisible into an infinite number of parts. There need be no limit to the process of division itself. And we can never run out of parts because any segment is always subject to further division. A part, no matter how small, never shades off into what has no spatial magnitude at all: the number of parts having magnitude is inexhaustible. This understanding of the relation of whole to part is expressed in the death event as the hypothesis that the world's supply of people is unlimited. Zeno's paradoxes highlight what the Eleatics claim cannot be thought: nonbeing. The death event expresses this structure in the form of radical annihilation.

In the case of the death event this logic is static and requires the propulsive force of a generative or sorting myth, a principle which determines how a group of people is to be divided. Two principal sorting myths dominate the death event: the myths of race and of ideology. These criteria have been ontologically interpreted: a rationale for distinguishing fullness of being from sheer nullity is provided in conformity with the sorting myths. The roots of these ontologized principles of purity are traced to an understanding of the world found in apocalyptic and gnostic literature.

It is all too easy to attribute this logical and mythic structure to the death-world, a dramatic flash point in the larger death event, without recognizing that it also functions in other forms of manmade mass death, for example, in war. Thus the true character of contemporary wars is covered over. All wars seem continuous, having the same ends and altering only in scale. But in fact, scale is the result of a new emphasis upon the annihilation of persons as an end in itself. This sets contemporary war apart from preceding wars, which were governed by values deriving from the heroic tradition and from just war theories.

This account of the death event, which now includes war, does not purport to be historical in the sense that a given set of facts supports an empirical generalization. At the same time the death event is involved in temporal process. Although there is an empirical fundament that requires historical study, the death event constitutes a new grid through which all experiencing now takes place, a new historical a priori amenable to phenomenological analysis. Since the idea of the a priori traditionally refers to the permanent unchanging structures of cognition, it is important to show the plausibility of the notion of a historicized a priori by examining recent revisions of this conception. The neo-Kantian philosophy of Ernst Cassirer interprets the a priori as the structure of forms expressed by a symbol-making consciousness; pragmatism, so far as it recognizes the possibility of a priori elements in experience, sees these as subject to change in conformity with the openness of cognition and modifications in the enterprise of science; phenomenological thinkers stress the culture and the lived body as the horizons of experience, whereas Wittgenstein speaks of propositions that stand fast for us, quasi-empirical propositions that highlight the taken-for-granted context in which meanings arise. This loosening of the a priori enable us to see the death event, not as a string of facts that together form the basis for historical generalization, but as a structural alteration in the character of all experiencing which has crept up on us without our realizing it.

III / Hegel and the Crises of Cognition

But when from a long distant past nothing subsists,
after the people are dead, after the things are broken
and scattered, still, alone, more fragile, but with more
vitality, more unsubstantial, more persistent, more
faithful, the smell and taste of things remain poised
a long time, like souls, ready to remind us, waiting
and hoping for their moment, amid the ruins of all the
rest; and bear unfaltering, in the tiny and almost
impalpable drop of their essence, the vast structure of
recollection.

—*Marcel Proust*

*T*HE DEATH EVENT WITH ITS VOR-
tex at the death-world seems to
have established once and for all the radical incommensurability of
reason and history. Yet the adequacy of reason to historical actuality
is a basic premise of Hegel's system. Why then should we look to the
philosophy of Hegel for insight into the meaning of man-made mass
death? What is living in the philosophy of Hegel, what speaks to us
as fresh and vital, is not his uncanny insight into such isolated pre-
cursors of the death event as the bloody aftermath of the French
Revolution but his recognition that the structure of Reason does not
somehow float above historical experience. This is true even if there
are grounds to doubt the converse, that the events of history can
somehow be deduced from Reason. The reciprocal relation between
historical actuality and critical intelligence results in Hegel's enlarged
conception of Reason, the entry into philosophical discourse of the
temporal succession of events so that, as John Dewey once noted,
"the here and now of life" is included in this historically nourished
rationality.

For Hegel, events *are* the fleshing out of the Idea in time, the self-
externalization or othering of Spirit or self-conscious mind as the
becoming of history.[1] The urge toward the reconciliation of critical

intelligence and historical experience is the dynamic of history, and history is the theater of this reconciliation.[2] Thus Hegel's own system allows for no lacunae in history, no dysteleological phenomena which remain outside the historical process. No wonder Benjamin Paul Blood is cited by William James as saying, "Contingency forbids any inevitable history, and conclusions are absurd. Nothing in Hegel has kept the planet from being blown to pieces."[3] It would seem therefore that, had he known of it, the death event of the twentieth century would have appeared to Hegel as merely another form in the series of moments that make up the history of Spirit, "the Bacchanalian revel in which no member is not drunk." Such at least is the intepretation Hegel gave to the limited phenomena of violence and destruction which belonged to his own experience.

Of course the possible destruction of all organic life by the newly developed lethal technologies of the present lay outside Hegel's ken. Even if he should have envisaged this possibility, on the grounds, as some would argue, that he believed historical events can be deduced from a priori principles, he did not. What is striking is not Hegel's failure to foresee the full range of phenomena included in contemporary man-made mass death but rather the extent to which Hegel's vision is useful in penetrating the postmodern culture of mass death. Multiple meanings of death play a critical role in Hegel's system. Because death is the existential expression of the prodigious power of the negative which does the work of Spirit, Hegel is able to glimpse aspects of postmodern thought forms that permitted the emergence of the culture of necropolis.

The purpose of the present chapter is to explore the meaning of negation in Hegel's system from a cognitive standpoint. I shall first consider the meaning of evil in Hegel, a phenomenon he interprets at least in part as a problem of cognition. I shall then assess Hegel's interpretation of the philosophy of reflection or analytic reason which, on the face of it, may seem far removed from the theme of the death event. But the philosophy of reflection is crucial for my analysis, since it opens up the logic of technique, thus foredisclosing the ethos of the technological society. I shall also examine the relationship between time and eternity in Hegel's thought, which provides unexpected resources for understanding how time is experienced in the death event.

Death and Spirit *D*EATH IS A BIOLOGICAL CIRCUM-
stance which man transforms into
an event of Spirit. Mere biological death, "which the individual *as
such* attains is [only] *pure being, death*; it is a state which has been
reached *immediately*, in the *course of Nature*." Such a death is "not the
result of an action *consciously done*"; it is a mere ceasing to be.[4]

But not only individuals die. Death also inheres in the historical
process, as cultures are organic entities which rise, flourish, and disappear when they become moribund. Death renders existentially explicit the inner conflicts potentially present in a moment of Spirit's
history. Through death, a cultural episode which can be canceled, is
canceled, allowing the work of spirit to proceed without becoming
stultified through repetition or endlessly sinking back into some immediate and, therefore naive expression of culture. But death does
not merely annul a decaying historical moment; it forces Spirit into
itself. This interiorization or self-reflection opens up a new dimension of conscious life which generates further activity and novel pro-
ductions of Spirit.[5]

Until now I have used the key term "Spirit" (*Geist*) without further
elaboration. It is impossible to do justice to the multifacted interpretations of Spirit in Hegel's thought within the scope of this book,
but some notion of its function in his system is crucial for understanding the phenomena generated by Spirit's negative acts. In a
representative passage which remains cryptic and elusive even for
Hegel, he states:

> That the True is the actual only as system, or that Substance is
> essentially Subject, is expressed in the representation of the Ab-
> solute as Spirit—the most sublime Notion and the one which
> belongs to the modern age and its religion. The spiritual alone
> is the *actual*; it is essence, or that which has *being in itself*; it is
> that which *relates itself to itself* and is *determinate*, it is *other-being*
> and *being-for-self*, and in this determinateness, or in its self-
> externality, abides within itself; in other words, it is in *and for
> itself.* (*Phen* 25, p. 14)

Spirit is both subject and object, a mobile and active oscillation
which is now one, now the other. When it *others* or alienates itself,
this externalization (*Entausserung*) is something finite, determinate,

and actual, yet Spirit remains what it is despite this alienated content. As a pattern of activity, Spirit relates what has been alienated from itself back to itself and is transformed as a result. Spirit enters into this process in order to bring out in its dynamic unfolding what is already implicit in Spirit. Yet Spirit does not transcend its activity, since Spirit *is* this alternation of motion and repose, the very process itself, as well as the aporias of consciousness created by its activities, and the breaching of those activities.

Spirit is not to be confused with the individual knower, the I, since for Hegel the personal subject is capable of eliciting only universals and therefore remains abstract. This point requires some explanation since the I familiar to common sense is the individual subject of experience, the unique existent, myself, with my personal quirks and habits. But for Hegel the term "I" refers to the power of intellect which abstracts universal meanings or the structure of the object from the conglomerate of experience. This meaning can be traced to the Cartesian *cogito*, "a substance whose whole essence or nature is to think" and which requires no place and depends on nothing material.[6] Kant transforms the Cartesian cogito into a formal and transcendental principle of unity, formal because it does not refer to a particular object or soul substance, and transcendental because this is required if its manifold representations are to belong to a single conscious stream. But, because Kant's transcendental "I think" abstracts from the content of consciousness, it remains, according to Hegel, an empty universal.[7] Hegel's own concept of Spirit absorbs the transpersonal dimension of the transcendental ego but does not make the mistake of separating thought from the concrete content of thinking.[8]

As a suprapersonal subject, Spirit expresses intersubjective meanings. Thus not only does Spirit attain the certainty of its object, but it also widens its field of inclusivity to encompass all historical experience. Spirit is free to roam over its past, to write it into a *Bildungsroman* whose subject is Spirit's transpersonal interiority, and to mull ceaselessly over this history. If Hegel's *Phenomenology* is in fact the autobiography of Spirit written from the privileged perspective of Hegel's own present, it is in a sense written pseudonymously, since it is not Hegel but the *viva vox* of Spirit which recounts its own story, "the I which is we and the we which is I."[9]

No analogy could do justice to the historical comprehensiveness of Spirit since its ultimate meaning lies in its being beyond representation. Still, it is possible to reach for an image of its structure. Proust's novel *Swann's Way* offers as fitting a metaphor as any for the pattern of the life of Spirit. The celebrated magic lantern given to the narrator in childhood can go proxy for Spirit's activity so long as we do not identify the lantern's beam of light with Spirit itself but remember that Spirit includes both the beam and the palimpsest of archaic and present images revealed in its light.

Thus Proust remembers:

> Someone had the happy idea of giving me . . . a magic lantern . . . in the manner of the master-builders and glass-painters of gothic days it substituted for the opaqueness of my walls an impalpable iridescence, supernatural phenomena of many colours, in which legends were depicted, as on a shifting and transitory window. But my sorrows were increased because this change of lighting destroyed as nothing else could have done, the customary impression I had formed of my room, thanks to which the room itself . . . had become quite endurable. For now I no longer recognized it, and I became uneasy, as though I were in a room in some hotel or furnished lodging where I had just arrived by train for the first time.[10]

Similarly, the life of the philosopher who has reached a vision of Spirit's full journey is expanded and transformed by his grasp of the whole.

Evil

*H*EGEL'S VIEW THAT EVIL IS OVER-come in the life of the Absolute is belied by twentieth century atrocities. Criticism of his denial of evil is fully justified, but it should not blind us to the power and depth of his grasp of the problem.

Hegel's optimism is connected to his view of religion's place in the life of the Absolute. Religion is Spirit's relation to the Absolute expressed in images or representations. The highest form of religious consciousness is revealed religion even if it is only the penultimate shape of Spirit itself because revealed religion is superseded by Absolute Knowledge. Hegel fails to see a crucial paradox generated by the transition from revealed religion to the final moment in Spirit's journey. It remains for his successors, Kierkegaard in particular, to bring out the full implications of the incompatible claims of revealed religion and Absolute Knowledge.[11] Hegel never ponders the fact that the consciousness of revealed religion considers itself final and unsurpassable. It represents itself to itself as that which cannot be superseded because it rests its case on the promises of the New Testament. Not only is the content of German Protestantism (the last pictorial form of revealed religion) eternal in its own eyes, but the form, from its standpoint, is also final. Either Absolute Knowledge must accept its own content, the faith claims of revealed religion, and thus cease to be knowledge, or New Testament faith itself is not merely pictorial as Absolute Knowledge alleges but a form of religion that is never superseded.[12] In that case Christian faith claims, and not knowledge, would be form and content of the last phase of Spirit's life. The fact that faith is the content of Spirit's *last* moment is important, since as such it cannot be sublated. Since Hegel thinks the phenomenon of evil belongs to this phase, evil will, like revealed religion, be overcome in the life of the Absolute.[13]

For Hegel, evil is a primordial expression of negation within religious consciousness prior to its transformation into Absolute Knowledge. Departing from the commonsense view of evil as something positive, a complex of undesirable doings or happenings which have independent existence, Hegel sees evil as annulling an unmediated unity and therefore as able to enrich the life of Spirit. Having defined evil as a form of negation, Hegel is driven to interpret it privatively as part of the speculative self-movement of thought.[14] Yet at the same time Hegel modifies this neo-Platonic reading of evil as nonbeing by depriving evil of its static character: evil is an activity of Spirit.

In *Lectures on the Philosophy of Religion*, Hegel develops the idea of evil in terms of the dialectical tension between God and world. For the worshipping consciousness of revealed religion, the Absolute is the object, yet the Absolute is thinkable only in terms of its opposite, the world, which appears as God's "garment, vesture, form or as something in contrast with Himself."[15] Once the world is released into independent being, the possibility arises of a purely cataclysmic negation of the world. Cosmic destruction over and against the sheer positivity of the being of the world is expressed as cosmic evil.[16]

This destructive force can acquire self-consciousness by linking itself to finite consciousness. In this case it appears as evil will, a split in the unity of will.[17] Individual religious consciousness has the power to overcome this psychic rift by imagining the infinitude of consciousness itself, a moment of "isolation" or "seclusion" of Spirit. Spared the vicissitudes of the world, this secluded form of Spirit avoids the disunity of a living will; thus evil is overcome in the idea of the immortality of the soul in which change can no longer affect the self. Endless existence in time is the pictorial expression of the self-reconciliation of an anguished consciousness. Wounded by its experience of the rift in God's nature—the othering of God as world—religious consciousness now attributes to itself the unity first imagined to belong to God, at the same time representing evil as self-separation, a disunity of psychic being.[18]

The expression of an evil will, from the standpoint of revealed religion, is sin. Only a being who both is the culmination of nature and reaches beyond it has the capacity for sin. But why should Spirit require the existence of a potentially sinning being or, in more familiar theological language, why should God need man, who is such a being? The finite human being is needed by the Absolute Idea so that it can manifest itself.[19] Man is the being through whom the truth of the Absolute Idea as Spirit comes into being. Human subjectivity exists as the need for truth. Thus the capacity for evil and the potential for truth belong together by necessity. Alienated from itself since it does not possess this truth, the subject lives in untruth and is split into good—the undivided unity of personality—and evil. So far as particular individuals are concerned, this dual nature remains since the natural being of man is ineradicable. Hegel's retention of the distinction between natural being and Spirit poses a difficulty for his idealistic metaphysics. But the difficulty vanishes if this distinction is seen as a tension within Spirit, experienced dialectically as the resistance of the real to the Concept.[20]

Hegel stresses the dual nature of man in the development of his philosophical anthropology. "What is meant by man," Hegel claims, "is a being who sets himself in opposition to his immediate nature, to his state of being in himself, and reaches a state of separation" (*PhRel* 3:47). For Hegel, the constitutive act which enables man to pass from purely animal existence to a human condition also creates him as a divided being with the potential for evil. One might of course argue, as does Nietzsche, that man is a transitional being who will be superseded, and that the overcoming of his duality rests on his recognition of himself as unhindered animal existence.[21] But so long as human existence is seen as a break with natural existence, the dialectical tension between Spirit and nature persists. Despite the work of Spirit, man as a natural being will be tempted to follow his passions and inclinations. When man's ends are animal ends, although he is no longer merely an animal, his acts are evil. "The primary condition of Man, which is superficially represented as a state of innocence, is the state of nature, the animal state. Man must be culpable; insofar as he is good, he must not be good as any natural thing is good, but his guilt, his will must come into play, it must be possible to impute moral acts to him. Guilt really means the possibility of imputation" (*PhRel* 3:48). What is required is that man should absolutely cease to be a natural being and natural will.

Since evil arises with the consciousness of Spirit, awareness of evil is intrinsic to evil itself. This is of paramount importance for Hegel. The knowledge of evil is a necessary condition for its expression. Indeed, Hegel goes even further to claim that knowledge in the most primordial sense is knowledge of evil. Hegel calls the knowledge which breaks into the original unity of man's being "reflection" (*Reflexion*), a structure of thought which persists and repatterns itself in various forms throughout the history of Spirit.

The mythological consciousness of revealed religion depicts the first act of reflective knowledge in the story of the Fall. Nowhere in Hegel's thought is the curious endorsement and reprobation of knowledge more evident than in the collision of innocence and reflection in the myth of the expulsion from paradise. Knowledge at once taints human nature and moves it forward in accordance with the Notion (*Begriff*), the goal of Spirit. In a passage reflecting this paradox, Hegel writes: "Knowledge as the disannulling of the unity of mere nature is the 'Fall' which is no casual conception but the eternal history of Spirit." This comment is followed by the striking observation that "the state of innocence, the paradisiacal condition, is that of the brute. Paradise is a park where only brutes, not men, can remain."[22] Natural will expresses itself in selfishness, in willing against the universal. This is the satanic dimension in man, hypostatized by Christian consciousness in the figure of Satan: "[Satan] as representing the Negative which wills itself is, because of this, self-identity, and must accordingly have the element of affirmation also in him, as he has in Milton, where his energy, which is full of character, makes him better than many an angel" (*PhRel* 3:49). Yet it is clear from this passage that human progress is envisioned as intertwined with the worst passions of man. In this sense Hegel's position continues in the tradition of Hobbes and Mandeville, except that the usual view of human depravity takes the contradictions in man's nature as ultimate, whereas Hegel offers a dialectical interpretation of these extremes.[23]

In the *Phenomenology*, Hegel attempts to resolve these contradictions by insisting that religious consciousness must unite with the moral spirit in the last phase of Spirit's development. The genuine self, Spirit, not only knows but also acts, "step[s] forth into existence" (*Phen* 796, p. 484). The withdrawal into self, the refusal to act, is, at this stage in the progress of religious consciousness, evil. Hegel appears to be criticizing the idea of that "beautiful soul," the pure religious interiority which cannot be the final phase of religious consciousness since it is not fleshed out in existence (*Phen* 665–69, pp. 403–07). For Hegel only Protestant Christianity has the capacity to inwardize the moral spirit so that the content of Christianity can be expressed in moral action and the diremptions of religious consciousness healed. But where evil persists, it is always signaled by a rent consciousness. As in Goethe's *Faust*, Hegel's paradigm for demonic presence—complexity of personality, anguish, and passion for power—are signs pointing to the presence of evil.[24] Evil is deeper, more itself, not because of the nature of the act committed or its consequences, but because act and consequence reflect the penetration of consciousness by negation.

From the standpoint of Hegel's analysis of religious consciousness, the death-world can only appear as a moment of naive immediacy, since it is precisely this dimension of self-reflective awareness that is absent in the consciousness responsible for ordering and implementing the massive annihilations of the twentieth century. Instead, the sense of evil expressed in feelings of guilt, a sense lacking in technological society, has been replaced by archaic traits of impurity, taint, and defilement. These traits are attributed by the sorting myths not to the apparatus of death and its agents but to the demonized other.[25] The victim's taint frees the agent of technological society for the work of the death-world. The representatives of the state can behave in accordance with the sanctions of the state without the feeling of torment which Hegel considers ingredient to all expressions of evil. It is this indifference of totalitarian man to suffering, this absence of a rift in consciousness—such that any act can easily slip into the structure of everyday life without disturbing its arrangement—that Hannah Arendt stresses in her analysis of the banality of evil. In considering the personality of Adolph Eichmann, Arendt observes:

> It would have been very comforting indeed to believe that Eichmann was a monster. . . . The trouble with Eichmann was precisely that so many were like him, and that the many were neither perverted nor sadistic, that they were, and still are terribly and terrifyingly normal. From the viewpoint of our legal institutions and of our moral standards of judgment this normality was much more terrifying than all the atrocities put together, for it implied—as had been said at Nuremburg over and over again by the defendants and their counsels—that this new type of criminal, who is in actual fact *hostis generis humani*, commits his crimes under circumstances that make it well-nigh impossible for him to know or feel that he is doing wrong.[26]

Arendt has grasped the absence of a rift in consciousness in the creators and implementers of the death-world, as well as the bureaucratization of the infliction of pain and death. She has also perceived the rational structure of the death world, which functions deductively on the basis of its own extraordinary mythicized premises.

But another aspect of the consciousness of the death-world is missing from Arendt's perspective: the world of myth placed in the service of power. Jean Amery writes:

Evil exceeds and overlays banality . . .[Arendt] knew Eichmann only from hearsay, saw him only through the glass cage . . . If one insists on it [my torturers] were only bureaucrats.

Yet they were, much much more. I saw it in their serious, tense faces, which were not swelling let us say, with sexual sadistic delight, but concentrated in murderous self-realization. With heart and soul they went about their business and the name of it was power, domain over spirit and flesh, orgy of unchecked expansion.[27]

Here too self-reflection is not, as Hegel alleges, a necessary condition of evil. Rather, the driving force of the death-world is pure power. The logic of Zeno's paradox, driven by the sorting myth, accounts for the exercise of power. According to the unconscious paradigm of the world of Amery's torturers, the reservoir of intended victims is imagined to be capable of infinite divisibility, and the power of the bureaucracy of the death-world is likewise imagined to increase exponentially as its victims are destroyed. The quanta of power can be made to grow infinitely by adding part on part, since the number of parts at one's disposal is seen as infinite.

For Hegel, once consciousness is born it is a for-itself (*Fürsichsein*); thus evil cannot be reduced to the expression of a natural force, as Nietzsche claims. Yet Amery interprets the structure of evil as the intention of consciousness to exist as *force*. Nietzsche's account of the will to power is instructive in this context. For Nietzsche the will to power is the basic form of affect from which all others are derived. The will to power exists as a striving to increase power. Every quantum of power desires only to grow stronger, since every center of force necessarily wills its own expansion. To be sure, when a quantum of power has been attained, pleasure ensues, but this pleasure is not power itself. The will to power is not the source of anything; it is not the cause of change but change itself.[28] Since power is inhibited by no proscriptions in the death-world, consciousness is not torn. Consciousness merely experiences a waxing and waning of power and imagines itself to derive this power from nature as its due, since it interprets relations of force as laws of nature. But for Hegel, power for its own sake, detached from its moorings in Reason, must in the end be sublated by the historical process.

Crime

*H*EGEL'S ACCOUNT OF EVIL IN THE *Lectures on the Philosophy of Religion* and the *Phenomenology* confines itself to a description of evil as a manifestation of reflection. The idea of crime belongs largely to the phenomenology of negation in its existential aspect, but the factor of reflection is also important to Hegel's theory of crime and punishment.

Hegel defines crime "as an initial act of coercion, as an exercise of force by the free agent . . . which infringes the existence of freedom in its concrete sense, infringes the right as right."[29] Crime is the refusal to honor the rights of any person in any regard whatsoever.[30] In contrast with civic wrong, the sphere of which is limited, crime attempts to set aside right as such but for Hegel, right is absolute and cannot be annulled. In this sense, "crime is in principle a nullity." Once this point is grasped, Hegel's celebrated definition of punishment as the annulment of crime, which may on the face of it seem absurd, can be seen to make sense. It is not the criminal act that is somehow erased by punishment. Instead, punishment which negates the crime is a negation of what is itself a negation, since crime— powerless to effect the extinction of rights—is itself a nullity. Crime may indeed do away with the existent object which embodies rights, but not with rights as such. The point is not the obvious fact that crime as an event has external reality, but that *qua* crime, it is the conscious purposeful intention of a criminal will. Punishment is also justified on the basis of an attribute of consciousness, in this case that of the criminal. The criminal is not "a harmful animal" who must be reformed or deterred but a rational being. He shows this when, by means of his actions, he makes freedom his own law—because even wrong acts express the principle of freedom. The state must vindicate the abstract rationality of the criminal will which accepts freedom as a universal principle (although of course not the crime) by exercising its own freedom. It does this by punishing him. The state "injures the injury" committed by the criminal (*PhR* 100–01, pp. 70–71).

For Hegel, an act guided by self-conscious awareness of a principle elevates its status; it is therefore preferable for the criminal not only to suffer punishment but also to interiorize the punishing authority. The sphere of law which embodies the principle of formal right is then raised to the sphere of morality.

Since crime infringes upon "right as right," Hegel takes a retributivist rather than a deterrence position on punishment. The issue for Hegel cannot be reform of the wrongdoer but "wrong and the matter of righting it" (*PhR* 99, p. 70). Hegel is careful to distinguish his position from "eye for an eye" retributivism since that leads to such reductio ad absurdum conclusions as justifying the punishment of theft with theft (*PhR* 101, p. 72). The annulment of the crime is retribution—the "injury of an injury"—but the two injuries are only implicitly equal. In actuality, making the punishment fit the crime is an infinite task. In Hegel's words: "In the field of the finite, absolute determinacy remains only a demand, a demand which the Understanding has to meet by continually increasing delimitation—a fact of the greatest importance—but which continues *ad infinitum* and which allows only of perennially approximate satisfaction" (*PhR* 101, p. 72).

Hegel's theory of punishment is based on the idea that the moral law violated in crime is rooted in the ethical life of a community. By establishing a context for the moral law in living institutions, Hegel hopes to remedy the detachment from actual life inherent in Kant's moral psychology. Kant pictures the moral life as a struggle between reason and inclination in which the actual will tosses helplessly between the moral law and the passions, because the will can only act rationally if inclination is suppressed. Hegel argues that reason split off from the wellspring of actual life is ineffective since it can issue imperatives but lacks the power to carry them out. If, on the other hand, a person obeys the rules of the community in which his life is bound up, as these are consolidated in a body of positive laws, he does not experience external constraints foreign to his own nature. Instead he feels his will is at one with the community's practices (*PhR* 151, pp. 108ff).

To assess Hegel's view of crime and punishment it may be useful to consider it in the context of some contemporary ethical theories. Recent discussion distinguishes between deontological and consequentialist or teleological accounts of moral acts. Deontologists believe that certain features of acts themselves make them right or wrong. "A deontologist contends that it is possible for an action to be the morally right or obligatory one even if it does not promote the greatest possible balance of good over evil for self, society, or universe."[31] Teleologists, on the other hand, appeal to the comparative amount of good brought into being. When an act is right it is likely to produce a greater balance of good over evil than any available alternative.[32] Only a sketchy answer can be given to the question of which, if any, of these views is Hegel's. If Hegel's view can be clarified it may be easier to assess the value of his view as it bears upon the death event.

As might be expected, Hegel's position shifts with context. If we begin with the standpoint of the citizen of an existing state, the perspective of *The Philosophy of Right* and the concluding sections of *The Philosophy of Mind*, Hegel applies deontological principles, though peculiarly restricted, in evaluating moral acts. Acts are the embodiments of will; as such they are right or wrong irrespective of their consequences. Moral decisions are not to be made by subjecting the agent's subjective maxim to the criterion of universalizability, as Kant claims, but rather by determining whether the agent's will is in harmony with the will of the community.[33] Hegel assumes that the collective will is, to a greater or lesser extent, the rational precipitate of its institutions and beliefs and so generates rules in accordance with rational norms.

This peculiar form of deontologism is obviously unsatisfactory. If rightness depends upon the values of communities, the worth of an act will be relative to the moral standards of a community. But if the rational component ingredient in the values of a community determines the rightness or wrongness of acts, then the community's particular expressions of value are irrelevant. In addition, Hegel's analysis tends to support the political status quo, a point not lost upon left-wing Hegelians.[34] It is hard to imagine that Hegel was unaware of these conspicuous difficulties. Only Hegel's faith in progress and its necessary concomitant, the interiorization of the rational precipitate of laws, lent credibility to this position.

Hegel's theory of crime appears ludicrously deficient from the standpoint of technological society and the history of the death event and holds up no better than his view of evil as a rift in consciousness. In the death-world, faceless bureaucracies, often deriving their authority from communal consensus, rule vast numbers of persons out of existence. The forces which Hegel expects to create a consciousness of guilt have now been harnessed to alleviate guilt feelings by consigning vast numbers of persons to death through the implementation of the metaphysics of impurity. Obedience to the will of the state is felt by the individual as acting in conformity with putative duty, or, more cynically, as self-interested conformity to authority or to a state apparatus of terror. To be sure Hegel thought modern states were becoming more rational (which for him meant acting in conformity with the Notion) and were therefore less likely to engage in barbarous acts. The death event has radically altered this perspective. Individual conformity to the will of totalitarian states continues to generate fresh episodes of annihilation.[35] In a striking passage, Hannah Arendt writes: "The frightening coincidence of the modern population explosion with the discovery of technical devices that through automation, will make large sections of the population superfluous even in terms of labor, and that through nuclear energy, make it possible to deal with this twofold threat by the use of instruments beside which Hitler's gas installations look like an evil child's fumbling toys."[36]

The present discussion arose in the context of my claim that Hegel's interpretation of moral acts changes depending upon context. In fact the deontological aspect of Hegel's view is sublated and superseded once we consider the dialectical structure of the *Phenomenology* and *The Philosophy of History*. Acts which take on one meaning from the deontological standpoint are seen differently when the higher interests of Spirit are taken into account. Since acts are much more likely to be judged in relation to their results, it is better to think of Hegel as a consequentialist in this context.

In the *Phenomenology*, moral acts are measured in terms of complexity and degree of self-consciousness, the richness acquired by Spirit as a result of their having been done. According to the *Philosophy of History*, acts are judged in terms of the rational freedom they produce. Hegel's consequentialism is peculiar in that agents need not be conscious of the consequences or long-term benefits of their acts. Acts may appear good to us retrospectively regardless of their motives. They may in fact have been undertaken in response to some overriding passion while at the same time serving the larger ends of history.

It would be odd indeed if, given the totalizing and systematic unity of his thought, Hegel did not have a theory of the good life in addition to a view of moral acts. For Hegel such a life must conform to the actualization of the Idea in accordance with which Spirit pursues its course through time. Man can realize this ideal by pursuing the two ends of life recommended by Aristotle in the *Nichomachean Ethics*: political excellence and contemplation.[37] But the Greek polis could never attain genuine moral excellence in Hegel's eyes, since it reached only an abstract understanding of freedom. True political excellence can only be achieved by the citizen of the modern Protestant state, whose "constitution and code . . . embody the principle and development of the moral life, which proceeds . . . from the truth of religion."[38] The moral life of the state and religious spirituality of the state are thus reciprocal guarantees of strength. Similarly, Hegel rejects such antecedent notions of the contemplative life as the static contemplation of the forms of Plato's metaphysics, Aristotle's vision of the unmoved mover, the neo-Platonic and Christian versions of the *unio mystico*, and the self-contemplation of Schleiermacher and Fichte.[39] Hegel, like his contemporaries, speaks of Spirit's retreat into self as an abandonment of its outer existence. Instead, Spirit contemplates precisely what Plato urged the true philosopher to forget in the simile of the cave: the dance of shadows on the wall, the fire, the puppets, the prisoners—the forms and shapes of becoming. For Hegel, actual, historical existence unfolds as the content of contemplation. In his words:

> [Spirit] gives its existential shape over to recollection. . . . Thus absorbed in itself, it is sunk in the night of its self-consciousness; but in that night its vanished outer existence is preserved, and this transformed existence—the former one, but now reborn of the Spirit's knowledge—is the new existence, a new world and a new shape of Spirit. In the immediacy of this new existence the Spirit has to start afresh to bring itself to

maturity as if, for it, all that preceded were lost. . . . But recollection, the *inwardizing* of that experience, has preserved it and is the inner being, and in fact the higher form of the substance. (*Phen* 808, p. 492)

We have had occasion to encounter a version of this position in connection with the modern view of the authenticity paradigm: Rilke's inwardization of the things vanishing in actuality, "they who so fleetingly need us" and solicit us for their very existence. Proust also sees reality as constituted by memory so that, paradoxically, the "first"—from the sensory point of view, the sharpest—experience is in fact the least significant. First impressions are for Proust necessarily superficial or, in Hegel's terms, "immediate." Only later, Proust says (speaking of his favorite sonata), "when these first apparitions have withdrawn," does memory reveal "what has thus been held in reserve for us, which by the sheer force of its beauty has become invisible and has remained unknown, this comes to us last of all."[40] But, for Hegel, the finite intellect raised up by contemplation is no longer merely finite, but attains to infinite knowledge of the infinite. The responses to so grandiose a vision by Hegel's immediate successors are proportioned to the magnitude of Hegel's claims. Kierkegaard retreats in horrified Christian humility before the thought of seeing with God's eyes what God himself sees; Nietzsche shatters the conformity of being to the Notion, the concept on which Hegel's totality is based, by remanding the appearances to the domain of multiple wills to power.

From the perspective opened up by the twentieth century phenomenon of man-made mass death, Hegel's version of the contemplative ideal collapses, since, even on Hegel's idealistic premises the natural world does not simply disappear when the self-consciousness of Spirit is totally and fully achieved.[41] Although the conquest of nature by Spirit entails the overcoming of an actual world, that world does not at the end of the process become an etiolated realm of shadows. The finite and contingent world must continue to exist even when the content of the history of Spirit is fully inwardized, if Spirit is not to become emptily transcendent. Spirit requires the continuity of the world; its destruction would leave Spirit without a field of actuality. The annihilation of human life would return the Absolute to the condition of God as Hegel describes Him in the *Science of Logic*, "in his eternal essence before the creation of Nature and finite Spirit."[42] But this is impossible since Spirit cannot be wound backwards, as it were. Twentieth-century man-made mass death threatens to destroy what the Absolute requires absolutely: humankind.

Kant and the Philosophy of Reflection   IN ONE OF HIS EARLY THEOLOGICAL writings, a fragment on love composed in 1797 or 1798, Hegel contrasts analytic intelligence, which divides existing reality without being able to reunite it, with love. "Genuine love," Hegel says, "excludes all oppositions," whereas the Understanding "always [leaves] the manifold of related terms as a manifold."[43] A year later, in his essay "On the Spirit of Christianity," Hegel revises his view of love as the ground for a unifying vision of the whole, since love, as mere feeling, excludes the rational element and falls back into subjectivity:[44] "This love [of the early Christian community] is a divine spirit, but it still falls short of religion. To become religion it must manifest itself in an objective form. A feeling, something subjective, it must be fused with the universal, with something represented in idea and thereby acquire the form of a being to whom prayer is both possible and due" (*ETW* p. 289). In 1802, in a long essay entitled "Faith and Knowledge," contributed to a journal edited by Hegel and Schelling, the distinctions of the earlier work are formulated in the context of a critical evaluation of the philosophy of reflection which, for Hegel, includes modern philosophy—British empiricism, continental rationalism (with the exception of Spinoza), and the philosophy of the French and German Enlightenment. But principally the essay refers to the philosophy of Kant, Fichte, and Jacobi, all of whom place the Absolute beyond the reach of reason.[45] These thinkers' views of the impotence of reason is, for Hegel, reflected in the piquant remark of Jacobi, "Reason is ashamed to beg and has no hands and feet for digging" (*FK* p. 56). Thus, despite his early flirtation with Kant's religion of reason, Hegel breaks once and for all with what he sees as the helplessness of reason in critical idealism, which he characterizes as "subjectivism" and "formal thinking" (*FK* p. 67). Hegel's critique of Kant is of particular interest since it provides a profound and far-reaching analysis of the philosophy of reflection, the thought form which dominates the ethos of technological society. Although complex, Hegel's analysis is indispensable to an understanding not only of the superficial manifestations of technique but of its metaphysical ground.

Kantian philosophy, for Hegel, represents an advance over its predecessors. Its great contribution lies in its systematization of the Enlightenment view of man. The thinking subject is an individual, but the individual is modeled on mankind in general (*HPh* 3:426. Since the Kantian philosophy views mind as consciousness, it remains, from Hegel's standpoint, hopelessly limited, a psychology rather than a philosophy of mind (*PhM* 415, p. 156). If for Kant the subject is a finite being, knowledge can only be finite and subjective. The question of what is true can never be settled, since knowledge is limited to the phenomena, the appearances of things, by the structure of the understanding. The ultimate reality of the thing, the *Ding-an-sich*, is beyond the grasp of finite intellect. For Hegel this reading of the limitations of knowledge only highlights what is really at stake in knowing: truth beyond the scope of reason, since things in themselves transcend the reach of the understanding. The solution to the problem of knowledge cannot, in Hegel's eyes, bypass Kant's analysis of the genuine contributions of the understanding which is able to uncover its own limitations. But philosophy must pass beyond this purely critical phase to recover the object which Kant consigns to an unreachable beyond. Hegel realizes that only if the object is a spiritual product from the first is its recovery by knowledge possible.

The limitations of Kant's conception of the subject are, according to Hegel, grounded in his view of the a priori elements of knowing, the determining conditions necessary for organizing experience. Since the objects of experience are given as extended and successive, Kant concludes that the understanding itself must work up the raw material of experience in the form of space and time. The understanding thinks the object of sensuous perception by deriving its matter from the sensuous faculty, but itself supplies the principle of its formal organization.[46]

Of course our thinking consists of relational elements, as well as the positing of objects and their sequential ordering. If we think away the perceptual content of objects, as well as time and space, which are the organizing forms of the understanding, what still remains is the schema of their thinkability—thing and property, force and effect. Kant gives an exhaustive account of these elements of thought or categories which bind together the empirical content of our concepts. Deriving the categories from the traditional logic of Aristotle based on the subject-predicate form of language, Kant develops a logic of judgments, what we would call propositions, which unite sensuous content with conceptual form.[47]

This systematization of the functions of reason founders in Hegel's eyes, since it remains merely subjective. The categories are features of synthesizing intelligence and therefore can only be subjective, whereas the putative object pole remains inaccessible, because the categories apply only to our own sense data.[48] Hegel writes:

> The first component of experience, sensation, is doubtless subjective, since it is connected with our organs. The matter of perception is only what it is in my sensation. I know of this sensation only and not of the thing. But, in the second place, the objective, which ought to constitute the opposite to this subjective side, is itself subjective likewise: it does not indeed pertain to my feeling, but it remains shut up in the region of my self-consciousness. (*HPh* 3:440)

Since its objectivity is limited to its own sensations, the finite epistemological subject loses the being of the thing. Hegel criticizes Kant for lacking a theory of objective reference, a difficulty made familiar in present-day philosophies of language in which linguistic transposition supplants objective reference, that is to say, one piece of discourse refers, within discourse, to another. It may appear odd for Hegel to fault Kant's critical idealism for its subjectivism when, after all, Hegel's own philosophy of the Absolute requires the in-itself or content of knowing to be transformed to an in-itself for a subject and thus seems to be equally vulnerable to the charge of subjectivism. Yet Hegel sees his own account of ontological reference as establishing strict objectivity in the only way possible. If an activity is to count as thought, the "other-being" of objects is ingredient in it. Thus the alterity of the object is constitutive of thought itself.

Not only is Kant's view of knowledge one-sidedly subjective but, for Hegel, it also falls short of being genuinely dialectical, since the faculty of the understanding flounders between two heterogenous elements: the raw data of sensation—the chaotic flux which cannot unite content and form—and the categories. This peculiarity of the understanding, the feature which makes it so fertile in the work of analysis, at the same time prevents the understanding from elevating what it has analyzed to a new level. Kant does distinguish between the mere understanding (*Verstand*) and reason (*Vernunft*) as a higher mode of cognition; indeed, Hegel concedes that it is Kant's achievement to have put the "beginning of the idea of Reason in the intellect itself," so that now the intellect produces transcendental ideas, such unconditioned principles of unity as the soul and God (*FK* p. 79). But for Kant there are no corresponding objects for reason; because sensuous intuition is a necessary condition for the production of objects, reason must remain emptily transcendent. The product of reason is the *mundus intelligibilis* of ideas which can have only a regulative function. In Hegel's view, only the fluid dialectical movement of Spirit could soar to a vision of reason sufficiently comprehensive to include genuine objectivity without engulfing it. He writes:

> Prior to Kant no distinction had been made between Understanding and Reason. But unless one wants to sink to the level of vulgar consciousness . . . the following distinction must be firmly established between Understanding and Reason: that for the latter, the object is determined in and for itself, is the identity of content and form, of universal and particular, whereas for the former it falls apart into form and content, into universal and particular, and into an empty "in-itself" to which the determinateness is added from outside; that, therefore, in the thinking of the Understanding, the content is indifferent to its form, while in the comprehensive thinking of Reason the content produces its form from itself. (*PhM* 467 add., p. 226)

Since reason for Kant yearns to know the infinite with a faculty the limitations of which are determined by the sensuous world, it becomes entangled in paradox and contradiction. Yet Hegel claims that Kant fails to grapple with the contradictions inherent in things themselves. Kant analyzes the antinomies and paralogisms or false syllogisms of reason, but he is blind, according to Hegel, to the depth of the negative, reason's ontological root. Thus Hegel says: "Kant shows here too much tenderness for things: it would be a pity he thinks, if they contradicted themselves. But that mind, which is far higher, should be a contradiction—that is not a pity at all" (*HPh* 3:451).

If reason's effort to penetrate the truth of the world of nature is futile, it might be argued that at least in the moral sphere reason can attain a deeper level of truth. But according to Hegel, the same bifurcation that is found in the realm of nature is also expressed in the realm of morality. Just as theoretical reason contains in itself the a priori structure of time, space, and the categories on the one hand and sensuous intuition on the other, so practical reason separates the moral law from inclination. The categorical imperative, the universal ought, is pitted against the desires of the individual. For Hegel the disclosure of the moral law "as within the human breast" gives practical reason an advantage over theoretical reason. But practical reason is also an abstraction lacking content. The will gives itself only the form of identity ("Act from maxims which are capable of becoming universal laws"), not its substance (*HPh* 3:460). The split between ought and is, between imperative and existence remains irreducible since concrete persons can never realize the demands of practical reason. The sensuous will can never be brought into conformity with the universal, and "the result is . . . that the aim of the moral will is to be attained in infinite progress only" (*HPh* 3:461). In order to create a sphere of actualization for moral progress Kant is obliged to postulate the immortality of the soul. To be sure, Kant attempts to reconcile the idea of a happiness commensurate with virtue by positing the idea of a highest good. But for Hegel this unification remains only "a beyond, a thought, which is not actually in existence, but only ought to be" (*HPh* 3:462). Hegel sees that if the gap between nature and law were closed on Kant's terms, "Nature would remain nature no longer . . . and thus there remains an utter opposition between the two sides" (*HPh* 3:463).

Only in the third *Critique* does Hegel find clues for overcoming the aporias of reflective philosophy. Kant's *Critique of Judgment* contains suggestions for overcoming a significant pair of oppositions in Kant's thought: the split between the phenomenal world of nature and the noumenal world accessible to practical reason. In the third *Critique*, Kant discovers in the idea of beauty and in our notion of the teleological structure of nature possibilities for mediating between the concepts of nature and freedom.[49] Hegel is quick to perceive an underlying common ground in these oppositions and the attainment of their unity through mediating judgment. He argues that, for Kant, "Understanding and practical reason have two different regulative systems on one and the same ground of experience, without the one being detrimental to the other" (HPh 3:464). Kant therefore seeks a connection between them. If experience teaches us that the world of freedom has an impact upon the world of nature, we must imagine a nature so constructed that its own laws allow for this realization. The mediator between the two realms of nature and freedom is the faculty of judgment. (HPh 3:464–68). In Kant's "Critique of Aesthetic Judgment," the antithesis vanishes in the conscious intuition of beauty, the experience of a supersensuous realm defined by Kant as an intelligible internal and external substratum of nature. Yet, in the end, the idea of beauty fails to bridge the gap between the concepts of nature and freedom, because it remains for Kant a mere representation of the imagination, an experience of the supersensuous, strictly speaking beyond conceptualization (FK pp. 86ff).

In the "Critique of Teleological Judgment," Kant comes closer to developing an approximation of Hegel's concept of Spirit which alone will transform these oppositions by uniting them at a higher level. Here Kant posits the idea of an archetypal (urbildlich) intellect as a necessary idea in which possibility and actuality are united and "the possibility of the parts" is dependent on a vision of the whole. But this insight remains empty because Kant's insistence upon the finite empirical subject drives him to abandon the idea of an archetypal intellect which may be logically necessary but which cannot exist in reality. Since Kant holds that the unification of possibility and actuality transcends human capacity, even the Critique of Judgment is flawed in Hegel's eyes and remains mired in the philosophy of reflection.

Death and Reflection   HEGEL'S CRITICISM OF THE PHIlosophy of reflection rests on what Wilfred Sellars has aptly called "the myth of the given." This myth, shared by rationalists and empiricists alike, assumes that "knowledge is either of the sort of entity naturally suited to be immediately present to consciousness, or of entities whose existence and properties are entailed by entities of the first sort (and which are entities reducible to those of the first sort)."[50] Hegel thought that the criteria of justification used in Enlightenment theories of knowledge, were reductionistic and fragmenting, and thus they lost the significance of the whole, which is for him the ultimate meaning of the Absolute. Like the recent work of Sellars and Quine—though from an altogether different point of view—Hegel rejects the artificial dichotomies created by Enlightenment epistemologies and seeks to reconcile (dialectically) necessity and contingency, form and content, even Kant's distinction between analytic or a priori propositions and synthetic propositions.[51] For Hegel the whole is united by a single grand purpose. His contemporary relevance consists neither in the vision of an absolute nor a fortiori in the particular absolute he describes, but in his insight into the historical breaching of its internal dichotomies, or (in our terms) the social construction of reality.

When Hegel turns in the *Phenomenology* from the critical analysis of the philosophy of reflection to the grand panorama of the history of Spirit, reflection takes on added meaning and plays a significant role in the dialectical progression of the moments of this history. In this new context subjectivity, reflection, and death are joined. By itself the understanding whose work is reflection can never rise beyond the creation of abstractions, but at the same time the understanding is described as an amazing power, capable of liberating the real from its immediacy. In a celebrated passage in which the understanding is linked to various powers of negation, Hegel says:

> The activity of dissolution is the power and work of the *Understanding*, the most astonishing and mightiest of powers, or rather the absolute power. The circle that remains self-enclosed and, like substance, holds its moments together, is an immediate relationship, one therefore which has nothing astonishing about it. But that an accident as such, detached from what circumscribes it, what is bound and is actual only in context with others, should attain an existence of its own and a separate freedom—this is the tremendous power of the negative; it is the

energy of thought, of the pure "I." Death, if that is what we want to call this non-actuality, is of all things the most dreadful, and to hold fast what is dead requires the greatest strength. Lacking strength, Beauty hates the Understanding for asking of her what it cannot do. But the life of Spirit is not the life that shrinks from death and keeps itself untouched by devastation, but rather the life that endures it and maintains itself in it. It wins its truth when, in utter dismemberment, it finds itself. It is this power, not as something positive, which closes its eyes to the negative, as when we say of something that it is nothing or is false, and then, having done with it, turn away and pass on to something else; on the contrary Spirit is this power only by looking the negative in the face, and tarrying with it. This tarrying with the negative is the magical power that converts it into being. This power is identical with what we earlier called the Subject, which by giving determinateness an existence in its own immediate element supersedes abstract immediacy. (*Phen* 32, pp. 18–19)

Subjectivity in this context is the understanding engaged in its negative work, the annulling of some positive content, without which this content cannot be superseded and Spirit cannot continue to increase in richness and complexity. At the same time, Hegel stresses the existential root of the annulling movement of understanding or subjectivity—death. This annihilating power converts the immediate object or raw material of consciousness into a finished product by refining its brute positivity, its lack of determinateness. This new object is, for a subject, a content inwardized by self-knowing mind.

It is tempting to think of the meaning of negation exclusively in connection with propositional truth. But for Hegel, opposition or contradiction (*Widerspruch*) is as much a determinant of things as it is of propositions. The basis for considering the false as an ontological determination, as well as a logical category, stems from the inseparability of being and truth. If it is granted that things contain polar oppositions, then the cognizing act is inseparable from this ontological root. Negation is deeply embedded not only in the subject but also in the substance or content of knowledge. This content—which is always in the process of becoming subject—is distinguishable negatively, first in its sheer distinctness from the subject, and second, insofar as this content is true, in its difference from the false. Of course Hegel understands very well that the ordinary meaning of falsity, as expressed in a simple correspondence theory of truth, interprets the false as a disparity between knowledge and its object, which, when recognized, is removed in order to establish the identity of knowledge and object. But for Hegel—and this is the main point—the moment of falsity is not irrelevant to the resultant truth: "It is not truth as if the disparity had been thrown away, like dross from pure metal, not even like the tool which remains separate from the finished vessel; disparity, rather, as the negative, the self, is still present in the True as such" (*Phen* 39, p. 23). Hegel does not mean to say that falsity is mixed up in truth "like oil and water," but that truth requires otherness and falsity in this otherness. When otherness is cancelled, it is inwardized, it is no longer false in the ordinary sense.[52]

The logic of truth and falsity as opposition belongs to the philosophy of reflection but, for Hegel, reflection itself is finite cognition as it stands opposed to infinite cognition or cognition of the Absolute. Finite cognition is incapable of relational thought, because it cannot see the interconnectedness of what intellect or the understanding isolates or abstracts from the whole, which can only be apprehended by reason. In an early fragment preserved by Rosenkranz, Hegel says that it is the task of logic to "cognize reflection completely and get it out of the way."[53] Thus logic keeps before us "a mirror image" or "pattern of the Absolute." In the *Lesser Logic*, Hegel expands upon this optical metaphor:

> This word "reflection" is originally applied, when a ray of light in a straight line impinging upon the surface of a mirror is thrown back from it. In this phenomenon we have two things— first an immediate fact which is, and secondly the deputed, derivated, or transmitted phase of the same. Something of this sort takes place when we reflect, or think upon an object; for here we want to know the object, not in its immediacy, but as derivative or mediated. (*L* 112, p. 163).

The act of reflection departs from the immediacy of things and shows them to be different from the way they first appear. Hegel connects reflection with the idea of essence, which lies behind the appearance and purports to give a deeper, truer account of the thing. For Hegel nonreflected immediacy, "an immediate fact which is," cannot supply the conditions for its own truth. At the same time, reflection, a necessary step in the attainment of truth, is equally helpless since it generates distinctions which can only be resolved at a higher level of rationality. In the absence of this higher level, the conclusions of reflection can only remain a last resort to which even naive immediacy may in some ways be preferable.[55] Thus Hegel objects to the proofs for the existence of God, not because they contain logical fallacies, but because reflection cannot produce conviction (*L* 2, p. 5). In a graphic passage Hegel writes:

> Reflection . . . has been often maintained to be the condition, or even the only way, of attaining a consciousness and certitude of the Eternal and True. . . . Metaphysical proofs of God's existence . . . have been treated as if a knowledge of them and a conviction of their truth were the only and essential means of producing a belief and conviction that there is a God. Such a doctrine would find its parallel, if we said that eating was impossible before we had acquired a knowledge of the chemical, botanical, and zoological character of our food; and that we must delay digestion till we had finished the study of anatomy and physiology. (*L* 2, p. 5)

The ethos derived from reflection presents striking parallels to the spiritual and material culture of technological society, the embedding matrix of the death world. Technological society depends upon the logic of quantification and the application of this technique to innumerable functions in the life of this society. The collapse of spatio-temporal nodes into mathematical expressions to create a system of conceptually transposable objects is applied mutatis mutandis to human beings. These strictly homogeneous entities are made to stand for one another and are treated as standard units in the functioning of a complex social "machine." Hegel could not be expected to foresee the full range of phenomena which would come into being in the technological society. Yet he is able to provide an astonishingly rich account of its characteristic mode of thought; the logic of reflection deprives objects of their relation to nature on the one hand and to historical existence on the other.

This double negation on the part of reflection, carried to its ultimate extreme, results in the conceptualization of man as machine. Descartes, whose thought provides an early example of the philosophy of reflection, raises this possibility in his well-known fantasy of the human automaton:

> I remember that, when looking from a window and saying I see men who pass in the street, I really do not see them, but infer that what I see is men ... And yet what do I see from the window but hats and coats which may cover automatic machines.[55]

Hegel draws out the full and ominous implications of Descartes' image by describing the impact of calculative thinking upon philosophical thought. In a passage of almost uncanny prescience, Hegel says:

> Calculative thinking (*Rechnen*) is an operation so external and consequently mechanical, one has been able to invent *machines* (*Machinen*) which perform arithmetical operations in the most perfect fashion. To judge from the nature of calculative thinking starting from this sole fact one would know enough to decide the worth of making calculative thinking the principal means for forming the mind and putting it to the torture in order that it pefect itself to the point of becoming a machine.[56]

Criticizing thought's tendency to split itself off from the wider range of experience has been the stock in trade of Romantic poets and philosophers.[57] Yet their observations almost always take the form of a yearning for paradisiacal innocence or the return of lost immediacy. But for Hegel only a vision of the whole which has taken reflective thought into itself can supplant reflection.

Although Hegel believes that his system has superseded the philosophy of reflection once and for all, recent criticism has placed critical idealism and Hegel's philosophy of the Absolute in the same stream of Western metaphysics, the history of onto-theology.[58] For Heidegger, Hegel belongs to the history of the progressive covering over of the meaning of Being. Derrida sees Hegel's thought as reflecting what Derrida calls the *logic of presence*. According to Derrida, *presence* is "the universal form of transcendental life" determined by the structure of consciousness and preserved by the capacity of language to fix concepts. The logic of presence rests on the belief that "before my birth and after my death . . . the present is."[59] Though I will die, the present will continue, not as this or that specific present, but as the now into which being can pour itself. Structurally, the logic of presence opens up because language retains something in ideal form and re-presents it. The terror of death is intrinsic to the logic of presence since I can maintain that, in spite of my death, the present will continue. The logic of presence functions as a spurious and largely unconscious form of immortality. This relation to my death is built into the very thought of myself since self-reference exists in the form of "I-am-present." Thus for Hegel, the individual is essentially related to the thought of his own death and to its sublation.[60] To the extent that death belongs to the whole, to the nature of the Absolute, and is ingredient in Spirit itself as the existential expression of its negating activities, Hegel cannot surmount the logic of presence.

The alternative for Derrida is the system of differences, that which cannot be brought into presence but can only be reached elliptically by strategies of detour and deferral.[61] Yet difference is not unrelated to the logic of presence. Difference, that which is past and cannot be reversed by re-presentation makes meaning possible since that which is present is related to that which cannot become present by way of negation. Presence becomes what it is by negating that which it is not. But if negation plays this all-important role, if, in fact, it is difference itself, then Hegel has given negation its most powerful modern formulation. Hegel has shown the force of the negative in the history of metaphysics but, at the same time, Reason recovers what has been sublated by negation as well as the process of negation itself. The negative must appear.[62] This bringing to presence of the negative places Hegel on this side of the logic of presence. Hegel therefore becomes the last representative of the philosophy of reflection, but also the first thinker to recognize the force of negation. Derrida says that in the *Phenomenology* Hegel establishes a system of equivalences among the appearances of negation—understanding, formality, mathematics, negativity, and death.[63] Negativity in Hegel is harnessed to the logic of presence so that the idea of the negative as reserve, pure loss, silence—that which is irrecoverable—is foreign to Hegel. Instead, the negative is brought into plenary presence carried forward by the dialectical activity of Spirit.

The possibility of man-made mass death adds a new dimension to Hegel's problematic in the context of Derrida's analysis of the logic of presence. For Hegel, the actuality of finite existents is necessary if negation is to find expression in phenomena. Without human beings, the Absolute is empty infinite possibility. If the idea of difference yields deeper insight into negation itself, difference acquires meaning only because we become aware of negation through the *play* of differences which leaves tracks or traces in that which is present; for example, the Freudian unconscious leaves its mark on conscious life. Such tracks allude to what is absolutely other than conscious content. But a negation so profound that all presence would be snuffed out would annihilate difference as well. Difference and presence alike depend upon the continuity of the world. Without it, alterity would be reduced to the same. Pure nothing which is pure being is the silent void, the celebrated Absolute of Schelling, described by Hegel as the night in which all cows are black.

Time and Eternity   H EGEL BOTH EXPRESSES AND brings to an end a metaphysical tradition which Derrida designates as the logic of presence. The structure of historical consciousness allows the past to become present while it expands in content in the course of time. The historical actualities of this reserve, this archeological field, can be fully recovered. This bringing to presence of the past expresses the triumphs of Spirit as it realizes the Notion in history.

Hegel develops the idea of time in detail in the opening section of the *Philosophy of Nature*. The placement of this discussion, which immediately precedes the section on inorganic nature, is not incidental to Hegel's interpretation of the relation of nature to Spirit. A grasp of the meaning of nature requires an understanding of time because in conformity with Aristotle's conception of *physis*, nature is the sphere of becoming.[64] For the same reason, the meaning of time is developed in dialectical relation to the concept of space. Hegel, in conformity with Kant, considers space and time in the context of phenomenality but, for Hegel, phenomenality is dependent on externality, Spirit's othering of itself. Time and space are not, as they are for Kant, contributions of the epistemological subject; instead, time is the outgrowth of space.

For Hegel space is the form of immediate externality. Our concept of space must take account of the double aspect of spatial existence: space as uninterrupted continuity makes it possible for things to exist *partes extra partes*, and the negation of this continuity, time's punctiform aspect, which makes the existence of discrete objects possible. Continuity alone cannot account for the discreteness of things, since the immediate form of externality lacks differentiation. The punctiform is the other of continuity so that together discreteness and continuity describe the way objects exist in space. The actuality of this abstract dialectical relation of point and continuity is the concretely existing material body. Since space cannot exist anywhere as a point, the punctiformity of space is expressed as line and plane. But—crucial for the analysis of time—line and plane are simply there without having undergone spiritual transformation; they express space as mere in-itself. Punctiformity must be expressed not only as in-itself but also as for-itself. How? If we resort to something visible we fall back upon lines and planes and so do not move the dialectical analysis to a new level. Only another dimension, time, can express the punctiformity of space as the truth of space. From the standpoint of space, punctiformity is the negation of continuity, and time the negation of the negation. What cannot spread out to become extended being—the point, the negation of continuity—can only be expressed as something other than itself, time. Time is what it is not, space, in the form of its ideality.

The necessity of the relation of time to space enables us to understand Hegel's otherwise odd interpretation of becoming. The commonsense view of contingent existence which comes into being and passes away imagines change as the alteration of the visible arrangement of some extended thing. But Hegel claims that extended things are temporal in the strongest sense: they are made of time, since time is the truth of space. Hegel claims that coming to be and passing away does not take place *in* time; rather, time itself is the *becoming*, this coming to be and passing away:

> Time is merely this abstraction of destroying. Things . . . do not pass away because they are in time, but are themselves that which is temporal. Temporality is their objective determination. It is therefore the process of actual things which constitutes time . . . The present makes a tremendous demand, yet as the individual present it is nothing, for even as I pronounce it, its all-excluding pretentiousness dwindles, dissolves and falls into dust. . . . If all stood still, even our thinking, we would be permanent, and there would be no time, but all finite things are temporal, as sooner or later they are all subject to change, and their permanence is therefore only relative. (*PhN* 1:258 add., p. 231)

The real is distinct from time, but it is also one with time as the destructive power of negation in things.

The Notion, on the other hand, is absolute freedom and negativity and so is free of time. Time has no power over the Notion; rather, the Notion has power over time. Only nature as the externalization of the Notion is subject to time: the Idea is eternal. Yet eternity must not be abstracted from time. Eternity is not something *outside* of time, as if it comes after time, for that would make eternity the future of time. Instead, it is something altogether different from time. Eternity is absolute timelessness (PhN 1:258 add., p. 231).

The standpoint of eternity belongs to the life of God "as He is in His eternal essence before the creation of nature and of finite spirit" (*SL* 1:50). The eternal life of the logos shows itself in the life of the Notion or in the element of logic. The structure of the eternal is circular, without beginning or end. To this extent, Hegel's conception of eternity conforms to Aristotle's view of the circular structure of cosmic being.[65] Not only is the totality of the logical process a circle but the logos unfolds into the categorial sequence of Being Essence, and Notion each of which is also circular in structure.[66] Were this all then Hegel would have added little to the classical conception of eternity. For Hegel the categorial sequence of Being, Essence, and Notion also reflects the dynamic structure of the relation of the persons of the Trinity to one another and thus points to the Christian basis of Hegel's analysis.[67] Eternity is not static: each category is the object of mediation, a reworking of the dynamic structure of the love of the persons of the Trinity which preserves their separation while uniting them in an eternal relation.[68]

Yet for Hegel the eternal does not exist apart from its relation to time. It must also be realized in history as the work of Spirit which externalizes itself and returns to itself in time. Thus eternity passes through the existential negation of time by entering the stream of time. In principle, eternity is present from the start and retains its circular structure, yet eternity will also absorb the process of temporalization by taking time up into itself and thereby altering both itself and time.[69]

For Hegel the present bears a special relationship to eternity since, like eternity, only the present truly exists. Of course the order of time is made up of past and future as well as the present: the nonbeing of the being replaced by the now is the past, whereas the being of the nonbeing which is contained in the present and which will replace it is the future. (*PhN* 1:259 add., p. 235) In the strict sense therefore past and future are nullities even if they impact upon the present. The nonbeing of past and future assures the primacy of the present. Although the now passes away and eternity is timeless, both the present and eternity are characterized by fullness of being.[70]

The structure of Hegel's analysis is Augustinian in that the concrete present exists in relation to the other dimensions of time, whereas eternity is not within time. On this view the completeness or fullness of eternity comes from its position outside time. But if the present is like eternity in this fullness, where does the fullness of the present come from? Why is the present not a whole, if it alone (among the modalities of time) truly is? Why is it not like Parmenidean being, everywhere complete? The answer for Hegel lies in the structure of contingency itself. Time is the coming to be and passing away of things. The truth of time must reflect the articulations of this structure. Thus the fullness of time must be a fullness different from the fullness of eternity. The truth of the present must preserve the past. It can only achieve this preservation through memory. The true present is not the immediate relation of consciousness to some given but, as for Proust, remembered content the cumulative weight of which continues to enrich the present. The past is the difference between ourselves—the content *for us*—and the in-itself of this content. Historical consciousness is memory as it is ingredient in Spirit. The celebrated passage in which Hegel elaborates this idea is worth citing at length:

> The evanescent itself must, on the contrary, be regarded as essential not as something fixed, cut off from the True, and left lying who knows where outside it, any more than the true is to be regarded as something on the other side, positive and dead. Appearance is the arising and passing away that does not arise itself and pass away, but is "in-itself" . . . and constitutes the actuality and the movement of the life of truth. The True is thus the Bacchanalian revel in which no member is not drunk; yet because each member collapses as soon as he drops out, the revel is just as much transparent and simple repose. Judged in the court of this movement, the single shapes of Spirit do not persist any more than determinate thoughts do, but they are as much positive and necessary moments, as they are negative and evanescent. In the *whole* of the movement, seen as a state of repose, what distinguished itself therein, and gives itself particular existence, is preserved as something that *recollects* itself, whose existence is self-knowledge, and whose self-knowledge is just as immediately existence. (*Phen* 47, pp. 27–28)

The idea that truth is remembered can also be found in Plato's doctrine of recollection. Yet for Hegel what is remembered is not the eternal, timeless, and unchanging truth of the forms, but the panorama of successive moments sublating themselves and being superseded by new moments. Like Augustine, who thinks man remembers through a glass darkly the happy prelapsarian state of Adam, Hegel believes memory is, roughly speaking, existential rather than logical. Memory functions to make that which was mere externality a possession of Spirit.

Hegel's comments on psychological memory are of interest in this connection, since in the process of individual remembering is writ small the archeological structure which characterizes the memory of Spirit. Through memory, the intuited content of experience becomes mine. The simplest form of imaginative possession is recollection, through which an image or picture is freed from conglomerate experience and enters my private space and time (*PhM* 452, p. 203). What is imaged gains permanence at the expense of clarity and freshness. The immediate individuality of what is intuitively perceived is gone: "The intuition, in becoming an image, is obscured and obliterated" (*PhM* 452 *Zusatz*, p. 203). But what is lost in freshness is gained in perdurance through time as a conquest of ephemerality. This content then enters the "mine or pit" of my inwardness. But the image in recollection (*Erinnerung*) is mine in only a formal manner. The dialectic must then pass to imagination (*Einbildungskraft*) so that the images of recollection which are mine only formally become actual possessions. "Intelligence," Hegel tells us, "emerging from its abstract inward being into determinateness, disperses the night-like darkness enveloping the wealth of its images and banishes it by the luminous clarity of a present image" (*PhM* 454 *Zusatz*, p. 208).

But the intellect does not work through images alone; it requires language which "aims at making itself be and be a fact." The intellect becomes "self-uttering, intuition producing: the imagination which creates signs" (*PhM* 457, p. 211). The relation of signs to language is a matter of some consequence for our analysis since signs make the logic of presence possible. Hegel distinguishes between symbols which use sensory material that directly suggests their intended meaning—for example the eagle as strength—and signs which bear no intrinsic relation to the signified. Memory (*Gedächtnis*), strictly speaking, has only to do with signs even if in popular speech it is confused with recollection (*Erinnerung*) (*PhM* 461, p. 219). In this connection Hegel expresses a preference for alphabetic writing, because it is abstract and flexible, over hieroglyphics, which remain merely pictorial (*PhM* 459, pp. 215ff). In Hegel's view we saw that time is the truth of space: on this premise, it is only reasonable to suppose that the audible, which depends upon time for its articulation, is preferable to the written. In Hegel's words:

Thus, while (with the faculty which transformed alphabetic writing ito hieroglyphics) the capacity of abstraction gained by the first practise remains, hieroglyphic reading is of itself a deaf reading and a dumb writing. It is true that the audible (which is in time) and the visible (which is in space), each have their own basis, one no less authoritative than the other. But in the case of alphabetic writing there is only a *single* basis: the two aspects occupy their rightful relation to each other: the visible language is related to the vocal only as a sign, and intelligence expresses itself immediately and unconditionally by speaking.— The instrumental function of the comparitively non-sensuous element of tone for all ideational work shows itself further as peculiarly important in memory which forms the passage from representation to thought. (*PhM* 459, p. 218)

Because for Hegel the patterns which appear in any given aspect of the development of Spirit recur elsewhere in the system, articulated at different levels of complexity, the role of the sign in memory as mediating between images and thought provides a clue to the significance of archeological memory in the history of Spirit. Memory inwardizes content not only in the immediate intuition of recollection (Erinnerung) but also and especially in the word as a sign in memory proper (Gedächtnis). This activity facilitates the transformation of substance into subject and then opens up the free play of content of the newly inwardized material. Memory preserves the sublated experiences and assures their availability.[71] Hegel claims "The realm of Spirits which is formed in this way in the outer world constitutes a succession in Time in which one Spirit relieved another of its charge and each took over the empire of the world from its predecessor." (*Phen* 808, p. 492). The process works in much the same way as some Buddhists imagine the activity of transmigration. A flame is passed along from torch to torch by soldiers of the night watch. The old one is extinguished as the new one is being lit so that, in a sense, all the flames are present in the last.[72] Similarly, William James in a rare burst of Hegelian insight writes: "who owns the last self owns the self before the last, for what possesses the possessor possesses the possessed."[73]

It is now possible to relate the complex dialectic of time and eternity to the mode of temporalization in the contemporary necropolis.[74] Hegel's analysis of eternity and time cannot be applied mutantis to the death event. Yet Hegel's problem—the difficulty of bringing eternity into genuine relation to time, the central philosophical problematic arising out of the Christian supersession of the classical conception of time and eternity—emerges in derailed form in the death event. The sorting myths of the death-world interpret the work of eternity in time as a negative, as the unending annihilation in time and history of the demonic other. But since eternity is now emptied into history in a fully realized immanentism, the death work becomes the unceasing task of the utopian societies patterned on the sorting myths. There is no superseding this negation since the work mandated by the myth is a pure and *final* negation.[75] In the sorting myth, ordinary time is suspended, whereas the present, pregnant with meaning, is seen as the fulfillment of the whole of the past and as that which the past prefigured. Standing in the way of this actualization are the impure, who are imagined to contaminate eternity and to threaten the fulfillment of the purpose of time.

Yet there is a jarring lack of harmony between the immanentized negative eternity of the myth and the time of technological society, the time of the saeculum. This disharmony comes about because myth requires profane time for its actualization. But how can mythic time penetrate the punctual time of technological society? Mythic time inserts itself into clock time by importing a sense of urgency into the saeculum which expresses itself as an acceleration of time. This sense of speed is captured by T. S. Eliot in *The Waste Land*. Describing the dessication of ordinary life, he punctuates conversations of terrifying banality with the pub-closing phrase: "HURRY UP PLEASE ITS TIME."[76] Quantifiable time from the standpoint of the myth is partially mythicized not by stopping time but by accelerating it, exaggerating its quantitative aspect. True, the new society is to lie outside of time, but the present, the split age of the interim, knows only the acceleration of time.

For the victims who acquire negative status through the myth, time is also greatly accented although not necessarily accelerated. Just as for Hegel time is the process of becoming itself, the "abstraction of destruction" in the death-world reaches a point where experience which ordinarily oscillates between a time-pole and a space-pole careens towards temporalization. This results from the shrinking of habitable space which is already present in technological society and is carried to its extreme in the death-world. Temporalization may express itself either as an acceleration or a slowing down of time in the concentration camps, but it is likely to appear as a lengthening of time in slave labor camps when a prisoner's sentence is extended. Time is destabilized and becomes the "truth of space," as Hegel had suggested, but this truth is the result of the impoverishment of space. This change may be marked by the mythicizing of geography, in which the meaning of place names changes from spatial to temporal signifiers. Siberia has become a term the denotation of which is no longer an actual territory but an ideal form, the complex of conditions whose primary mark is an indefinite extension of time.

The time of the sorting myth belongs to what might be called "bad eternity." For Hegel, true eternity is "absolute timelessness," something altogether different from time, while bad eternity is that which is put in front of time as the future of time. This future eternity imagined as just ahead is in fact the time of the death-world, which sees itself as the penultimate phase of an end-time which in actuality is continually deferred. Paradoxically, the sorting myths of the death-world posit an infinite supply of persons when actually the supply is exhaustible, but a finite quantity of time when in fact time is inexhaustible.

Is Hegel's standpoint then our own? Does the for us (*für uns*) of the *Phenomenology*, the distance achieved by the philosopher from the panorama of history, coincide with the place we now occupy as observers or demythologizers of the sorting myths in order to elicit their hitherto unperceived annihilatory implications? Did Hegel foresee the relation of bad eternity to a newly emergent death event? Something like such foresight is attributed to Hegel in Kojève's interpretation of Hegel's Concept as time. Kojève thinks that for Hegel "History itself must be essentially finite; collective Man (humanity) must die just as the human individual dies; universal History must have a definitive *end*."[77] but even in this radical reading of Hegel, Kojève goes on to acknowledge: "We know that for Hegel this end of history is marked by the coming of Science in the form of a Book—that is by the appearance of the Wise Man or of *absolute* Knowledge in the World. This absolute Knowledge being the *last* moment of Time, that is a moment without a *Future*—is no longer a temporal moment."[78] Such knowledge *is* for Kojève what Hegel means by eternity.

Yet the most that Kojève can argue is that universal history is fragile and will, like other moments, be sublated. But finite beings do not just disappear. If the logos is to retain a grasp of the whole it cannot dispense with one of its dialectical poles. Transfigured he may be, but finite man, as T. S. Eliot has written, "woven in the weakness of the changing body," endures.[79]

In this chapter I have examined the congitive activity of Spirit as it goes about its work of sublating and raising what is actual to a new level of ideality. Spirit achieves its results by bringing what is merely implicit in any given moment to self-conscious awareness. In its work as reflection, Spirit creates a series of oppositions in the form of paradoxes and antinomies. These are cognitive crises of Spirit.

The problem of evil is one such crisis. Departing from the commonsense understanding of the meaning of evil, Hegel analyzes the question of theodicy as a crisis of knowing embodied in phenomenological shape. Evil is necessary to the history of Spirit as annulling unmediated unity, an unwarranted innocence that fails to take account of its own implicit meanings. This for Hegel is the real significance of the myth of the fall. The depth of evil is measured by the degree to which it penetrates consciousness. Yet this depth is precisely what is absent in contemporary manifestations of evil. Bureaucratic structures and distancing technologies blunt the awareness of the machinery of death, as well as of the magnitude of annihilating acts.

Hegel's analysis of crime is structurally related to his interpretation of evil and is therefore treated as phenomenologically similar, although the context of crime is no longer theological but is expressed in the relation of the individual to the state. Crime is less an event than a phenomenon of conscious life, of the intentionality of a criminal will. Hegel locates the moral law violated by the criminal in the consensus of the community. The difficulties of Hegel's view are assessed in relation to the distinction, drawn by contemporary ethical theorists, between deontological and consequentialist positions. Hegel is able to relate these positions dialectically. In the context of his political theory he offers a deontological analysis, but from the standpoint of the system as a whole, the consequentialist or teleological position prevails. From my point of view, Hegel's version of deontological ethics with its appeal to community consensus, is bankrupt since communities have all too willingly participated in the destruction of untold numbers of persons.

Hegel does not separate what we would call "decision theory" from his vision of the good life as a whole. Individual decisions are related to the goals of life which Hegel derives from the Aristotelian view of the proper ends of man: political excellence and contemplation. The contemplative ideal undergoes modification in Hegel's hands to become the backward glance of history, whereas Hegel's political ideal reflects the precipitate of rationality in the laws and institutions of existing states.

While problems of ethical and religious life are cognitive crises for Hegel, these are expressed phenomenologically. But the crisis of cognition comes to a head only in Hegel's own time in the work of Kant, Fichte, and Jacobi. For Hegel, the system of oppositions generated by Kantian thought—what Hegel calls the philosophy of reflection—fails to accommodate the character of the transpersonal subject which alone can reach truth. In Hegel's eyes Kant has developed a psychology of the understanding in which the scope and limits of knowledge are seen in terms of a finite subject rather than a genuine philosophy of mind. The special limitations of the individual epistemological subject force Kant to exclude the thing-in-itself from the field of knowledge. Hegel must overcome this difficulty by recognizing that the subject of knowing is transpersonal, and that the object is a spiritual product from the first. Only a dialectical philosophy can breach the aporias which were brought to light by the understanding and which remain unresolved in critical philosophy.

Hegel detects instances of the philosophy of reflection elsewhere in the history of thought, particularly in the attempt to make mathematics and the physical sciences paradigmatic for philosophy as a whole. Here Hegel's interpretation of the ethos of reflection provides a theory of culture that anticipates culture's fragmentation in technological society. This strain of Hegel's thought recurs as the seldom-noticed backdrop for Heidegger's view of technology.

Despite this fruitful approach, Hegel's analysis is dominated by what Derrida calls the logic of presence, the possibility for bringing to view the totality of the content of consciousness. The logic of presence is expressed in Hegel's view of the dialectical relation of time and eternity. The becoming present of the past activity of Spirit is the work of time. Hegel contrasts the destructive process of becoming which is time with the timelessness of eternity. He makes the further mystifying claim that time is the truth of space. Yet this claim makes sense in the context of the dialectical requirement that the in-itself or actuality of space must give way to a higher degree of ideality. It must become an in-itself for-itself, a work that can only be accomplished as time.

If eternity is timelessness, then the present is a form of eternity in time. The criterion which unites them is comprehensive content or fullness. The present is full because it is an archeological structure: the past is ingredient in the present and the true present is memory. The logic of presence comes to fruition in this vision of the present. Hegel rejects Kant's categorial view of time and instead interprets time as destruction and becoming, an important ingredient of the experience of time in the death-world. Even if Hegel is a philosopher of radical finitude and can imagine the end of universal history as Kojève claims, Hegel does not envisage the coming-to-an-end of all human existence. The most that can be said of negation within the framework of Hegel's system is that the standpoint of time is overcome in the ultimate knowledge of the philosopher.

IV / Hegel and the Aporias of Existence

The inner freedom from the practical desire,
The release from action and suffering, release from the inner
And the outer compulsion, yet surrounded
By a grace of sense, a white light still and moving
Erhebung without motion concentration
Without elimination, both a new world
And the old made explicit, understood
In the completion of its partial ecstasy,
The resolution of its partial horror.

—T. S. Eliot

*T*HE MEANING OF DEATH REQUIRES an understanding of man not only as a self-conscious existent, a subject, but also as a natural being. Even if man transcends nature, the human existent is also "the most fundamental type of organism." This means that the conquest of nature by Spirit does not entail the end of finite existence. Instead the sheerly contingent aspects of finite existence are transformed by the actions of Spirit and taken up into its larger design so that the overcoming of nature remains a perpetual challenge to Spirit. This would be true even if this overcoming belonged only to the content of recollection as the remembered moment of man's sublation of mere species being, as one moment among many in a gallery of images, since Spirit relives its history in recollection. But this overcoming of nature is not only a relation of man to his past displayed before the remembering eye of Spirit. Hegel's claim is far stronger: nature is the object of a perpetual reconquest. The tensions of human existence are continual since man must continue to sublate natural existence, which reappears in protean guises.

Paradoxically, the more knowledge grows, the more intense is our awareness that human existence is also natural existence. This awareness deepens because it is impossible to ignore mortality. What makes man a creature of Spirit from the start is his capacity to kill the animal side of his nature by transcending it. At first man merely recognizes himself as a being who dies. The foreknowledge of death catapults him out of the natural world and creates him as a spiritual being. But once man possesses his death, this knowledge weaves itself into the texture of his existence and affects the mode in which he experiences temporalization, relations to other people, and the building of cultures. Memory, the signature of Spirit's life, forces these death-related changes to become cumulative, eternalizes them by holding fast to the work of time.

I will examine how Hegel thinks the crises in existence come about and will try to determine their bearing upon man's relation to his own death, as well as to the death event. These crises become more comprehensive and include ever larger spheres of existence as the life of Spirit develops. The first crisis of mortality occurs when man becomes a conscious subject through awareness of the inevitability of death. The second crisis is enacted in a struggle between two antagonists, one willing to risk life, the other quaking in the depths of his being before death the sovereign master. The relation of mastery and bondage is established as the outcome of this combat through reciprocal recognition of the other's status. The widening circle of death is expressed in the context of social existence as war, a repetition of the struggle to the death which takes place in the sphere of culture and polity. The final crisis in the life of Spirit occurs when man recognizes the goal of Spirit as embodied in the spiritual life of the Christian community. This new crisis is initiated by the destruction of transcendence, or deicide, without which the truth of Spirit as fully immanent cannot be realized. This truth, for Hegel, is expressed in the death of God or, in the pictorial language of Christianity, as crucifixion. But the self-emptying of God is succeeded by resurrection and the continuing work of the Holy Spirit, which, for Hegel, lives eternally in the spiritual community of Christ.

Death and the Transcending of Nature NATURE FOR HEGEL IS THE IDEA in the form of pure externality, the negation of the Idea which is subjective existence or Spirit. This externality exists in the mode of time and space. Thus for Hegel space and time are not (as they were for Kant) forms of the understanding through which phenomenal existence is grasped but, since nature is the externalization of Spirit, they are the modes in which nature others itself. Since the life of the Absolute is an oscillation between Spirit's self-disclosure as other and the progressive interiorization of this otherness there is no noumenal residue or thing-in-itself behind the appearances to constitute nature's true being. Nature is the limit of Spirit; at the same time, Spirit reappropriates nature, which is an alienated portion of itself.[1] As a product of Spirit, nature is from the beginning rational, although this rationality is merely implicit and must be brought out in the life of Spirit. Nature is not free in its manner of being but exists as a combination of necessity and contingency. To be a sheer natural being is to exist unreflectively. Nature is Spirit's sacrifice of its primal unity in the interest of a freedom to be achieved by Spirit in the process of its becoming. In Hegel's eyes:

> The self-knowing Spirit knows not only itself but also the negative of itself, or its limit: to know one's limit is to know how to sacrifice oneself. This sacrifice is the externalization in which Spirit displays the process of its becoming Spirit in the form of *free contingent happening*, intuiting its pure Self as Time outside of it, and equally its Being as Space. This last Becoming of Spirit, *Nature*, is its living immediate Becoming; Nature, the externalized Spirit, is in its existence, nothing but this eternal externalization of its *continuing existence* and the movement which reinstates the *Subject*. (*Phen* 807, p. 492)

The development of culture cannot nullify the existence of nature—Spirit cannot do away with nature *tout court*. Hegel is emphatic on this point. At the conclusion of the *Phenomenology*, describing the coincidence of Spirit with its object, Hegel speaks of external nature as ongoing, an "*eternal* externalization" and reinstatement of the subject. This is a matter of considerable importance since it establishes the necessity, not to be surpassed at some higher state, of man's mortality.

The sundering of the primal unity of Spirit and its othering as a nature which grows ever more complex is the central problem of Hegel's philosophy of nature. Viewed in this light Hegel's discussion can be seen as a reworking of Plato's response in the *Timaeus* to the Eleatic philosophy of the One which considers why there are many (a world of multiplicity) rather than One. Hegel's version of this puzzle can best be stated in the form of Schelling's question (later made familiar by Heidegger): "Why is there something rather than nothing?" The identity of these questions may not be self-evident unless one remembers that, for Hegel, the One, pure Being without determinations, is tantamount to Nothing so that multiplicity begins as soon as there is anything at all. In answer to this question Hegel claims that being which lacks determination may have formal perfections but in the end is unproductive. Arthur O. Lovejoy describes the problem and its solution in his unsurpassed account of the great chain of Being:

> A self-sufficient being who is eternally at the goal, whose perfection is beyond all possibility of enhancement or diminution *could* not be envious of anything not itself. Its reality could be no impediment to the reality in their own way, of beings other than it alike in existence and in kind and in excellence; on the contrary, unless it were somehow productive of them, it would lack a positive element of perfection, would not be so complete as its very definition implies that it is. . . . The concept of Self-Sufficing Perfection, by a bold logical inversion, was—without losing any of its original implications—converted into a concept of Self-Transcending Fecundity. A timeless and incorporeal One became the logical ground as well a the dynamic source of the existence of a temporal and material and extremely multiple and variegated universe.[2]

Hegel also discusses a second and related question: What rule governs the ordering of this multiplicity? His response is characteristically Aristotelean: nature is hierarchically ordered along lines of complexity beginning with matter and ending with man. Yet Hegel modifies Aristotle's naturalistic frame of reference, since the hierarchy of nature is governed by the interests of Spirit—the growth of subjectivity and freedom. He writes:

> Nature is *implicitly* a living whole; more closely considered, the movement through its series of stages consists of the Idea pos-

iting itself as what it is implicitly [dead matter]. . . . It does this primarily in order to take on living being, but also . . . to bring itself forth into the existence of Spirit, which constitutes the truth and ultimate purpose of nature, and the true actuality of the Idea. (*PhN* 1:251, p. 216)

The work of Spirit in nature becomes particularly obvious in Hegel's discussion of animal life and is important for an understanding of the death event, since death plays a central role in Hegel's account. Both Aristotle and Hegel agree that the animal is self-moving and can spontaneously determine its place, but Hegel gives animal motion a unique interpretation by introducing the negative into purely natural existence. The animal, according to Hegel, posits itself as the negation of place, a negation which it accomplishes through self-mobility. "In all things apart from animals . . . singularization is fixed, for it is only in the animal, that the self has being-for-self. . . . It posits its own place" (PhN 3:351 add., p. 105). More, the animal has voice which gives utterance to self-feeling while sound production itself exists in the abstract ideality of time. This means that the animal can express its inwardness, and in some sense, though by no means fully, take cognizance of its own death. This stands to reason since hierarchical ordering is, for Hegel, determined by the degree to which Spirit penetrates a given natural form. If animal being fails fully to apprehend its mortality, still less can the animal reach the level of subjectivity achieved in the use of language. Only man, the being who recognizes his mortality, can abstract from conglomerate experience repeatable elements which can function as signs.[3]

Yet if animal being fails to express the Notion conceptually, it does so in the lived pattern of its existence. To be an animal is, for Hegel, to experience lack. Animal life is a perpetual alternation of lack and its overcoming, the tension between its subjectivity and an external reality. This means that even animal being is, in a rudimentary sense, aware of the "unity of itself and its specific antithesis" (PhN 3:359 remark, p. 151). The alternation of lack and repletion is a basic structure which recurs at every level of existence. It provides a counterpoint to cognition and accounts for such ineradicable features of corporeal life as nutrition, sexuality, and, ultimately, violence and destruction.

This structure first appears when externality is conquered by the animal through assimilation, devouring the external world and thus converting it to something inner. The animal eats in order to live. Yet the particular animal can only attain satiety, never significance, through the chain of need, since it is mortal. Although animal consciousness may be sated in this way, meaning is secured for individual life only when it can express something universal. This universality is expressed through the individual animal's membership in a genus (*PhN* 3:351, pp. 170ff). Through participation in the being of the genus the animal attains universality and also a certain immortality. Although the particular animal dies, the genus endures. The presence of the universal, the genus, in the individual prompts it to seek another like itself, "to integrate itself in union" with another in order to reproduce itself (*PhN* 3:368, pp. 172ff). The immortality of the genus is maintained at the expense of the individual, for the particular being works in the interest of the genus. When the individual has reproduced itself it has fulfilled its objective and dies.

The situation of man is, however, altogether different from that of mere animal existence. Man, like the animal, is mortal but, unlike the animal whose immortality depends upon species being, man has the capacity to organize the universal in himself, to transform mere existence into logos. Thus man transmits to his progeny far more than the stamp of the genus. To be sure, he reproduces and dies in accordance with the laws of the organism. But the function of recollection, of inwardized experience, permits the generations to carry a *remembered* identity rather than the mere stamp of external likeness. This subjective continuity negates mere animal being. The parents see themselves in the child and in this act of recognition the generations are linked.[4]

In order for this chain to be fashioned, self-recognition must take the place of mere genus identity. The animal must die and Spirit must be born. Hegel explains:

> The negation of the immediate singularity of natural being [the death of a particular being] consists in the positing of the universality of the genus. . . . In spiritual *individuality*, this movement of the two sides is the self-sublating progression which *results in consciousness*, i.e. the unity which is in and for itself the

unity of both, [the single natural creature and the genus] and which is this as self, not merely as genus in the inner Notion of the singular. It is in this way that the Idea exists in the independent subject, which as an organ of the Notion, finds everything to be fluid and of an ideal nature, i.e. it thinks, appropriates to itself all that is spatial and temporal, and so contains universality, i.e. itself. . . . As this universal which has being for itself, thought is *immortal being*, while mortal being consists in the universality of the Idea being inadequate to itself. (*PhN* 3:376 add., pp. 211–12)

But why import the idea of the Notion into a purely natural process? Most animals die of disease. For Hegel any particular disease *is* the capture of the organism by one of its organ systems (for example, the digestive), which disturbs the vital unity of the whole (*PhN* 3:374, p. 208). Hegel acknowledges the obvious fact that organic disease exists, but he insists that the disparity between singularity and universality constitutes the true disease of animal existence, and for this disease there can be no cure. Thus in a remarkable passage Hegel claims: "The *original disease* of the animal, and the *inborn germ of death*, is its being inadequate to universality." He adds: "The organism can recover from disease, but it is because it is diseased from its very nature that death is a necessity" (*PhN* 3:375, p. 209). The implications for Hegel's anthropology are considerable. Human existence is poisoned root and branch: man as animal being is the disease of nature because he cannot avoid death, and as spiritual being he knows that he is this disease. For Hegel, man can overcome this dilemma only by transforming actual existence, by taking charge of death, by the willingness to risk life and thus give meaning to death.

Culture itself contains elements that represent nature. The conflict of nature and Spirit is expressed within the sphere of culture in an opposition between the family—which represents blood ties, takes charge of death rites, and substitutes for nature—and the state, a rational community governed by discourse and therefore capable of expressing universal moral norms. This conflict is expressed in Greek tragedy. In tragedy the laws of the family, the custodian of death, cannot be reconciled with those of polity.[5]

For Hegel, nature and its substitutes—animal, woman, and family—are sticking-points, "ironies" in the life of Spirit (*Phen* 475, p. 288). The sublated aspects of Spirit not carried forward by the progress of Spirit, become dead nature, the detritus of civilization in which Spirit has lost interest. Since the natural is required as the pole of opposition for the life of Spirit, it retains its place in the larger history of Spirit. But only those aspects of nature which play a role in a living dialectical moment hold the interest of Spirit at any specified time.

The Theft of Immortality

FOR HEGEL THE TELEOLOGICAL development of nature expresses itself in two ways. As the externalization of Spirit in space, it moves toward complexity; as the unfolding of the Notion in time, it seeks immortality which it finds in thought. "As this universal which has being for itself, thought is *immortal being*" (*PhN* 3:376 add., p. 212). This understanding of natural existence has direct bearing on the death-world. The objective of the death-world is to create an enclave stripped of cultural meanings in order to return to sheer animal existence. Terence des Près sums up this abrasion of meaning in concentration camps: "All were places in which the human self was stripped of spiritual as well as physical mediations, until nothing was left to persist through pain and time but the body itself."[6] Hu Nim, the information minister of democratic Kampuchea after 1975, whose confession was obtained by means of torture, writes: "I am not a human being—I am an animal."[7] In Hegel's terms he has regressed to "the immediate singularity of natural being"; he is only his body or space and nothing else. In the context of culture the body becomes a vehicle of meaning, but to reduce the individual to mere bodily existence is to make the body itself the whole of space as well as the whole of consciousness. Such an existence is as near as possible to a life deprived of logos, since thought exists in the form of time. The present of the least complex consciousness is like Proust's magic lantern which both retains and projects the past. Technological society reduces memory to information retrieval. The death-world, retaining this perspective, cuts away the symbol systems which create ties to the past and options for the future. Two things persist, paradoxically: the information systems which are the

end products of the philosophy of reflection derived from technological society, and the naked organism stripped of symbolic meaning, the unique contribution of the death-world itself.

The existence of man in Hegel's eyes culminates in the realization
of Spirit as thought. The key to thought is ideality, which has the
power to fix the pulse of time: "Thought is immortal being." To steal
the symbolic expressions of culture is to steal immortality. The death-
world is created and maintained to rob its victims of immortality,
the power to transcend time.

It is not enough to kill all victims outright. The scheme of annihilation must exhibit to a token number of victims the nullity of their
symbolic structures, to force them to comprehend their loss. The
quest for eternal life is a common element in widely differing religious traditions, but it has been observed less often that immortality
can be stolen.[8] By reducing victims to animal status the death-world
strips them of the symbolic truths of their existence and consigns
them to death forever. This must be confirmed in the minds of victor
and victim alike. Viktor Frankl illustrates the point in his description
of an episode which occurred on his arrival in Auschwitz. Frankl tells
a long-time inmate:

> "Look, this is the manuscript of a scientific book. I know what
> you will say; that I should be grateful to escape with my life,
> that should be all I can expect of fate. But I cannot help myself.
> I must keep this manuscript at all costs; it contains my life's
> work. Do you understand that?" Yes, he was beginning to
> understand. A grin spread slowly over his face, first piteous,
> then more amused, mocking, insulting, until he bellowed one
> word at me in answer to my question . . ."Shit!" At that mo-
> ment I saw the plain truth and did what marked the culminating
> point of my psychological reaction: I struck out my whole for-
> mer life.[9]

Hegel's view that time is the truth of space takes on unanticipated
meaning in this context. The body is a prison not because, as Plato
alleges, the soul is its captive, but because the body cannot express
meanings which depend upon temporal existence. In technological
society, the homogenization of space creates an experience of con-
densed temporal intensity. This is possible because the body is not

itself a source of pain and cannot obstruct inner experience or fantasy. But the sense of time approaches a breaking point when it is made to bear both temporal and spatial meaning. In the *death-world* even this atomizing structure is precluded because everything that belongs to consciousness is stolen.

Spirit in Ashes

*H*EGEL'S VIEW OF THE RELATION of nature and culture brings to light the relevance of Hegel's thought to the structures of the death-world. But the death event includes other manifestations of contemporary man-made mass death. These are phenomena which entail total annihilation—nuclear, chemical, and biological warfare. Hegel's philosophy of nature is useful for understanding these phenomena, although Hegel's arguments relevant to this theme are complex and grounded in anachronistic nineteenth-century scientific theories.[10] For Hegel, nature is organized hierarchically; its development proceeds along lines of increasing complexity. Each stage proceeds necessarily from the preceding stage and is its truth. Nature is not "a natural engendering of one out of the other," but an engendering within the inner Idea which constitutes the ground of nature (*PhN* 1:249 remark, p. 212). Thus Hegel rejects the idea of evolution as a chronological sequence of forms which emerge without inherent necessity from lesser to greater complexity. He argues: "To think of the genera as gradually evolving themselves out of one another is to make use of a completely empty concept; the time-difference is completely devoid of interest for thought" (*PhN* 1:297 add., pp. 212–13). To follow the course of nature one must not merely systematize its complexity but remain attentive to its aspiration to become Spirit. Thus Hegel says:

> The thinking view of Nature must note the implicit process by which Nature sublates its otherness to become Spirit, and the way in which the Idea is present in each state of Nature itself. Estranged from the Idea, Nature is merely the corpse of the understanding. Nature is the Idea, but only implicitly. That is why Schelling called it petrified intelligence which others have

even said is frozen. God does not remain petrified and moribund however, the stones cry out and lift themselves up to
Spirit. (*PhN* 1:247, p. 206)

It is the task of the philosophy of nature to bring this process to
light. Its proper method is metaphysical, which means for Hegel
using "the range of universal thought determinations, [which are] as
it were the diamond-net into which we bring everything in order to
make it intelligible" (*PhN* 1:246 add., p. 202). In contrast to the
view "that Nature is implicitly a living whole," the physical sciences
are instances of the philosophy of reflection which can distinguish
relations but lacks an intuition of the whole. Hegel's view of nature
is not a simplistic intuitive one. Intuition lacks thought and can only
be restored at a higher level in the unity of the Notion which can
also hold difference in itself (*PhN* 1:246 add., p. 203). But intuition
is set above reflection as a necessary stage in raising the philosophy
of nature to "the immanent and self-moving unity . . . the diaman-
tine identity" Hegel believes it to have.

Although the subject matter of the physical sciences has altered
radically, the grounds upon which Hegel criticizes them remain pertinent. Hegel acknowledges two criteria widely accepted to characterize adequate scientific hypotheses: parsimony and comprehensiveness. Parsimony is the more important since it is a standard for
evaluating hypotheses. The entities which modern particle physics
postulates as the basic constituents of the universe are virtually infinite in number while a maximum economy of statement governs the
understanding of their activity.[11] The principle of parsimony in the
statements of science and reductionism in relation to its fundamental
units appear to be what Hegel has in mind when he speaks of abstraction or formal universality in the scientific grasp of Nature. He
says:

> The inadequacy of the thought determinations used in physics
> may be traced to very closely connected points. (a) The univer-
> sal of physics is abstract or simply formal; its determination is
> not immanent within it, and does not pass over into particular-
> ity. (b) This is precisely the reason why its determinate content
> is external to the universal, and is therefore split up, dismem-
> bered, particularized; separated, lacking in any necessary con-

nection within itself; why it is in fact merely finite." (*PhN* 1:246 add., p. 202)

The postulated entities of the modern physical sciences are distributed throughout the world of natural forms, what Hegel calls organic and inorganic existence. These entities represent the limit of structure and function at present available to us for understanding the way the universe works, but they give only indirect evidence of their actual existence. This perspective is elaborated in what is perhaps the most convoluted section of the *Phenomenology*, the section on force and the inverted world (*Verkehrte Welt*). Although Hegel criticizes the physicists' understanding of nature from the standpoint of the scientific mechanism of his time, his conclusions remain remarkably fresh.

Hegel begins by introducing the idea of force to explain some problems in the naive empiricist's theory of perception. The empiricist claims that we know things only together with their individual qualities; for example, sugar with its whiteness, sweetness, granularity, and so on. But qualitative understanding must give way to an explanation in terms of the relationship of forces, the object as it appears to scientific analysis, since the play of forces accounts for the properties of the thing. The laws which govern the play of forces come much closer to the truth of things, since as the work of the understanding they give a much better picture of the thing's interior than does mere perception. If this is so, a supersensible world is affirmed as the true world, one which recalls Plato's theory of forms. The peculiar character of the world of laws is its constancy, whereas the real world is in flux. True, yet unlike Platonic forms the laws of force redeem the appearances; they are the truth of the appearances. Unlike Platonic forms they are not different from the world that appears since the laws of force are nothing but the laws of pure appearance.[12] "The supersensible world is thus an inert realm of laws" (*Phen* 132, p. 90).

There is still another difference between the perceived and ideal worlds as they are pictured in Plato's view and in Hegel's conception of physics. The inverted world, Hegel argues, unlike the Platonic world of forms, contains the principle of motion. This means that the "tranquil laws" are not (dialectically) static after all but are dynamic principles. In a play on the word *Verkehrt*, this world is also topsy-turvy in a different way; it is perverse or distorted in its invertedness. Commenting on the inverted world, H. G. Gadamer writes: "What is found in the topsy-turvy world is not simply the contrary, the mere abstract opposite of the existent world. Rather this reversal in which everything is the opposite of itself makes visible in a kind of funhouse mirror the overt perversion of everything as we know it."[13] Hegel's proposals for overcoming the limitations of the inverted world are characteristically Romantic: "Spirit cannot be confined to this procedure of the reflective understanding . . . [whereas] an alive and open mind . . . feels the life and universal relatedness within Nature; it has a presentiment of the universe as an organic whole, a rational totality" (*PhN* 1:246 add., p. 202).

Hegel's view of scientific reason is intrinsically embedded in the ontology of science. For Hegel the dialectical method demands that Spirit actualize its cognitive structure always and by necessity. Hegel sees the stunted firstfruits of the philosophy of reflection in the ethos created by the Enlightenment. But he does not anticipate (and could not have anticipated) the extent to which the content of science, a creation of Renaissance and Enlightenment rationality, requires existential expression. The cognitive work of Spirit demands actuality (*Wirklichkeit*). But how is actualization attained in regard to the theoretical structures of physics? It is by no means farfetched on a Hegelian reading of the relation of theory to practice to suggest that physics acquires existential import by reducing the phenomenal world of experience to the level of homogeneity and atomicity: to the truth of the inverted world. Just as Plato put forward the notion of ideal forms to account for the appearances, modern science alters the process: it reduces the relative ideality of appearances to the "real" if postulated entities of physics. Science provides the generative metaphors of negation which culture actualizes in the events of extinction which have come to characterize twentieth century existence. Culture brings into existence the closest possible approximation of science's picture of the world as homogenous and uniform matter. Unhindered by the backdrag of life which does not yield to theoretical elegance, science, wedded to the culture of reflection, sets out to destroy the appearances in order to *duplicate* its own consciousness in actuality.

Of course there is no conspiracy on the part of scientists to do away with the life-world. To the contrary, the scientific community has often been self-critical. But moral constraints appear futile once the technology of destruction has gained a foothold. Science offers a picture of cosmic infrastructure but no moral vision of the world. It is therefore appropriate that J. Robert Oppenheimer, watching the explosion of the first atomic bomb test, cited not a moral apocalyptic vision of cosmic disaster, but a purely cosmological display of cataclysm. Like Krishna's devotee, Arjuna, "filled with amazement, his hair standing erect," Oppenheimer could only stammer the words of the *Bhagavad Gita*: "Time [death] am I the destroyer of worlds, matured, come forth to subdue the worlds here."[14]

Death the Sovereign Master   THE BASIC STRUCTURE OF ANIMAL existence is the dialectical relation of need and satisfaction. The animal feels lack and satisfies this lack by assimilating its environment. Similarly, the animal experiences the urge to unite with another of its kind to maintain what is universal in animal life, the species. In these natural relations the animal has no image (*Vorstellung*) of what it requires; it cannot overcome the endless repetition of the cycle of need that ends only with death. Lack must be transformed into human desire (*Begierde*) in order to transcend animality. But, if desire is to be something more than mere lack, its object must also change. This can only come about when sheer animal velleity becomes the acknowledgement of the existence of other beings like itself who are not to be destroyed and who do not fulfill merely reproductive functions but, to the contrary, solicit recognition. This change marks the transition from mere life to reason.

Hegel develops this idea in the celebrated section of the *Phenomenology* entitled "Lordship and Bondage." We have already seen that the first halting steps across the threshold separating animal from human life occur when the necessity of death is acknowledged. But even if death is recognized how is what Hegel has called "the disease of the animal . . . the inborn germ of death" sublated when the living being knows that death is unavoidable? Man, in Hegel's eyes, must possess his death, take charge of it, find a way to make himself master of death "the sovereign master." For Hegel this cannot come about by imagining human existence as continuing in a beyond, although Spirit does pass through this stage of death. Mastery can only be realized by risking life itself, and life must be wagered in the interest of something above death. Though the sovereign master is victor in the realm of nature, in the realm of Spirit death is subordinated to something higher—recognition of one's mastery by another consciousness.

Hegel's account of the struggle to the death begins with an analysis of natural being absorbed in the task of sheer living. But natural existence lacks the validity of self-consciousness, since no being, knowing only itself, has had its existence confirmed by another. Such acknowledgement can only be achieved in a combat to the death. But the mere willingness to risk life is not yet a sufficient condition for the emergence of independent selfhood: if one or both combatants die, no consciousness is left to affirm the selfhood of the survivor. Life is necessary if the dialectical progression is to continue. In order to preserve the significance of the struggle both antagonists must survive. "In this experience," Hegel says, "life is as essential to it as pure self-consciousness is" (*Phen* 189, p. 115).

In making the fear of violent death rather than the certainty of the cogito the foundation of self-consciousness, Hegel follows Hobbes rather than Descartes. For Hegel, consciousness must experience the vicissitudes of concrete existence, as well as epistemological doubt, if Spirit is to mature. This is made clear in the structure of the *Phenomenology*. The history of Spirit begins with the deceptive epistemologies of naive empiricism and simplistic scientism. Unable to gain access either to the object or to itself, the subject must penetrate these deceptions. It can only flounder painfully until it turns in desperation from cognition to life. The subject cannot overcome its dilemma through further reflection but only in the pain of actual existence, which culminates in the struggle to the death. This organization not only contradicts any obvious principle of chronological ordering, but seems to fly in the face of Hegel's own claim that philosophy does not precede but supervenes upon experience. Although the task of philosophy is reflection upon immediate experience which passes for knowledge, philosophy's full actualization as self-consciousness also requires existence. Genuine philosophy therefore includes both thought and existence.[15]

Hegel's choice of Hobbes over Descartes in the pivotal episode of the struggle to the death, and the bifurcation of Spirit into consciousness of lordship and bondage, affirms the importance of existence in Hegel's system. For Hegel knowledge which does not sear the flesh is naive, lacks the true mark of the negative without which genuine knowledge cannot come into being. Thus self-consciousness can be born only at the point where life itself is at stake. In a celebrated passage Hegel writes: "For this consciousness has been fearful, not of this or that particular thing or just at odd moments, but its whole being has been seized with dread; for it has experienced the fear of death, the absolute Lord. In that experience it has been quite unmanned, has trembled in every fiber of its being, and everything solid and stable has been shaken to its foundations" (*Phen* 194, p. 117).

To see this one must imagine man merely as a natural existent. For Hegel, Hobbes is right to claim that man in the state of nature is a predatory creature whose desires are limited only by his power to satisfy them. "In the first place I put for a general inclination of all mankind a perpetual and restless desire of power after power that ceaseth only in death," Hobbes writes.[16] In the Jena lectures of 1803–04 Hegel sees the object of the struggle as the delineation of property rights:

> The two adversaries who recognize each other and want to know themselves as being recognized mutually as this totality of particulars confront each other as this totality. And the significance and importance that they give mutually to each other is: that each appear in the consciousness of the other as the one who excludes him from . . . everything that this latter possesses.[17]

But for Hobbes *death* is the supreme evil, and this is confirmed by the terror man feels in anticipating death. The preservation of life (rather than property) becomes a primary good in the light of this all-consuming fear.[18] Death may, on occasion, come as a relief, as in the case of painful disease, but violent death is always an unequivocal evil which arouses pure terror. It is a sign of superiority, therefore, to be willing to risk violent death on the belief that life which prefers humiliation to death is not worth living.[19] The victor in a struggle to the death establishes his superiority and can afford to restrain his passions. Once his reason for killing has vanished, he can afford the luxury of magnanimity.[20] The one who generously spares the life of the other becomes master, the other servant. For Hobbes, the despotism which results from the struggle is merely a natural state and not a true polity. The artificial state (which is preferable) arises for Hobbes when reciprocal fear of death leads man in the state of nature to recognize that safety lies in all men uniting against death.[21] But for Hegel the struggle to the death gives birth to reciprocal recognition and to self-consciousness.

The tutelary society thus created is unstable since servile consciousness begins to transcend itself as soon as the servant produces things for the enjoyment of the master. The whims of the master are dependent upon the will and the productive capacity of the bondsman. The dependence of the master upon the servant for the products of his labor is not enough to free the bondsman. The master also seeks recognition from the bondsman and thus finds the truth of his existence through the consciousness of the bondsman. Work establishes the independence of servile consciousness from natural existence by deferring desire, which in nature obtains immediate satisfaction. In this way servile consciousness places its stamp upon nature. The consciousness of mastery, on the other hand, is grounded in desire rather than in the universality of reason. But for Hegel consciousness that is based upon caprice must collapse. Since desire remains individual and idiosyncratic, it can never provide the ground for freedom and self-consciousness. For Hegel, the consciousness of mastery cannot be fully rational, since it is dependent upon servile consciousness and is still captive to natural existence.

Since Hegel claims that desire and reason are sundered in the consciousness of mastery and bondage, does his analysis of lordship and bondage, for all that it owes to Hobbes's idiosyncratic account, deviate from more traditional analyses of the proper role of desire in social existence? Is there actually little difference between Kant and Hegel in regard to the relationship between desire and reason? If we forget that Hegel is a historical thinker it might be tempting to envisage his interpretation of rationality in Kant's terms as excluding inclination. But the cunning of reason is something it acquires in the course of its history. For Hegel, therefore, desire is integral to Spirit's development. Rational desire is an oxymoron expressing the necessity of both reason and desire. It is not difficult to see from the preceding description of the play of terror and desire in the consciousness of master and servant the reflection of a purely feudal conception of society imported into an archetypal form of existence.[22]

Though the image is disguised in the *Phenomenology*, we can still see the motif of knightly combat and behind it a version of the authenticity paradigm. If the courageous management of natural death is the test of a virtuous life, willingness to risk violent death must be the sign of an even nobler nature. This point of view governs Hegel's concept of war. Hegel insists in his lectures of 1805–06: "The soldier condition and war are the objectively real sacrifice of the personal Self, the danger of death for the particular . . .[but] it is in war that this is permitted to the particular; [since] it is a crime committed *for the Universal.*" Hegel knows that in war the passions of knightly combat are attenuated: "This alienation of the Particular to the Universal must be received and given coldly; not by a deliberate struggle, in which the particular perceives the adversary and kills him in an immediate hatred; no, death is given and received in the void—*impersonally*, in consequence of the smoke from the powder."[23] Hegel appears in this passage to have achieved an uncanny insight into the impersonality of contemporary man-made mass death and, what is more, to have placed his stamp of approval upon it, since he sees war as the forward-moving impetus of history. The point is that, whether in the heat of passion as in knightly joust or coldly as in the wars of Hegel's day, self-transcendence is assured only by the willingness to risk life. Struggle must of course be freely engaged in, for if one is swept up in the movement of history one cannot create historical change; rather, history sublates free individuality.

The dialectic of mastery and servitude can be directly related to the problem of war; it is also relevant to our grasp of the death-world. Consider first the cumulative and accelerating structure of technological society as an interlocking system of references which reinforce technique and in which the death-world arises as a node. Within this postmodern structure of technique, the discourse of the death-world expresses an archaic metaphysics of purity. The death-world cannot be the existential expression of the Hegelian paradigm, since in the death-world the categories of mastery and servitude are predetermined by the metaphysics of purity without recourse to combat. Bureaucratic and technological means are set in place to serve the sorting myths' prearranged categories. The authenticity paradigm collapses when the results of combat are preordained.

The authenticity paradigm belongs to a more comprehensive structure quite different from the conception of defilement or taint which sustains the metaphysics of purity. Most versions of the authenticity paradigm presuppose a divine logos either as first mover or as intelligible principle which creates or runs the cosmos. Actions that imitate divine detachment perfect life, whereas actions that swerve from this norm degrade it. Taking charge of death affirms the logos hidden behind the contingencies of natural existence and expresses in microcosm the divine order of things. Existence tests the true lover of logos by providing opportunities to risk life in its behalf. Freedom and contingency are ingredient in this structure since the logos can only be freely affirmed.

The death-world excludes this freedom both in theory and in practice, in theory since the outcome of combat is decided in advance and in practice since the vast machinery of technological society bears down upon the impure, making resistance futile. Yet the myth used to justify the death-world puts forward the authenticity paradigm in quasi-Hegelian form by suggesting to the victim that a struggle of sorts has already taken place and has revealed his inferiority. At the same time the myth is cynical since it is clear that any genuine conditions of egalitarian combat have been precluded. Thus the myth exhibits all the characteristics of false or double consciousness: it knows what it pretends not to know and does not know what it pretends to know.

Although the warlike existence of the master is intrinsic to Hegel's account of Spirit's development, it would be misleading to see mastery as pivotal for the dialectical understanding of mastery and servitude.[24] The simple use of force is barbarism for Hegel and comes closer to the violence of animals than to the human ideal of courage.[25] When the martial ideal is dominant in culture, nature rather than Spirit rules existence. Thus Hegel would have seen Nietzsche's premodern warrior as reflecting an unmediated relation to ethical life, the static consciousness of mastery which defines good on the basis of its own whims. Hegel's statements on the warrior have given rise to conflicting interpretations. But, in the present context, Spirit is represented not by the victor in the primal combat but by the consciousness which sustains historical memory. Servile consciousness, the consciousness which remembers, is the vehicle of Spirit. It is no accident that Nietzsche extols the purgative powers of forgetting. The contrast between Hegel and Nietzsche can be interpreted as a difference between the value placed upon Nature and upon Spirit, bearing in mind that Nature forgets and Spirit remembers. The place of servile consciousness begins by making the master's ephemeral desires permanent through labor. Thus the slave is custodian of the future because through labor he learns how to leave his mark on history. Hegel says this explicitly in an overlooked passage in *The Philosophy of Mind*: "In place of the rude destruction of the immediate object there ensues acquisition, preservation, and formation of it, as the instrumentality in which the two extremes of independence and non-independence are welded together. The form of universality thus arising in satisfying the want creates a *permanent* means and a provision which takes care for and secures the future" (*PhM* 434, p. 174). The trembling before death establishes the master's hegemony in the present, but the future belongs to the one who gives an account of the present. In the moment of mastery and bondage this account is not yet mediated by a fully developed historical consciousness, but it nevertheless establishes the principle that events belong to their interpreters.

It is by now a commonplace in the literature of survival that, once the possibility of victory in any conventional sense is foreclosed, the desire to live is tied to the desire to bear witness to the structure and the day-to-day events of the death-world. Hegel's analysis provides a systematic and persuasive account of this impulse by suggesting that servile consciousness is the vehicle of recollection. The action of the slave bypasses what might seem a preferable alternative—stoicism. Hegel demonstrates that the passivity of stoic consciousness ends in the cul de sac of resignation, whereas servile consciousness leaves its mark on history.[26] A dynamically self-transcending and imaginative consciousness recognizes the power of memory to control history by becoming narrative consciousness. This is illustrated in a comment made to Alexander Donat by a fellow inmate of the Maidenek concentration camp: "Should our murderers be victorious, should *they* write the history of this war . . . their every word will be taken for gospel. Or they may wipe out our memory altogether, as if we had never existed. . . . But if *we* write the history of this period . . . we'll have the thankless job of proving to a reluctant world that we are Abel, the murdered brother."[27]

The Slaughterbench: War and History   *H*EGEL'S UNDERSTANDING OF war is already implicit in his analysis of the primordial struggle to the death, but it acquires its full meaning only in his description of the development of the state (*PhR* 328 *Zusatz*; pp. 211–12). Although bloody conflict is ingredient in many aspects of the history of Spirit as the existential ground of negation, it achieves its highest rational expression in war, when it is freely undertaken on behalf of the state. For Hegel war plays an essential part in the lives of individuals and states. He says:

> War is not to be regarded as an absolute evil and as a purely external accident, which itself therefore has some accidental cause, be it injustices, the passions of nations or the holders of power etc., or in short, something or other which ought not to be. It is to what is by nature accidental that accidents happen, and the fate whereby they happen is thus a necessity. Here as elsewhere, the point of view from which things seem pure accidents vanishes if we look at them in the light of the concept and philosophy, because philosophy knows accident for a show and sees in its essence necessity. (*PhR* 324, p. 209)

The individual does not go to war for the preservation of either life or property. If the interest of war were the preservation of life, one would be risking life in order to preserve it, a patent contradiction. Similarly, the goal of war canot be protection of property, since common sense dictates that property can only be enjoyed if one is alive (*PhR* 324, p. 210). If the preservation of life and property are not the goals of war then how do these aims stand in relation to the state? If this can be determined, it will be easier to see what Hegel believes are the legitimate ends of war.

In Hegel's eyes life and property do not belong to the sphere of polity at all; instead they organize a nexus of institutions around themselves that Hegel calls civil society (*die bürgerliche Gesellschaft*). Hegel defines civil society as the sphere for the realization of individual interests: "an association of members as self-subsistent individuals in a universality which, because of their self-subsistence, is only abstract . . . brought about by their needs, by the legal system—the means to security of person and property" (*PhR* 157, p. 110). Civil society is organized into families or individuals who, "while independent and free, as private persons," fall short of genuine ethical substance. Their aim is not "absolute unity," Hegel says, "but their own petty selves and particular interests" (*PhM* 523, p. 256). Despite the cooperation required for the satisfaction of needs, civil society can never provide the basis for establishing the general interest for which wars are fought. The state must reintegrate the particularized self of economic existence into the actuality of concrete freedom. Hegel writes:

> The state in and by itself is the ethical whole, the actualization of freedom; and it is an absolute end of reason that freedom should be actual. The state is mind on earth and consciously realizing itself there. In nature, on the other hand, mind actualizes itself only as its own other, as mind asleep. Only when it is present in consciousness, when it knows itself as a really existent object is it the state. In considering freedom, the starting-point must not be individuality, the single self-consciousness, but only the essence of self-consciousness; for whether man knows it or not, this essence is externally realized as a self-subsistent power in which single individuals are only moments. The march of God in the world, that is what the state is.[28]

Hegel has in mind not this or that particular state but, rather, an ideal toward which existing states tend depending upon the degree to which they embody the Notion. Thus, Hegel claims:

> In considering the Idea of the State, we must not have our eyes on particular states or on particular institutions. Instead we

must consider the Idea, this actual God by itself. On some principle any state may be shown to be bad, this or that defect may be found in it. . . . The state is no ideal work of art; it stands on earth and so in the sphere of caprice, chance and error, and bad behavior may disfigure it in many respects. But the ugliest of men, or a criminal or an invalid or a cripple, is still always a living man. The affirmative life subsists despite his defects, and it is this affirmative factor which is our theme here. (*PhR* 258, p. 279)

The state is still the "hieroglyph of Reason," however defective any individual state may be. The individual who risks life on behalf of the state does so in the interest of a higher ideality.

But why should states go to war against other states? Are not all states rational entities, thus precluding bloody combat as a means to settle disputes? Borrowing the structure of the relation of mastery and servitude as they function in individual consciousness, Hegel claims that states require other states for recognition. He says: "A state is as little an actual individual without relations to other states . . . as an individual is actually a person without *rapport* with other persons. . . . This authority should receive its full and final legitimation through its recognition by other states" (*PhR* 231, p. 212). States are individuals and exist as particular wills; when they disagree their disputes can only be settled by war. The welfare of individual states governs the relation of states with one another. States enter into relations with each other as particulars. It is not surprising that these relations "are a maelstrom of external contingency and the inner particularity of passions, private interests and selfish ends, abilities and virtues, vices, force and wrong. All these whirl together, and in their vortex the ethical whole itself, the autonomy of the state is exposed to contingency" (*PhR* 340, p. 215). But even if states are individuals we may think that one is wrong and another right. Impossible, Hegel insists, since each state always represents a genuine right and a breach of right is inherently indeterminable (*PhR*, 334 p. 214). He says: "Right is the advantage of one state acknowledged and settled by treaties." In this case war decides "not which of the rights alleged by the two parties is the genuine right—since both parties have a genuine right—but which of the two rights is to give way."²⁹

But if the state is a particular will, why can disputes not be submitted to an international body for settlement? This was Kant's solution to the problem of war and the ground of his hope for perpetual peace. But Hegel rejects this. For him states are the final form of political existence; they are by definition individual and sovereign.³⁰ Hegel tells us: "The nation state is mind in its substantive rationality and immediate actuality and is therefore the absolute power on earth. It follows that every state is sovereign and autonomous against its neighbors. It is entitled in the first place and without qualification to be sovereign from their point of view, i.e., to be recognized by them as sovereign" (*PhR* 331, p. 212). Sovereignty thus understood can never pass to an international body. Even if an international authority were both legitimate and effective, it, like individual states, would have to be prepared to fight. In Hegel's eyes, "Even if a number of states make themselves into a family, this group as an individual must engender an opposite and create an enemy" (*PhR* 324 *Zusatz*, p. 295). The only recourse left for resolving disputes which may arise between sovereign states is war.

Hegel's indifference to the loss of individual life in the interest of historical progress has been frequently and justifiably criticized.³¹ Indeed, not only in the light of contemporary war, but even in the context of the wars of Hegel's day, his perspective appears bizarre and extreme. Yet it should not be confused with a justification of violence for its own sake or with a feudal conception of combat. In fact, Hegel affirms Machiavelli's view that "there are two ways of fighting: by means of law and by means of force. The first belongs to man, the second to animals."³² Hegel makes this view plain in his unusually acid criticism of von Haller's *Restauration der Staatswissenschaft*. Von Haller (cited by Hegel) writes: "Just as in the inorganic world, the greater dislodges the less and the mighty the weak . . . so in the animal kingdom, and then amongst human beings, the same law appears in nobler forms . . . this therefore is the eternal unalterable ordinance of God, that the mightier rules, must rule and will always rule." Hegel replies: "It is clear enough . . . in what sense 'might' is taken here. It is not the might of justice and ethics, but only the irrational power of brute force" (*PhR* 258n, p. 158). Von Haller's position anticipates in far cruder form Nietzsche's analysis of the origin of morality, whereas Hegel's response could apply to Nietzsche's interpretation of the origin of good and bad as a difference of force.[33]

Nowhere in Hegel's system does the necessity for negation, as it is expressed in existence through death or bloody combat, conflict more with his support for law and reason. The strained resolution of this tension in favor of war appears to be dictated by Hegel's insistence on the ineradicable natural foundation of human life—man's mortality. Hegel is driven by this to defend in however bizarre a fashion what he takes to be natural in all aspects of man's existence, historical, cultural, and political. The only way negation can be overcome (since it is in any case ineradicable) is, in Hegel's eyes, to imbue it with Spirit, to place reason in charge of it and thus bring the natural into conformity with the Notion.

Hegel also thought that as wars were brought under the aegis of Spirit, their severity, in terms of their duration and their effect upon social institutions and civilian populations, would be mitigated. Hegel says:

> The fact that states reciprocally recognize each other as states remains, even in war . . . Hence in war, war itself is characterized as something which ought to pass away. It implies therefore the proviso of *jus gentium* that the possibility of peace be retained (and so, for example, that envoys be respected), and, in general, that war be not waged against domestic institutions, against the peace of family and private life, or against persons in their private capacity. (*PhR* 338, p. 215)

Hegel imagined that the modern world would be united by "thought and the universal" which would become more and more evident as the European peoples who "form a family in accordance with universal principles underlying their legal code, their customs, and their civilization" would modify their international conduct "to exclude hatred as a principle of action" (*PhR* 339 *Zusatz*, p. 297). Hegel had an uncanny grasp of technological sophistication and impersonality towards which modern warfare was tending, but he believed these characteristics would make wars more humane. Describing them with chilling accuracy, he writes:

Courage is the maximum self-subsistence of individuality, yet only as a cog playing its part in the mechanism of an external organization; absolute obedience, renunciation of personal opinions and reasonings, in fact complete *absence* of mind, coupled with the most intense presence of mind and decision in the moment of acting; the most hostile and so most personal action against individuals, coupled with an attitude of complete indifference or even liking towards them as individuals. (*PhR* 328, p. 211)

The marks of contemporary combat which Hegel describes so vividly were in their infancy in his day. Karl Barth's astute observation that "the age of Hegel and the age of superseding Hegel are related as the Battle of Sedan to the Battle of Marne" applies a fortiori to the conditions of the contemporary death-world.[34] This is true not only for the obvious reason that the techniques of man-made mass death have grown beyond what Hegel could recognize, but because the totalitarian state as a long-range, perhaps permanent, political structure has contradicted Hegel's idea of the state by fashioning death-worlds. The death-world does not reflect war between two existing states. Its victims do not represent one state and its architects and maintainers the other. Rather, the death-world is an artificially contrived return to the state of nature, in which every man is at war against every man. The death-world is not merely a collapse of polity, because it is embedded in a functioning state. The death-world has its being as paradox: it is a state of nature that exists not only de facto but also (per impossible) de jure, a Janus-faced beast artifically created and maintained by an all-powerful existing state.

This contrived state of nature is characterized by shortage. In the death-world goods are insufficient to satisfy needs, resulting in a brutal scramble for the means of subsistence. But at the same time the state also enforces cooperation of the competitors by forcing them to engage in socially organized slave labor until they die of starvation or exhaustion. This complex mesh of need, competition, and enforced cooperation is illustrated everywhere in the literature of the death-world. In *One Day in the Life of Ivan Denisovitch*, a camp commander in the wastes of the Siberian taiga comments: "It is the law of the jungle here fellows." Each individual is forced to exercise self-interest without restraint yet, at the same time, each is compelled to work as a member of a unit in the interest of the larger society. Thus the slave laborers "heard a lot of talk of switching their gang to a new job, building a new Socialist Community Development." At the same time the communal enterprise is being built to sabotage the interests of those who labor on it. Solzhenitsyn goes on to detail the gang's new job: "So far it was nothing more than bare fields covered with snowdrifts and before anything could be done there, holes had to be dug, posts put in and barbed wire put up—by the prisoners, for the prisoners, so they couldn't get out. And then they could start building."[35]

It is impossible to fit the contrived state of nature Solzhenitsyn describes into Hegel's view of the state as the actualization of freedom and rationality. Hegel's conception encompasses many forms of polity, some of which are defective in his eyes. Yet Hegel's idea of the state can never include an enclave within itself in which the state of nature prevails. In the light of the death event the incongruity between Hegel's description of the state as the expression of freedom and rationality and the conduct of existing states requires no comment. In a rare sortie into mythological expression, Hegel speaks of Jupiter as "the political God who produced a moral work—the state."[36] It never occurred to Hegel that, through the state, man might return to the age of Chronos, an age, he declares, "without moral products."

The Terror

THE STRUGGLE TO THE DEATH which establishes autonomous consciousness does not come to an end with the emergence of mastery and bondage but is repeated in new forms whenever consciousness seeks to attain freedom since, in Hegel's words, "freedom has died from the fear of dying" (*PhR* 324, p. 210). Fear of their lord and master would again enter men's hearts, for life would continue to be risked in the interest of the sovereignty of the state. In Hegel's day the phenomenon of the French Revolution and the Jacobin Terror which was its aftermath shook the world. Events the novelty of which Hegel was quick to perceive revealed entirely new structures. Here was the annihilation of an entire social order; death was everywhere. But unlike death resulting from natural disaster, it was humanly conceived and executed—yet, Hegel believed, utterly meaningless in the end. In what is perhaps the most chilling passage of the entire *Phenomenology* Hegel writes: "The sole work and deed of universal freedom is therefore *death*, a death too which has no inner significance or filling, for what is negated is the empty point of the absolutely free self. It is thus the coldest and meanest of all deaths, with no more significance than cutting off a head of cabbage or swallowing a mouthful of water" (*Phen* 590, p. 360).

It was useless to turn to ancient paradigms in seeking to understand the purely modern structure of Jacobinism. Here was the existential expression of the primacy of the present with a vengeance. Hegel tells us:

> Amid the pressure of great events, a general principle is of no help, and it is not enough to look back on similar situations; for pale recollections are powerless before the stress of the moment and impotent before the life and freedom of the present. . . . In this respect there is nothing so insipid as the constant appeals to Greek and Roman precedents we hear so often, as for example during the French Revolution. Nothing could be more different than the character of those nations and that of our times.[37]

But if Hegel perceived the unprecedented significance of the phenomenon, he was persuaded that it could not endure. The ideal of permanent revolution would have been to Hegel monstrous and unimaginable, for it would mean thinking the negative over and over again, like a phonograph needle stuck in the groove of the present. For Hegel the Revolution and the Jacobin Terror are not the first skirmishes of the death event but an extraordinary temporary intermezzo between the decadence of the ancien régime and the birth of Kantian morality. It would, like other historical moments, be sublated and finally superseded. Thus Karl Barth writes: "Hegel could even speak of the Devil in tones of unfeigned admiration . . . *Tout comprendre, c'est tout pardonner!* From the height occupied by the concept a soft and reconciling light can be shed upon everything and everyone, and even more than that, *tout comprendre c'est tout admirer* might be added to the saying to embrace Hegel's meaning."[38]

Yet Hegel's insight into the Jacobin Terror may well be the reason for his ambivalence—disguised somewhat by the movement of the dialectical process—toward the theory and practice of the Revolution. Hegel often speaks glowingly of the Revolution because he saw it as the first attempt in history to achieve the freedom of each and every individual. It would be difficult to find praise of the Russian Revolution more fervent than Hegel's panegyric for the French:

> Never since the sun had stood in the firmament and the planets revolved around him had it been perceived that man's existence centers in his head; in thought, inspired by which he builds up the world of reality, Anaxagoras had been the first to say *nous* governs the world; but not until now had man advanced to the recognition of the principle that thought ought to govern spatial reality. This was accordingly a glorious mental dawn. All thinking beings shared in the jubilation of this epoch. Emotions of a lofty character stirred in men's minds at that time. A spiritual enthusiasm thrilled through the world, as if the reconciliation between the Divine and the secular was now first accomplished. (*PhH* p. 447)

But behind this praise one can discern the canker in "the rose in the cross of the present." For if "man's existence centers in his head" then the French Revolution has tried to bring into actuality something based upon a mere abstraction and such an enterprise must in the end founder.

This caveat is made explicit in Hegel's criticism of Rousseau, whose social contract theory Hegel believes to provide the intellectual basis of the French Revolution. Unlike those which are grounded on gregarious instinct or divine authority Rousseau's theory acknowledges will as the principle of the state (*PhR* 258, pp. 156–57). This represents an important advance to Hegel and provides a link with Kant's view of ethical life based on the principle of universalizing acts of will as the foundation of morality. Yet Hegel also traces the frenzy and destruction which followed the French Revolution to Rousseau's conception of the general will.

According to Rousseau, the social contract stipulates that "each of us puts into the common pool, under the sovereign control of the general will, his person and all his power. And we as a community . . . take each member unto ourselves as an indivisible part of the whole."[39] The trouble with this conception is, according to Hegel, that Rousseau in "reducing the union of individuals in the state to a contract" bases the state on "their arbitrary wills, their opinion, and their capriciously given express consent." (*PhR* 258, p. 157). The difficulty lies in the conception of the general will. For Hegel, this is an aggregate of individual wills. Rousseau distinguishes between the will of all—the sum total of particular wills each legislating in the private interest—and the general will which looks to the common interest.[40] But the common interest is not intrinsic to the rational element in will, since it issues from the "numerous small differences of opinion" among the citizens. For Hegel the general will can never become genuinely universal.[41] Why then should Hegel think of general will as Rousseau understood it as belonging to atomized individuals who cannot form a permanent social bond? The answer depends on the impact of the Jacobin Terror upon Hegel's sensibility and Hegel's need to find in the theoretical underpinnings of the Revolution harbingers of the fissure in consciousness which would result in the Terror itself.

Certainly Rousseau's conception of the general will is capable of a quite different interpretation. Two remarks by Rousseau suffice to make the point. First, Rousseau insists that in order to be truly general, the general will must be general not only in its essential character but in its object as well. It must emanate from everybody and apply to everybody, so that it divests itself of its inherent rectitude the instant it looks to a particular object.[42] Hegel in faulting Rousseau's conception of will for its lack of universality may have in mind Rousseau's contention that "if everybody wills uninterruptedly the happiness of each, surely this is because there is no one who fails to seize upon that word (each) as his very own—so that when he votes on matters concerning all he is thinking only of himself."[43] But Hegel could certainly have read this as compatible with his own view by arguing that only by envisioning one's own happiness—in what Hegel might call a Vorstellung—does the general will become internalized for the individual. Rousseau insists that "what generalizes a will is not so much the choices that speak out in its favor as the common interests that harmonize them."[44] For Rousseau the general will is not a universal will in the Kantian sense. It does not legislate the moral law binding upon all of humanity but founds and sustains an actual polity together with its complex of positive laws. But for this very reason Rousseau's remark seems perfectly in harmony with Hegel's view that will mired in abstract universality remains merely formal, and that will requires concrete embodiment for its full realization. Hegel writes:

> That personal individuality and its particular interests not only achieve their complete development and gain explicit recognition for their right (as they do in the sphere of family and civil society) but also pass over of their own accord into the interest of the universal . . . they take [the universal] as their end and aim and are active in its pursuit. The result is that the universal does not prevail or achieve completion except along with particular interest and through the cooperation of particular knowing and willing. (*PhR* 260, pp. 160–61)

It is now possible to see the relation between Hegel's interpretation of the general will and the Terror. On the one hand, the idea of expressly given consent which characterizes the social bond in Rousseau's theory opens up the possibility of integrating the Christian ideal of freedom, of "infinitely free personality" into the idea of the state, freedom even if only in principle. This is a matter of cardinal importance to Hegel and should lead him to treat Rousseau's analysis of will at least as favorably as that of Kant. But, at the same time, Rousseau's idea of the general will clears the way for every man to transform his private will into a political actuality. This transformation dialectically creates the need for society to concentrate the general will in a single head, a government, since only something integral and undivided can act. Yet a government which comes into being in this way is necessarily opposed to the aggregate of combined individual wills which together constitute the general will. Government therefore can only express its will in dictatorial rule: absolute power is required as a counterforce to absolute freedom. Hegel's worry in this context may also be a practical expression of his fear of popular will. Speaking against the creation of a representative body,

Hegel remarks: "What can one begin to do with such a rabble . . . which does not lead a public life and which has not been educated to the consciousness of the common will and to action in the spirit of the whole?"[45]

In a brief section of the *Phenomenology*, Hegel directly addresses the theme of the Jacobin Terror not in terms of the political theory which buttresses it but rather in the wider context of the demythologizing tendencies of Enlightenment thought, especially its war against superstition upon which its critique of faith is based. Regarding faith as the consciousness to be transcended, the Enlightenment tries to show faith that its object, the transcendent other, is something which has merely been alienated from itself. In his celebrated description of God as a projection of human imagination, Feuerbach only extends and deepens Hegel's characterization of the skepticism of the Enlightenment which has declared the object of its faith to be a fiction. In Hegel's words: "The beyond [of the individual's] actual existence hovers over the corpse of the vanished independence of real being, or the being of faith, merely as the exhalation of a stale gas, of the vacuous *Être Suprême*" (*Phen* 586, p. 358). Yet the Enlightenment forgets that it is itself dependent upon that which it negates, forgets that in negating the object of faith it is obliged to turn to the world which faith has forsaken, *this* world, and to seek its ends in the here-and-now by finding satisfaction in this-worldly utility. In Hegel's words, "Heaven is transplanted to earth below" (*Phen* 581, p. 355).

The world Hegel describes in the dense language of the *Phenomenology* is one we can recognize all too clearly as having much in common with our own. The philosophy of the Enlightenment tries to ground the burgeoning new science at the expense of the picture-consciousness of naive faith. The object of faith is, in turn, demythologized. Too weak to withstand the onslaughts of skeptical attack, the world-picture of faith collapses, leaving nothing to take its place. Ancient skepticism awaited the advent of Christianity but post-Christian skepticism can only hope for a reconciliation with faith. Without myth, the new world takes shape around what Hegel calls "the Useful"—a nexus of techniques in which "means ceaselessly circulate" but, in the absence of ultimate purpose, permit only proximate aims to be realized. Hegel writes: "Just as everything is useful to man so man is useful too, and his vocation is to make himself a member of the group of use for the common good and serviceable to all" (*Phen* 560, p. 342).

Yet Hegel's suggestive remark may be misleading, since the utility belonging to objects does not automatically become a property of Spirit as subject. Instead, when Spirit tries to wrest utility from the object Spirit becomes not an object but the subject that wills their use. Such a subject is a purely impersonal will whose identity is determined by the alienated objects it uses. This will is the same in all, a general will. Why is Spirit not merely transformed into the useful? Hegel tells us indirectly in his account of the useful: "What is useful, is something with an enduring being in itself, or a Thing" (*Phen* 580, p. 354). Man can be made useful, but consciousness itself cannot become a thing; it can only turn into radical, ever more compulsive willing.[46] In the light of its ideal of utility Spirit now recognizes a will that has real force in the world, "not the empty thought of will which consists in silent assent . . . but a real general will, the will of all *individuals* as such" (*Phen* 584, p. 357). Spirit is now pure will and exists as absolute freedom.

Individuality as will recognizes no class distinctions. Thus Hegel says: "In this absolute freedom . . . all social groups or classes which are the spiritual spheres into which the whole is articulated are abolished; the individual consciousness that belonged to any such sphere, and willed and fulfilled itself in it, has put aside its limitation; its purpose is the general purpose, its language universal law, its work the universal work" (*Phen* 585, p. 357). In his analysis of the Jacobin Terror, Hegel has sketched the main features of the postmodern phenomenon of totalitarian rule (although he could not have predicted its ancillary institutions designed to destroy persons and cultures): a vast police network and censorship system which penetrates the entire fabric of a society in order to "quarantine" or destroy outright its suspected detractors. In a strikingly contemporary passage, Hegel describes the transformation of ideological passion into the actuality of Terror:

> This is the freedom of the void which rises to a passion and
> takes shape in the world as . . . the Hindu fanaticism of pure
> contemplation, but when it turns to actual practise, it takes

place in religion and politics alike as the fanaticism of destruction—the destruction of the whole subsisting social order—as the elimination of individuals who are objects of suspicion to any social order, and the annihiliation of any organization which tries to arise anew from the ruins. Only in destroying does this negative will possess the feeling of itself as existent. (*PhR* 5, p. 22)

For Hegel Jacobin Terror is incapable of producing a positive work. From the standpoint of the history of spirit, this form of Terror is superseded when universal and individual will are reconciled in Kantian morality, the next stage in Spirit's progress. But within the framework of Terror itself, consciusness as will can only affirm its existence by engaging in annihilatory action. Terror, once unleashed, can have no positive productive content. It is not surprising that long-lasting postmodern Terror can only seek to negate internally what has already been negated and surpassed in external reality. For Hegel the demoralized ancien régime, a culture of wealth and flattery which sustained a tottering monarchy, is swept away once and for all. But were Terror to continue, impossible according to Hegel but a fact in our own world, vestiges of the ancien régime would be imagined to exist in even the most innocuous manifestations of culture. Thus, for example, the aim of the Red Guards in China's Cultural Revolution was to destroy the four olds: old ideas, old culture, old customs, and old habits.[47] But the institutions in which these olds were embodied and transmitted has been effectively destroyed by the successful Revolution. Only the bureaucratic apparatus of Terror could possibly imagine their lingering presence. The vagueness of these categories made it impossible to describe the olds accurately or to embody them in legal codes. Thus any reality designated as old called down the wrath of negation on the part of an elite cadre.

No aspect of culture is exempt from fanatical acts of destruction. Even music, which seems to harbor no ideological content, is in the postculture of Stalinist Russia imagined to express counter-revolutinary tendencies. An account of composer Dmitri Shostakovich's description of a conference of Ukrainian folk poets, "blind musicians who wandered around the countryside singing of the past," called in the Soviet Union in the mid-1930s, illustrates the point: "From tiny villages all over the Ukraine, these Lirniki and Banduristy as they were called gathered at the First All-Ukrainian Congress to discuss their future in the Soviet Union under Stalin's guidance. It was . . . Shostakovich says 'the country's living history . . .' There at the Congress the poets were subjected to the 'highest measure of punishment' for their singing—they were executed."[48] The instances of Terror are archetypal forms which could be expanded indefinitely. It is unlikely that their structure would have seemed alien to Hegel. True, the irreversibility of Terror and the creation of death-worlds, the "widening gyre" of death, are absent from Hegel's thoughtful and otherwise perfectly contemporary description of Jacobin Terror: "'absolute fear,' abstract freedom undeterred by an institutional limit."[49] As J. N. Findlay remarks: "A philosopher who can smell out an identity between the Guillotine and the Categorical Imperative is obviously *capable de tous*."[50]

The Death of God　　　　N OWHERE DO THE APORIAS OF EX-
istence make themselves so strongly felt and find so problematic a resolution as in Hegel's treatment of Revealed Religion. Nowhere do the promises of Reason to fulfill the expectations of revelation meet so clearly with the rebuffs of existence. The claims to comprehensiveness and self-certitude that Hegel attributes to Absolute Knowledge are not based upon the structures of inference themselves; they are not empty abstractions, but claims justified by a richly actualized historical content. In religious consciousness this historical content is realized in the truths of religion: in God's self-emptying into history in the incarnation of Christ, and in the internalized meaning of his coming through the work of the Holy Spirit in the hearts of Christian believers. This means that the truth of Reason now rests squarely upon the shoulders of bourgeois Christendom.

As Kierkegaard would insist, Reason tricks out the claims of revelation in speculative garb and by opening its meaning to philosophy destroys the paradoxes of Christian belief that are at the heart of Christianity. For Hegel, philosophers form a new priesthood of Reason. The new tablets of Spirit are entrusted to them. In a statement which could reflect as easily the positivism of Auguste Comte as the last, best fruit of Spirit's development, Hegel comments: "Philosophy forms . . . a sanctuary apart, and those who serve in it constitute an isolated order of priests, who must not mix with the world, and whose work is to protect the possessions of Truth" (*PhRel* 3:151). Of course Hegel realizes that philosophy is not for the masses, whereas Christianity appeals to every heart. "When the Gospel is no longer preached to the poor, when the salt has lost its savour, and all the foundations have been tacitly removed, then the people, [for whom] every solid truth can exist only in a pictorial conception, no longer know how to assist the impulses and emotions they feel within them" (*PhRel* 3:150). But, Hegel confesses, "How the actual present day world is to find its way out of this state or disruption, and what form it is to take, are questions which must be left to itself to settle, and to deal with them is not the immediate practical business of philosophy" (*PhRel* 3:151). By making thought the absolute judge of content, the scandal of Christian claims which had heretofore been anchored in faith is mitigated. The way is open on the one hand for an existential theology which will cling to paradox as the logical form in which its content will be cast, and on the other for liberal theology which—once the Hegelian system appears to fall apart—will turn back to the Enlightenment philosophy of reflection for its principles.

Yet Hegel was only trying to construct a master synthesis of the competing claims of the nineteenth century, a gift for the age through which it would become transparent to itself. Had Hegel, as Karl Barth declares, not given the age what it wanted: faith and reason, historical relativity and eternal truth, freedom and necessity? Yet would the age not come to despise itself when it measured its achievements against its reflection in the mirror of Spirit, because it would prove impossible, starting from Hegel's vision, to settle every question of truth? Thus Karl Barth, intending to highlight the scandal of Christianity whitewashed by Hegel, remarks in a curious aside: "The rejection of Hegel might have been the fig-leaf with which man at this time sought to hide what he himself was aware of as his pudendum from the sight of others and from the sight of God."[51]

Yet Hegel's philosophy of religion is no mere superficial patchwork of faith and reason, but a sustained attempt to bring the mystery of faith into the sunlight, to do for the religious vision of the inner Christ, the vision of Eckhart and Boehme, what had been done for the inhabitants of Plato's cave—to make rational truth the prize of the ascent. But, curiously, in Hegel's eyes, the content of religion is not overriden once speculative truth is attained. He writes: "Philosophy has been reproached with setting itself above religion; this, however, is false, as an actual matter of fact, for it possesses this particular content only and no other, though it presents it in the form of thought; it sets itself merely above the form of faith, the content is the same in both cases" (*PhRel* 3:148).

I have already pointed to the difficulty posed by the relation of form to content in Hegel's thought and exhibited uniquely in the case of revealed religion. If philosophy supersedes religion and accepts as true the faith claims of religion, does it cease to exist as philosophy? If on the other hand it rejects the faith claims of religion, what will be left of the content that it intends to make its own?[52] Philosophy is (as Heidegger later recognizes) conceivable for Hegel only as an onto-theology. For Hegel, Christianity is the crucible through which Greek thought must pass in order for it to become true (fully reconciling all oppositions) and genuine (having passed through and interiorized objectivity) thinking. In a terse statement of what he means by *thinking* in this context, Hegel writes:

> But insofar as thought begins to place itself in opposition to the concrete, the process of thought then consists in carrying through this opposition until it reaches reconciliation. This reconciliation is philosophy; so far as philosophy is theology, it sets forth the reconciliation of God with Himself and with Nature, and shows that Nature, Other-Being, is divine, that it partly belongs to the very nature of finite Spirit to rise into the state of reconciliation, and that it partly reaches this state of reconciliation in the history of the world. (*PhRel* 3:149)

And yet for Hegel, despite the superseding of religious consciousness as form, absolute knowing itself is haunted by the scandal of Christianity, that God would become man, transformed in Hegel's eyes to the scandal of finitude itself. For Hegel the infinite must after all include and encompass the finite. Were they to remain apart the infinite would be limited by the finite and would become the bad

infinite. Yet because Hegel does not wish to destroy finitude it becomes ingredient in the infinite itself. Finitude means mortality; the
inclusion of finitude in the infinite makes the death of God—the
crucifixion and passion—eternal elements in the history of Spirit.

> God Himself is dead, as it is said in the Lutheran hymn; the
> consciousness of this fact expresses the truth that the human,
> the finite, fraility, weakness, the negative is itself a divine mo-
> ment, as in God himself; that Otherness or Other Being, the
> finite, the negative, is not outside of God, and that in its char-
> acter as otherness it does not hinder unity with God; otherness,
> the negation, is consciously known to be a moment of the Di-
> vine Nature. The highest knowledge of the Idea of Spirit is con-
> tained in this thought. (*PhRel* 3:98)

This outward negative changes in this way into the inner negative.
Regarded in one aspect the signification attached to death is that in
it the human element has been stripped off, and the divine glory
comes again into view. But death is at the same time also the negative, the farthest point of that experience to which man as natural
being and consequently God himself are exposed. This view is borne
out by the penultimate line of the *Phenomenology*: "History and the
Science of Knowing, the two together . . . form alike the inwardizing
and the Calvary of absolute Spirit" (*Phen* 808, p. 493).

But if Christian consciousness retains the passion, it is consum-
mated in the joy of resurrection. Yet Spirit cannot fully come to know
itself or the joy of the resurrected Christ until it passes through the
crucible of unhappy consciousness, the most deeply polarized moment in the history of Spirit. As Unhappy Consciousness, Spirit
knows itself as both the unchangeable God who is the essential consciousness and the protean human consciousness which remains ines-
sential. Hegel is describing the relation of man and God as it is experienced in the asceticism of medieval Christianity. Unhappy
consciousness repeats the duality of mastery and servitude, but now
the consciousness of mastery lies beyond the experienced world. Asceticism seeks to negate the individual ego in order to become a
deeper consciousness, to enrich its inwardness. The Church as the
agent of God mediates between the kingdom of man for whom the

world is as nothing and the kingdom of God, the realm of ontological fullness.

But revealed religion can never reach the Notion until the lacerations of Spirit are healed and God once again comes down to earth in the consciousness of the community to become the eternally present God. For Hegel the historical Jesus belongs to the past but must continually be made present by the presence of the Holy Spirit in the community of believers. Jesus as the Christ is rescued from the immediacy of Jesus' historical circle so that his atoning death takes on universal significance. The person of Jesus must become the Comforter. Thus Hegel tells us "Christ—man as man—in whom the unity of God and man has appeared, has in his death, and his history generally, himself presented the eternal history of Spirit—a history which every man has to accomplish in himself, in order to exist as Spirit, or to become a child of God, a citizen of his kingdom" (*PhH* p. 328). For Hegel the circle of the history of Spirit retraces the trinitarian circle of the history of the divine life. The eternal idea as mere universality is represented in the life of God the Father. The second stage reflects the othering of the eternal idea in time so that God becomes manifest in the temporal process. In the final phase God is eternally present in the consciousness of the community. The mystery of the Father as Abgrund, the veiled and hidden source of the divine life, is made fully immanent in Christ who is revealed through the Holy Spirit in the life of the Christian (Lutheran) community.[53]

Yet has Hegel really come to grips with the implications of God's self-emptying into culture? Should not the fully immanent God also be subjected to the terrifying process of negation? What could the complete absence of an immanent God mean for the culture of the West? For Hegel negation is never merely the contrary of what has been affirmed, since negation always brings something new into the world. How is this new work of the negative to be achieved? It can, as we have seen, appear, become manifest in a work, by virtue of difference—the difference between what has been sublated and what comes into being. The negation of the Absolute, therefore, must itself be absolute, and the difference generated by this negation must itself be an absolute difference. Hegel all too quickly passes over the uniqueness of the negation when what is negated is the Absolute itself.

Negation of this sort is without voice; it can only be interpreted as silence and therefore mystery.[54] Of course, for Hegel nothing lies outside of intelligibility. If an unsurpassable negation could be imagined *within* the Hegelian system it can only be thought of as transconceptual, transymbolic, and translinguistic.[55] For Hegel such a negation is unthinkable. But if it could be imagined, it could only become actual in the annihilation of man as it has begun to occur in the death event. The extermination and extinction of man is the negation of the Absolute, not the Biblical Absolute, but Hegel's fully immanent Absolute. No further revelation, no Divine Word is now possible, since there is no beyond. This negation is manifest as unique and ultimate silence—not the awesome quiet of cosmic space to which Pascal alludes but a historical absence of speech, the silence that supervenes upon speech.[56]

The traces of this silence are to be found in language, in the speech of the death-world and its survivors where death attaches to every signifier. Were we to imagine this negation in the language of traditional religion, we could only use the language of religious mystery. From this point of view the death event, with its nadir at the death-world, would necessarily become the ultimate mystery and resist inclusion into an Absolute which could no longer be a positive Absolute. Thus Arthur Cohen writes in relation to the death-world as it manifests itself in the extermination of the Jews of Europe:

> *Tremendum* is used by me for the mysterious only, in precisely the sense which Rudolph Otto originally intended it. In my usage, however . . . the phrase is reversed, my emphasis falling not upon the mystery as such but its immensity. It is the immensity of the event that is mysterious but its nature is not mystery.
>
> If the holocaust is allowed to stand as a *mysterium*, indeed *mysterium tremendum* unavailable to thought . . . the profound risk is run that an historical event is made absolute and therefore necessary, overturning all other historical events whose occurrence is contingent and whose meaning is tributary. Or the

holocaust is allowed to stand as a mysterium . . . precisely because it is not historical and derives its force and arbitrariness from the metaphysical structure of the universe, no less absolute and necessary, overturning thereby all other metaphysical structures including God whose existence is claimed by classical theism to be absolute and necessary. If the project of absolutizing the holocaust is pushed much further than it has been already, it is made twin of the divine. . . . Such a radical extension of the argument from holocaustal ontologies ends by making the tremendous no different from the divine truth.[57]

Cohen's vision of the holocaust is Hegelian in an important sense: he finds in the holocaust a negative concrete universal, an existential support for negation itself. Yet for Cohen the holocaust drives a wedge in Being which cannot be overcome since Evil becomes a second Absolute. This Manichean interpretation without hope of supercession departs from any vision which could be embraced by Hegel's system.

The intellectual implications of Hegel's radical vision are first realized in Nietzsche's depiction of the madman who not only declares the death of God, but makes the equally important and unthinkable claim that man is his killer. A culture emptied of transcendence can only be apocalyptic: "There will be wars the like of which have never yet been seen on earth," Nietzsche cries. "We shall have upheavals, a convulsion of earthquakes, a moving of mountains and valleys, the like of which has never been dreamed of."[58] To be sure, Nietzsche only wishes to hasten the prospect of decay in order to usher in a new type of human being: one who can not only endure the collapse of culture but indeed will it over and over again. Yet Nietzsche's vision does not project the final annihilation of all life but "existence as it is, without meaning or aim, yet recurring inevitably without any finale of nothingness: *the eternal recurrence*."[59] Hegel imagined that morality (*Sittlichkeit*) could, like a mighty steed of Plato's *Phaedrus*, be hitched to the inner spirituality of the community of believers and that together they would ascend into the sunlight. But Neitzsche saw that postmodern, post-Christian culture leads not to the transcendental unity of an Absolute Subject but to residual selves which ooze away leaving faceless anonymity. Seen from the point of view of a culture held together by the vision of an Absolute, the death event is mystery, the obverse of the ontological fullness of the Absolute, a negation which appears and opens up a phenomenology of nonbeing. Nietzsche understood that this culture has a structure and language which can be brought to light only obliquely, for its thought follows the contours of a purely negative phenomenality. Nietzsche unmasks not only the false consciousness of the Enlightenment's celebration of the new saeculum, but also the culture of bourgeois Christendom that Hegel believed would rescue faith from irrationality. Thus Nietzsche writes: "Disintegration characterizes this time. . . . Everything on our way is slippery and dangerous, and the ice that still supports us has become thin: all of us feel the warm uncanny breath of the thawing wind; where we still walk soon no one will be able to walk."[60]

For Hegel natural existence is unsurpassable; man remains mortal though Spirit becomes ever more complex. Yet nature is the othering of Spirit and so is itself also Geist. Man is the goal of nature, the end toward which natural existence tends. Since he can sublate his animal existence, man is a diseased creature, unnatural in his foundations. Unlike animals, man attains his universality not through the being of his genus, but through consciousness. Man is the being who thinks, who appropriates temporal and spatial existence and becomes a for-itself. Thought gives man immortality. The death-world attempts to cut away the spiritual acquisitions of man, the symbolic structures of his life. It attempts to divest him of the complexity of consciousness and reduce him as far as possible to animal status. By stripping man of thought so far as possible the death world, in an inverse Promethean gesture, steals man's immortality. Cutting off his symbolic systems, it creates a spurious present: a present without past or future. The immortality of a present which includes recollection and anticipation are precluded.

Hegel's view of nature is holistic and resists reduction to the homogeneous entities of the physical sciences both of his own day and of our own technological society which shares the world view of the physical sciences and thus runs counter to holistic interpretation, instead this society is bent on destroying appearing entities by reducing them in actuality to those which science theoretically posits.

This law of parsimony is the logic which underlies mass destruction by sophisticated weapons, nuclear, chemical, and biological. This is not to say that a conspiracy exists but that the law of parsimony can be seen after the fact to operate in the death event. In a movement contrary to Plato's saving the appearances by positing ideal forms, science reduces nature to its homogeneous but invisible constituents whether considered as elements or relational fields. The annihilation of the death event consists in leveling the appearances and returning (from a phenomenological point of view) to formless matter.

Hegel traces natural existence through its various cultural transformations. Death is the sign for natural existence. But death can become a work of Spirit if man takes charge of death by showing his willingness to risk life. Hegel describes an archetypal struggle in which life is risked by one antagonist while the other trembles before death the sovereign master. This struggle results in the consciousness of mastery and bondage.

But Hegel, unlike Nietzsche, does not automatically validate the consciousness of mastery. Instead he turns to servile consciousness which learns through labor to defer the gratification of desire. Servile consciousness is memory. Efforts to structure the death-world in terms of the consciousness of mastery and bondage reflect the attempt of the totalitarian mind to reintroduce (unconsciously) a spurious version of the authenticity paradigm to a situation in which it is inapplicable. Since there can be no combat of equals in the death-world there is no genuine struggle and resistance can only lead to death. But Hegel's model is still important: it suggests that the spiritual advantage of servile consciousness is memory and that recollection sublates the consciousness of mastery. The psychological weight of this Hegelian insight is attested in the desire of survivors to bear witness to the events of the death-world.

Using the struggle to the death as a paradigmatic pattern of Spirit's activity Hegel tries to show that war is necessary for the sublation of individual ego on behalf of the state, which he considers to represent a higher form of reason, and for states themselves, whose honor depends upon their willingness to risk their sovereignty. For Hegel war is not absolute evil but necessary to the life of polity. The state is the actualization of freedom, "the hieroglyph of reason" and as such demands the surrender of life on its behalf. Hegel rejects the idea of an international body which would have authority over individual states since he believes that the sovereignty of states is inalienable. But Hegel did not foresee that states would create enclaves or death-worlds modeled after man's existence in the state of nature. Hegel foresaw that in the future wars will be less personal but he did not imagine that this depersonalization would increase rather than diminish the brutality of war.

Hegel analyzes the Terror which followed the French Revolution and distorted the ideas of the Revolution but was nevertheless implicit in it. The Terror is warlike but its structure ought not to be confused with that of war. Meaningless death is suffered for an empty ideal, in this case absolute freedom, which lacks content and expresses itself as arbitrary will. This is the result of the interpretation of "general will" developed in the work of Rousseau. Although Hegel astutely analyzes the Terror, he could not imagine permanent revolution and the persistence of Terror as a form of life. Yet in the twentieth century Terror becomes archetypal, a form of life which cannot be superseded.

Hegel's analysis of religious consciousness introduces the concept of the death of God. In Hegel's view, revealed religion—for him, Lutheran Christianity—is the content though not the form of Absolute Knowledge. Christian consciousness develops from the incarnation, God's self-emptying into history in the final universalization of the meaning of the Resurrection of Christ in the community of believers. But Hegel does not see the consequences of the moment of negation of a fully immanentized Absolute. The negation of such an Absolute can only be the annihilatory impulse of death that is manifest cognitively as silence and mystery and existentially in the death event. At the same time the culture of the death of God (as described by Nietzsche) is the embedding culture of the death event.

V / Finitude and the Structures of Existence: The Early Heidegger

Why, he could not but hear unless he had plugged up the tube Understanding (which he had not done). For through that tube he saw that he was in the land of Phenomenon where he must for a certain one day die as he was like the rest too a passing show. And would he not accept to die like the rest and pass away.

—James Joyce

IN A REMARKABLE PASSAGE IN HIS Logic, Hegel describes the character of finite being: "They *are*, but the truth of this being is their *end*. The finite not only alters, like something in general, but it *ceases to be*; and its ceasing to be is not merely a possibility, so that it could be without ceasing to be, but the being as such of finite things is to have the germ of decease as their Being-within-self: the hour of their birth is the hour of their death."[1] Finite things are what they are because it is impossible for them not to come to an end. To be finite means to exist as self-destructing being. Thus finite things are not *in time*; instead, they exist *as temporal*: "The process of actual things makes time."[2]

Two important conclusions emerge from a close reading of this passage which furnish a point of departure for assessing Heidegger's view of death in his early work *Being and Time*. First, in the passage cited, Hegel attributes "the germ of decease" to finite things as their ontological mark. Second, because no passage in Hegel can be interpreted without considering the system as a whole, Hegel's analysis of finitude is subject to dialectical reversal, the process through which something is driven beyond what it immediately is into its opposite. Thus finitude must become its other. But this becoming other occurs not by way of an external cause but by virtue of what is already inherent in its own nature. Thus Hegel's analysis is not a poignant description of the transiency of all finite things even if the finite will disappear *tout court*. In the context of the *Phenomenology*, the historical process itself is transcended. Spirit, its alienation overcome, looks back at its journey through time and is at last at home with itself.

It is unlikely that Heidegger would wish to deny that things perish. But for Heidegger any account of finite being must distinguish the manner of being of things from that of the being whose truth is its finitude: human being. Thus "human being" is not a species of the genus "finite being." Instead, man is the only being to whom his own demise and the coming-to-an-end of the thing are revealed as altogether different: "Any entity is either a 'who' (existence) or a 'what' . . . and each requires a different mode of explication."[3] Whether consciously reflecting upon the matter or not, the human existent foresees his own death: it is this anticipation that opens out man's relation to the destruction of things.

Hegel was well aware of man's anticipation of his own dying and had, in his *Philosophy of Nature*, made it the centerpiece of his account of the transition from animal to human being. But for Hegel death is a deficiency: "Thought is *immortal being*, while mortal being consists in the universality of the Idea being inadequate to itself" (*PhN* 3:376, p. 212). Thus, even if man dies, it is possible to transcend this death conceptually at least, for death has no place in the truth of Absolute Knowledge, in thought thinking itself, except as something which is overcome. But Heidegger, having appropriated the stress upon death in the work of Kierkegaard, Nietzsche, and others, recognizes that the individual thinker's finitude is unsurpassable and that deathless thought without a thinker is absurd. Properly understood, the structure of man's finitude alters the meaning of man's existence and indeed of truth itself.

The second point, gleaned from the passage cited earlier on the nature of the finite thing in Hegel's thought, alludes to the dialectical sublation of finitude for Hegel. But, since Heidegger holds fast to human finitude, he believes that time can never be overcome. Instead, he claims, time constitutes the horizon—the range of visibility that determines what can be seen from some given perspective of Being.[4] By defining Being in terms of time, Heidegger defies the mainstream of the Western philosophical tradition, what he calls onto-theology, which subordinates time to eternity. Heidegger shows that Hegel's view of time is a logical outcome of the very tradition that Hegel criticizes:

> On occasion Hegel characterizes time as the "abstraction of consuming" the most radical way in which time is ordinarily experienced and interpreted. On the other hand, when Hegel really defines time, he is consistent enough to grant no such priority to consuming and passing away as that which the everyday experience of time rightly adheres to. . . . Hegel understands this "becoming" in an abstract sense. . . . Thus the most appropriate expression which the Hegelian treatment of time receives is as the "negation of a negation." (*BT* 432, pp. 483–84)

Heidegger contrasts this with his own view: "Our existential analytic of Dasein, on the contrary, starts with the 'concretion' of factically thrown existence itself in order to unveil temporality as that which primordially makes such existence possible" (*BT* 435, p. 486). For Heidegger man is thrown into time, a situation which founds man's historical being.

If man's historicity cannot be sublated, we must take our sighting from the world in which human beings find themselves; the people of our generation and the events which surround us and in which we are coimplicated. This chapter begins with clues derived from ordinary habits and experiences which, when properly interrogated, open up the primordial structures of man's way of being in the world. The starting point is important since the transcendental framework is related pari passu to the clues with which the analysis begins. The clues Heidegger chooses determine the course of his reflections, but if another feature of contemporary existence is selected—the death-event in particular—this initial choice has far-reaching implications for a grasp of the ultimate meaning of human existence in the present age.

The Question of Being

*T*HE PRIMARY PURPOSE OF HEIdegger's major work, *Being and Time*, is "to work out the question of the meaning of *Being* and to do so concretely. Our provisional aim is the Interpretation of *time* as the possible horizon for any understanding whatsoever of Being" (*BT* 1, p. 19). Heidegger hopes to rescue this question from the neglect into which it has fallen in the Western philosophical tradition by peeling away the presuppositions and prejudices which have come to surround it. He believes these prejudices are incipiently present in the first formulations of the issue by Plato and Aristotle and their predecessors even if they could still think through the meaning of Being more primordially than does contemporary philosophy, which is by now overgrown with historical accretions.

We no longer know how to inquire into the meaning of Being. In fact, the present age has lost the capacity to ask significant questions about anything whatever. Thus Heidegger directs our attention to the meaning of "asking" itself: "Every inquiry is a seeking. Every seeking gets guided by what is sought" (*BT* 5, p. 24). Genuine questioning attempts not only to find out the manner of being of an entity but also to discover what it means to say that the entity exists. Inquiry is always about something but it is also "a questioning of something." More, it is a way of being of the questioner. Even if we do not take these matters fully into account, Heidegger claims, we have a *"vague average understanding of Being"*—of the meaning of that which our inquiry is about. (*BT* 5, p. 25). We already think of Being as that which "determines entities as entities," something which already belongs to them insofar as they are said to exist. But "the being of entities is not itself an entity" (*BT* 6, p. 26) alongside the others. If Being somehow belongs to entities, although we do not yet know how, then should we not turn to entities themselves and interrogate them in regard to their being? But there are many different kinds of entities. We ourselves are in fact beings of a certain kind. Does it matter which entities we interrogate in our quest for the meaning of Being? Is our starting point optional if we are to gain access to the meaning of Being?

The procedures in which we have just engaged—searching for something, asking, inquiring—are the structural elements of inquiry—are also comportments which belong to us, the inquirers. We must make ourselves transparent to ourselves, since we, the ones who ask, are the access routes of the inquiry. Asking is our own mode of being; through inquiry human beings are as we are: "This entity which each of us is himself and which includes inquiring as one of its modes of possibility we shall denote by the term *'Dasein'"* (*BT* 7,

p. 27). Until now I have refrained from using the neologism Dasein and have spoken instead of man or human being. Now we are pre-pared to drop the older terms, the historical accretions of which Hei-degger believes lead us astray, and inquire into Dasein's manner of being. It may seem that Heidegger proceeds by way of circular rea-soning, defining the being of Dasein first and only later inquiring into the meaning of Being. For Heidegger, formal objections of this type are meaningless in this context. We have always spoken mean-ingfully of beings although our knowledge remained conceptually unclarified. Some conception of Being arising from an ordinary grasp of Being belongs to us as Dasein. It might be argued that a more precise way of articulating the problem of Being occurs in the specialized sciences of nature, language, and man. But Heidegger insists that our taken-for-granted notions of Being prepare the ter-rain for scientific inquiry and are therefore more primordial, al-though the sciences themselves are unaware of their ontological pre-suppositions (*BT* 12, p. 32). This theme is already well-formulated in Heidegger's early work. In the present context the important point is that Dasein's distinguishing trait remains that, in its very constitution, Being is an issue for it. Dasein is an aperture for the disclosure of Being. "*Understanding of Being is itself a definite char-acteristic of Dasein's Being.* Dasein is ontically distinctive in that it is ontological (*BT* 12, p. 32). Dasein does not make the question of Being a central focus of its daily life, but comports itself in some fashion toward its own existence: "Dasein always understands itself in terms of its existence—in terms of a possibility of itself: to be itself or not itself. Dasein has either chosen these possibilities itself, or got itself into them or grown up in them already. Only the particular Dasein decides its existence by taking hold or neglecting. The ques-tion of existence never gets straightened out except through existing itself" (*BT* 12, p. 33).

Heidegger designates this mode of self-understanding *existentiell* in contrast to an ontologically clarified or *existential* analysis of exis-tence. To arrive at the meaning of Being in a fundamental way we must first begin with Dasein's existentiell comportments. Now the difference between Hegel's and Heidegger's understanding of the meaning of finite things becomes clearer. For Heidegger, Dasein is a being for whom existence is determinative and "*with equal primor-*

diality Dasein also possesses—as constitutive for its understanding of existence—an understanding of all entities other than its own" (BT 13, p. 34). Of special significance to the theme of man-made mass death, it must be remembered that "the roots of the existential analytic, on its part are ultimately existentiell, that is, ontical" (BT 13, p. 34). This means that the ontic clues, the clues taken from Dasein's usual comportments, are the root from which ontological analysis grows: the transcendental framework arrived at depends upon our preliminary observations of Dasein's comportments, because these fundamentally affect the course of our inquiry.

The Dailyness of Life HEIDEGGER HAS IN THE DEVELopment of his analysis established important protocols which are useful in considering the death event. By observing our everyday comportments (what Virginia Woolf called "the dailyness of life"), Heidegger elicits the general structures of existence, because Dasein's way of being is best brought out if it is exhibited as it is "proximally and for the most part—in its average *everydayness [Alltäglichkeit]*" (BT 370, p. 421). What is discovered in this way is provisional and awaits further clarification. Yet these findings are not false in the sense in which falsity is ascribed to the proposition "England is east of France" because it gives us inaccurate information about the respective locations of these countries. Nor is it vague in the way the proposition "Paris is somewhere in Europe" seems to someone who wants to get there from Nancy. Rather, we learn something essential about Dasein even if what is learned is not yet clear. It is something like seeing that one is in a particular neighborhood but has not yet located the house he is looking for there.

Heidegger uses the term "everydayness" to refer to Dasein's usual or average way of being, something of which Dasein is rarely conscious. It expresses Dasein's manner of being in the presence of others, not any specific others but the public in general. Everydayness is the way Dasein "shows itself for Everyman not always but 'as a rule'" (BT 370, p. 422). Dasein feels comfortable in its habitual mode of behavior, remaining more or less the same from day to day. This average way of being is unsurpassable, though "in the moment of vision . . . existence can even gain the mastery over the everyday" (*BT* 371, p. 422).

Who is this public self from which Dasein takes its orientation? The *They* (*das Man*) sets the standards by which we live, assures us that nothing gets out of hand, that Dasein see itself in a certain way. Yet it relieves Dasein of responsibility for its behavior by providing an excuse for doing merely what is done, what conforms to general standards. "Distantiality [concern with the way one differs from others], averageness, leveling down" are characteristic behaviors of Dasein absorbed in the They. The They which dominates our everyday existence "is an *existentiale*; and as a primordial phenomenon, it belongs to Dasein's positive constitution," even if the manner in which the They displays itself varies historically (*BT* 129, p. 167). Although Dasein can, on occasion, be made aware of the They, can penetrate its disguises, nevertheless it is always given proximally to itself by way of the They. These proximal comportments of the Dasein lost in the They can be used to assess the veracity of Heidegger's account in the light of the death event. Since Dasein is given to itself through the They, Dasein cannot avoid the They, which therefore functions as a transcendental structure.

How does the They show itself in Dasein's everyday activities? How does Dasein maintain itself in the being of the They? Heidegger thinks of Dasein as falling or becoming absorbed in the They. The idea of falling suggests that there is a more primordial mode in which Dasein relates to itself, the world, and other persons. But falling also implies that the Dasein forgets these deeper modes of connectedness. Thus Dasein encounters the world in its ontological wholeness through "discourse, sight and interpretation" but each of these relations can be lived in the manner of the They (*BT* 167, p. 210). I shall turn first to the way each comportment is lived in its average everydayness.

For Heidegger the primary function of discourse is to disclose the matter talked about, the meaning of whatever is under consideration, whereas the communicative function of language is secondary. Once the meaning of the matter at hand no longer predominates, discourse degenerates, becoming mere gossip or idle chatter (*Gerede*), "the possibility of understanding everything without previously having made it 'one's own'" (*BT* 169, p. 213). Such talk precludes genuine understanding by gearing discourse to its lowest level of intelligibility: the They is the arbiter of discourse. Idle talk also cuts off new channels of inquiry by pretending to settle matters, by bringing questions which are actually open to artificial closure. We can place Heidegger's analysis of the degeneration of language in the context of the sweeping indictments of mass culture which begin with Nietzsche and Spengler and culminate in the accounts of the *Massenmensch* (the mass personality) in the work of Marcel, Ortega y Gasset, and Pareto. The same phenomenon is also expressed by a whole generation of poets including Pound, Eliot, Auden, and Spender.

Just as speech falls into idle chatter, penetrating sight has its own form of everydayness. Sight turns into idle curiosity, a seeing just in order to see, so that Dasein flits from one distraction to another in quest of perpetual novelty. The type of existence Heidegger describes is anticipated in the nineteenth-century Bildungsroman, for which Goethe's *Wilhelm Meister* is paradigmatic, and is later exemplified in Kierkegaard's depiction of the aesthetic personality. In its archetypal expressions, the hero craves erotic adventures, a theme which is remarkable for its absence from Heidegger's published work.

Another expression of everydayness, ambiguous interpretation, is a mixed form that depends on curiosity and idle chatter. Because nothing is serious in mere talk, matters under discussion are leveled down to become accessible to everyone and therefore open themselves to a multiplicity of readings. The interpreter is in a quandary: matters present themselves as ambiguous (*zweideutig*). People try to anticipate the latest fads, to guess "where things are at" in order to import novelty into existence. But the moment these fads are on the way to realization, they move on to the next thing: "Thus Dasein's understanding in the "they" is constantly *going wrong* (*versieht sich*) in its projects, as regards the genuine possibilities of Being. Dasein is always ambiguously "there"—that is to say, in that disclosedness of Being with one another where the loudest idle talk and the most ingenious curiosity keeps "things moving," where in an everyday manner, everything (and at bottom nothing) is happening" (*BT* 174, p. 218–19).

From the perspective of the death event, Heidegger's investigations into the everyday comportments of Dasein have the advantage of a certain concreteness. Heidegger analyzes the social being of Dasein in its commerce with others and with the world and uses his findings as clues for penetrating into the deep structures of Dasein's existence. But the chief strength of his analysis is also a major weakness.[5] The world Dasein inhabits is a materially rich and complex structure dense with social exchange. Although Heidegger's description applies (at least in part) to Western societies, it does not reflect the everyday conditions of Communist or Third World countries. In totalitarian societies (of both the right and the left) language is not corrupted by idle talk, but in a quite different fashion. Language in such societies is *double*—real meaning is opposed to surface signification.[6] The official language (unlike Heidegger's idle chatter) is duplicitous, disruptive, a parody of factual discourse. It arouses suspicion rather than soothing by seeming normative. Consider Andrei Platonov's picture of bureaucratic language and a peasant's astute hermeneutic in a passage from his novel *The Foundation Pit*:

> The activist . . . began to write out a report on the exact fulfillment of the measure for total collectivization and on the liquidation by means of a raft, of the kulaks as a class; but while doing this the activist was unable to put a comma after the word "kulak," since there was none in the directive. . . . The activist would have liked for the district to proclaim him in its decree the most ideological person in the entire district superstructure, but this desire subsided in him . . . because he recollected how, after the grain procurements for the state, he had had occasion to proclaim himself to be the most intelligent man in the given stage, and how, on hearing this, a certain peasant had declared himself to be a woman.[7]

Heidegger concedes that the way everydayness expresses itself varies historically, but if the existentiell comportments of Dasein are to be used as ontic clues or access routes to the structures of Dasein, historical differences are not innocuous. Thus a distinction between idle chatter and the double discourse of totalitarian societies is significant because the deeper framework and the mode of gaining access to it are inseparable. Heidegger's conclusions concerning the inauthentic comportments of Dasein are grounded neither introspectively nor intuitively but are based on empirical observation. Despite his effort to avoid the appearance of a scientific anthropology, an empirical residue remains in his account of the basic structures of Dasein (*BT* 51, n. 11, p. 490). The utility of the clues we lean on depends on the universality of their dispersion in societies and cultures. The behaviors opened up by the death event (unlike the comportments of Heidegger's everydayness) are universal. They do not define an eternal essence of man but, in the age of the death event, they have become the "propositions that stand fast for us," a historical a priori structure which dominates our seeing, discourse, and interpretation.

The Basic Structures of Dasein

THE AUTHENTIC STRUCTURES OF Dasein from Heidegger's perspective open a vista or human being different from that which begins with the phenomenon of man-made mass death. For Heidegger, authentic existence is not something that floats above everydayness; existentially it is a modification of the way in which everydayness is grasped (*BT* 179, p. 224). Thus our consideration of the They has laid the ground for an analysis of Dasein's authentic modes of existence. However, it would be misleading to take these authentic behaviors as virtues which are the counterparts of Dasein's everyday activities in their fallenness. Heidegger claims his analysis lies outside the moral domain because from his perspective the moral is a derivative sphere.

Before fallenness and Dasein's authentic manner of being in the world can be compared, the exact meaning of Being-in for Dasein, as well as the signification of the term world, must be considered. If the being of Dasein is unique, how is the way in which we speak about Dasein differentiated from the way in which we designate other entities? Heidegger claims: "Because Dasein's characteristics of Being are defined in terms of existentiality, we call them *"existentialia."* These are to be sharply distinguished from what we call *"categories"*—characteristics of Being for entities whose character is *not* that of Dasein" (*BT* 44, p. 70). Now we are prepared to define Being-in: "[it] . . . is a state of Dasein's Being. It is an existentiale" (*BT* 54, p. 79). This means Dasein exists in the world in a manner

different from that of all other entities. The others lend themselves
to categorial description. The entity to which Being-in pertains is an
I-myself, and Being-in-the-world is an essential state of that entity's
existence (*BT* 54, p. 79–80). Being-in also means that we are not
primordially spectators of the world but involved in it; Dasein exists
as already implicated in the world. To see this we are forced to interpret not merely Dasein but also the world in human terms: world is
itself an existentiale (*BT* 64, p. 92). Thus the world is not something
which Dasein is not, but arises as a characteristic of Dasein. This may
seem to fly in the face of the fact. How can the world have the character of Dasein? Is the world not the sum total of existing entities
taken together? It is just this sort of objective definition that Heidegger seeks to avoid. Instead, he thinks of world as a *wherein* in
which Dasein lives and which it first encounters as environment. In
this context, things are not merely alongside each other *partes extra
partes*; rather, they are entities we reach for, use, or make. In such
encounters with things we invoke a noncognitive kind of knowing,
a familiarity or conversance with things. Heidegger calls the ensemble of entities with which we have such concernful dealings *equipment*: "To the Being of any equipment there always belongs a totality
of equipment, in which it can be this equipment that it is. Equipment
is essentially 'something-in-order-to'" (*BT* 68, p. 97). Thus equipment has some purpose beside itself; it reaches beyond itself and
exists as part of a referential totality. Heidegger calls this manner of
being *readiness-to-hand*. Dasein relates to what is ready-to-hand
through active involvement but this does not mean that equipment
is not also something seen. The way we see is atheoretical; it is a
concernful seeing. Heidegger calls this manner of seeing *circumspection*. At the same time, we can also relate to entities from the point
of view of the spectator, looking at them as objects *present-at-hand*,
the manner of being of those things which are simply there, which
merely occur (*BT* 69, pp. 98–99).

Dasein's capacity to alternate between circumspection and theoretical apprehension of things is mystifying unless the peculiar character of Dasein's spatiality is understood. By elaborating the meaning
of *Da*, Dasein's manner of existing spatially can be brought out. The
primordiality Heidegger attributes to the There is particularly significant for our own problematic:

The entity which is essentially constituted by Being-in-the-world *is* itself in every case its "there." . . ."Here" and "yonder" are possible only in a "there"—that is to say, only if there is an entity which has made a disclosure of spatiality as the Being of the "there." This entity carries in its ownmost Being the character of not being closed off. In the expression "there" we have in view this essential disclosedness. By reason of this disclosedness, this entity [Dasein], together with the Being-there of the world, is "there" for itself. (*BT* 132, p. 171).

It is only as I-here, that is, something spatial, that Dasein relates itself to something yonder; because of the There (*Da*) of Dasein it is "deservant, directional and concernful" (*BT* 132, p. 171). So strategic is the There to the being of Dasein that it is on the There that Dasein's self-disclosure (a self-disclosure which makes Dasein human) is founded. For Heidegger the traditional term *lumen naturale*, which makes the self transparent to itself, can be explicated in terms of the There:

To say that it is "illuminated" ["erleuchtet"] means that *as* Being-in-the-world it is cleared ["gelichtet"] in itself, not through any other entity, but in such a way that it *is* itself the clearing. Only for an entity which is existentially cleared in this way, does that which is present-at-hand become accessible in the light or hidden in the dark. By its very nature, Dasein brings its "there" along with it. If it lacks its "there" it is not factically the entity which is essentially Dasein; indeed it is not this entity at all. *Dasein is its disclosedness.* (*BT* 133, p. 171. Emphasis mine.)

It is significant that Heidegger thinks of Dasein as *Lichtung*—a clearing in the woods, something spatial. Dasein is a clearing through which the Being of beings can become manifest, and this self-disclosing possibility is grounded in its There.

Dasein is most primordially its orientation as a spatial being, its relation to the worldhood of the world, to the referential totality of equipment. Even its self-reflexivity is founded on its spatiality rather than the converse. Heidegger's analysis of authentic discourse also reflects the primacy of this spatiality by way of the readiness-to-hand of equipment (*BT* 161, p. 203ff). Genuine discourse is understanding, a projection of the being of Dasein upon possibilities (*BT* 148, p. 189). But what is thus explicated in interpretation is something ready-to-hand: "To say that 'circumspection discovers' means that the 'world' which has already been understood comes to be interpreted. The ready-to-hand comes explicitly into the sight which understands" (*BT* 148, p. 189).

The primacy of Dasein's spatial being and Dasein's relation to equipment to that which is ready-to-hand, as the framework for grasping interpretation can be contrasted with the perspective opened up by the death event. For Heidegger, meaning is grounded in Dasein's relation to things organized as a referential totality. But if we begin with a different set of clues, with what is disclosed primordially in the age of the death event, the dead themselves and the disposable masses open up the way the world shows itself. Thus the necropolis of the twentieth century constitutes the referential totality. If we begin with the space of the death-world or the moonscapes of nuclear devastation, the readiness-to-hand of equipment cannot determine the self's way of being or its modes of behavior, authentic or inauthentic. What haunts those spaces still free of omnipresent death is only secondarily the absence of things, but primarily the absence of persons. Yet human beings resist thinking or conceptualizing this "no one." Instead they substitute some proper name to designate the one who is absent or Everyman, an anonymous subject. Odysseus, when asked who had put out the eye of the one-eyed giant Polyphemus, answered, "Nobody." The cunning of Odysseus' answer lies in its power to fool the other cyclopes into believing no one was responsible for this act. But the cyclopes are beings who do not know the laws of gods or men, and only such beings can accept this astonishing answer; they are unable to conceptualize the relation of being and nonbeing in regard to persons. When the Cyclops episode is taken up in Joyce's *Ulysses*, Nobody becomes the anonymous narrator, Everyman, who speaks with the violent voice of the demos of Dublin and of modern man against Bloom's teaching of peace. By contrast, Heidegger does not see inauthenticity as the voice of bloody nationalism, but as that of a bored novelty-seeking middle-class European society.

Since the being of equipment or readiness-to-hand cannot orient space in the various domains of the death event, we must look else-where for the primordial revelation of space. In this context corpo-reality itself becomes the bearer of signification.[8] This is not only because objects of use are lacking in the death-world or because in the death-world (using Heidegger's language) the here suppresses the yonder. Signification is based on the positive presence of anni-hilation rather than upon the lack of equipment in that world. Mean-ing opens out from absence, from the unthinkable nonbeing of the innumerable existents who were but no longer are There. Even the body, which is spatial, expresses this destitution as a sign. The body conveys meaning through sexuality, hunger, and other primordial human behaviors which are drastically altered in the death-world. The paucity of reference to the body in Heidegger's work has often been noted.[9] Heidegger's analysis of death ignores the question of the body and does not break with the perspective of the primacy of things over persons but reinforces it.

From the perspective of the death event, space is not grasped pri-mordially by way of equipmental being but is intersubjectively con-stituted as that which lies between persons separating them or draw-ing them together. Human beings or selves are encountered as the ultimate referents of moral acts. If we put these considerations to-gether—that space is constituted as what lies between persons and the self is defined as having a moral dimension—then primordial space also has a moral character. The closer one approaches the nadir of the death-world the more perceptible the moral dimension of space becomes. The old saw "iron bars do not a prison make" reflects this meaning. The application of this truism in the age of the death event is reflected in the language of Eva Kubasiewicz, a Polish polit-ical prisoner and member of the illegal trade union Solidarity. She writes:

And if you are capable of mean calculation, you have your first reason for not signing [a document which would secure her release]. It isn't worth it. Here no one can "detain" you for "explanations." Here you have nothing to fear. It is paradoxical, I know, but if in the morning you are awakened by someone banging on the door, you are not afraid of uniformed guests. You know it is only your kindly jailer bringing you your morn-

ing coffee. Bialoleka [the prison] is a moral luxury and an oasis
of freedom.[10]

The point at issue here is not to determine the character of the prisoner's act. Rather, the emphasis is on the prisoner's experience of
space as moral space. The moral articulation of space is not an a priori
structure of existence, a transcendental framework through which
experience is filtered come what may. In fact, only now, with the
advent of man-made mass death, is this structure disclosed. But this
new character of space is a sea change, the consequences of which
are revolutionary. In a world fast losing differentiated space, this new
meaning supersedes the aesthetic and utilitarian significations of
space. Space becomes the mise-en-scène for transactions which fos-
ter, deplete, or annihilate the relations between persons.

Being-with   *F*OR HEIDEGGER THE I IS NOT A SO-
                        lidary monad; we cannot be Dasein
without a world. But does Heidegger not also affirm that we can no
more be Dasein without other persons? If so, is it not misleading to
claim that Heidegger asserts the primacy of the being of things?
Despite Heidegger's separate explication of Dasein's social existence,
Being-with is in the end parasitic upon Being-in in three crucial con-
texts: the manner in which Being-with is originally established, the
function of language, and the meaning of the *call of conscience*.

Explicating the social being of Dasein, Heidegger asserts that
Being-with others is not incidental to Dasein but is an essential aspect of its existence. The other is encountered in all Dasein's comportments even when Dasein is alone, for then the other is experienced as missing, but in the presence of many Dasein can still feel
isolated and lonely. But how does Dasein express its relation with
others? Just as we engage the being of equipment through circumspection, so too there is an appropriate way of encountering other
persons. Since these others also have the being of Dasein and not
that of things, we encounter them in a manner which expresses this
difference—through solicitude (*BT* 121, p. 157). For the most part

Dasein lacks solicitude and expresses its Being-with negatively: "Being-for, against, or without one another, passing one another by, 'mattering' to one another" are deficient or indifferent modes of solicitude which treat the other as if he or she were merely present-at-hand (*BT* 122, p. 158). Heidegger also mentions two positive modes of solicitude: first, "leaping in and taking over for the other," and second, helping the other to face up to what it means to be authentically as Dasein but without taking away the other's care. Thus we can help the other to become transparent to himself, to assume his own cares. This is authentic solicitude characterized by forbearance and considerateness. Heidegger also rejects empathy (*Einfühlung*) as the basis of one's relations to others since in empathy the other is merely another self (*BT* 124, p. 162). One does not begin with the self and then move towards others; rather, being is already social.

To the extent that Heidegger's account of Being-with assumes that our relations to others belong to us essentially as human beings and that others are encountered in solicitude, the present analysis of sociality is in agreement with Heidegger's account. But even here, if we attend closely to the explication of Being-with, we can once again discern the primacy of equipmental being for the understanding of social existence. Heidegger opens his discussion of Being-with by showing that we already encounter it in connection with the world of the craftsman: there is always someone, a human being for whom the crafted product is intended. Dasein's primordial sociality expresses itself through the world of things: Dasein encounters others against the ground of a shared referential totality. Yet, in designating the world as the mise en scène for man's encounter with things, the force of the "with" in Dasein's Being-with others is not fully accounted for.

We have already seen that the other is neither present-at-hand nor ready-to-hand in the manner of things but that he or she is there as having something of the being that I-myself have. But what is this manner of being? First and foremost it is Being-in. Thus the analysis leads back to the referential totality of equipmental being which defines the There of Dasein and determines the manner of its Being-in. Heidegger expresses this by noting that the others are the ones who are *there too* although not as present at hand. But then how are they There? The "with" of Being-with means "too," and the too, in turn, "means a sameness of Being as circumspectively concernful Being-in-the-world. . . . By reason of this *with-like* [*mithaften*] Being-in-the-world, the world is always one I share with Others" (*BT* 118, pp. 154–55). The other is for Heidegger the one with whom I share the world: my relation to the other never bypasses the world; rather it passes through the circuit of the world. Thus, for Heidegger, in solicitude, I help the other with some matter, with work or in seeing his or her ownmost task. (This is particularly important in the death-world since all work, indeed any task which its victims may do in common, is coerced and therefore meaningless to its inhabitants.) But such relations as love, sexuality, and friendship, which occur primordially as relations between persons, circumvent the world, and represent a sphere of limited freedom, play no part in Heidegger's analysis.

The primacy of the thing is also expressed in Heidegger's view of language: interpretation is making plain what has been anticipated by circumspection, the manner in which Dasein links up with things. Thus Dasein relates to what is to be interpreted as something ready-to-hand. If we follow another path language takes for Heidegger, there is further evidence that Being-with is not equiprimordial with Being-in but, instead, depends upon it. This is attested in the manner in which Dasein frees itself from the They and shows itself to itself in its authenticity (*BT* 268, p. 313). Dasein is called to itself, to its own potentiality for being, by the voice of conscience. For Heidegger "calling is a mode of discourse," and as such it rouses Dasein, lost in the They, to itself (*BT* 271, p. 316). Heidegger seems to think of Dasein's condition in the They as something like the blindness of the Homeric hero overcome by *ate*, the mist cast over insight by the gods. The "call asserts nothing, gives no information about world events" nor does it "set going a soliloquy with itself" (*BT* 273, p. 318). Yet it summons Dasein to itself. The call is not a voice from elsewhere: caller and called are aspects of Dasein's own being. The call does not take propositional form: the language of the call is silence. Then what does the call convey? Dasein is called to its own being guilty, not as the result of some moral failing, but rather because the who of Dasein is negatively defined as the possibility of its not existing. Heidegger grounds Dasein's guilt in the fact that it is explicated as a not; in Dasein's being the basis of a nullity (*BT* 284, p. 329). Thus guilt is not tied to our relations with others: "Dasein need not first load a guilt upon itself through its failures or omissions; it must only be guilty *authentically*—'guilty' in the way in which it is" (*BT* 287, p. 333).

Some of the more obvious difficulties of Heidegger's position are already anticipated in traditional objections to the concept of original sin, which Heidegger's view of the structure of guilt resembles. If human nature is corrupt, how can human beings be made responsible for their acts? If guilt is universal and human beings are already guilty, can guilt still accrue for wrong acts? Does it then accrue as something different from original guilt, or does original guilt admit of degree, deepen when one commits certain acts? [11]

The principal point remains the question of Heidegger's explication of Being-with in relation to the call of conscience. For Heidegger Dasein calls itself and its language is silence. Thus Dasein's turn to authentic acceptance of its unfoundedness, of its being thrown into existence, bypasses the sphere of the other. Dasein remains a monadic existent at its most profound level, because Being-with is irrelevant to Dasein's self-calling. This aspect of Heidegger's analysis is especially odd since it dissociates guilt both from the sphere of acts and from Dasein's sociality. Even in the pre-Socratic tradition, in which guilt can be cosmic as well as human, "things make reparation for their injustice" but they do not bypass the sphere of acts.[12] Yet Heidegger separates the question of guilt from that of justice as it was understood in the classical tradition from the pre-Socratics to Aristotle. In the context of the death event the universality of primordial guilt offers no ground for distinguishing morally between victim and agent. It does not preclude distinguishing people on such other grounds as intelligence and race. Nothing in this position prohibits separating people on natural or protonatural grounds. Thus this analysis of guilt offers no frame of reference for making moral determinations and is fully compatible with the manner of grouping that is mythologically determined by the sorting myths. In spite of its difficulties the Christian doctrine of original sin at least acknowledges individual guilt and works out a scheme of responsibility for acts committed. Heidegger, to the contrary, leaves the sphere of facts vague and indeterminate, indicating merely that immoral acts are secondary phenomena parasitic upon primordially guilty existence.

Care

DASEIN'S GUILT ARISES FROM ITS being thrown into existence, in being the basis of a nullity. This claim can be elaborated by studying how Dasein reveals itself in its totality. For Heidegger such revelation does not come about in some behavior of Dasein but rather through mood or state of mind *(Stimmung)*. Dasein always has some mood even if it is expressed as lack of mood. Cognition cannot tell us why this is so since it cannot reach into mood: "A mood makes manifest how one is faring. In this, 'how one is,' having a mood brings Being to its There *(BT* 134, p. 173). In its everyday comportments Dasein tries to elude what mood discloses. But this very evasion reveals something about Dasein: the being of Dasein reveals it as "a naked 'that it is and has to be'" *(BT* 134, p. 173).

Its whither and whence are hidden but "that it is" is all the more strikingly revealed as Dasein's *thrownness*, its being delivered over to its There. Dasein expresses this thrownness in mood or state of mind *(BT* 135, pp. 174–75). This self-disclosure is independent of cognition or will *(BT* 136, p. 175). Moods simply assail Dasein and are not the result of introspection. The mood basic to Dasein's self-disclosure is anxiety or care: "Anxiety . . . provides the phenomenal basis for . . . grasping Dasein's primordial totality of being" *(BT* 182, p. 227). But why is Dasein anxious even in the absence of any ascertainable ground? That in the face of which one has anxiety is Being-in-the-world as such. This is always something indefinite: "What threatens is *nowhere*." But this nowhere is not nothing, but something already there, even if without spatial locale. It "stifles one's breath, and yet it is nowhere" *(BT* 186, p. 231). This nothing and nowhere are brought into view by anxiety. They bring the world as such before Dasein because in anxiety the specificity of persons and things vanishes. But with their disappearance fallenness also disappears so that Dasein can no longer hide from itself. Thus anxiety is the linchpin of Dasein's self-disclosure: through anxiety Dasein is thrown back upon itself, individualized. Dasein sees itself as free, able to project itself upon pure possibilities, as "choosing itself and taking hold of itself" (*BT* 188, p. 232). Here the disclosure and what is disclosed merge: Dasein discloses itself to itself. This pure anxiety should be distinguished from fear, which is "anxiety fallen into the world, inauthentic, and, as such, hidden from itself" (*BT* 189, p. 234). In fear, mood is directed to something we actually encounter in the world—persons or objects—something which actually threatens a specific region of Dasein's existence. Although we may know precisely what we fear there is still something uncanny in fear. Fear is not added on to our experience of something imminently threatening but is the manner in which we grasp what threatens us. Fear discloses Dasein as abandoned to itself (*BT* 141, p. 180). Other fears derive from Dasein's primordial fear for itself as a being thrown into existence without support.

A point of considerable importance for the analysis of mass death follows from this. For Heidegger, Dasein's fear for the other derived from a more primordial fear for itself. "One can fear about others, and then we speak of 'fearing for' them. . . . One can 'fear about' without 'being afraid'" (*BT* 142, p. 181). I may be apprehensive about the other who can be torn away from me but fearing-for is possible only in regard to my own being. This analysis anticipates Heidegger's view of Dasein's death, but this view is inadequate before the possible extinction of all human life.

My analysis agrees with Heidegger's view that mood reveals something about the existent. Yet I differ in regard to what and how mood reveals. For Heidegger, anxiety opens up the possible nothingness of the world, the impingement of the world upon Dasein, whereas fear is a derivative mood and refers to something specific that threatens Dasein. But faced with the possibility of total annihilation of persons and things, anxiety and fear coalesce, collapse into one another: the disappearance of persons and objects is not something vaguely disclosed through state-of-mind but is the object of a realistic apprehension about the human future. Alongside this fear is another which points backward rather than forward: the fear of losing a personal and collective past. Heidegger speaks of Dasein's being as it already was, that is, being as the past. The past is not a property Dasein drags along behind it. Instead, Dasein's "traditional way of interpreting itself, its own past and that of its generation," is intrinsic to Dasein's way of being (*BT* 20, p. 41). But the death-worlds have shown that it is possible to erase the past. The phenomenon of cultural revolution, in which cities are emptied and their inhabitants sent to the countryside to perform agricultural tasks with rudimentary technology sometimes under conditions of extreme terror, attests this feature of the death-world.

My Death   FOR HEIDEGGER, CARE IS DASEIN'S primordial disposition. But has Dasein as a fully articulated unitary being yet been brought into view? Is it in fact ever possible to bring Dasein as a whole into view? As long as Dasein is alive there is a portion of time left over to Dasein—that which Dasein can and will become (*BT* 233, p. 276). Aristotle argued that we could not judge whether a person's life had been happy until the moment of death because only then could we bring the whole into view. Must Dasein die then before we can apprehend it as a whole? If death were merely something that befell Dasein as an event after all the other events that make up Dasein's life, then we could only get hold of Dasein at its last moment. Nor could we grasp our own deaths, for if we begin by thinking of death as the terminal event of life then the only way to catch a glimpse of death is through the death of another. Only then could we observe the transition from human being to thing, from Dasein to something present-at-hand. But even here we distinguish between the being of a corpse, something that had once been a human being, and a thing. We show this by way of rites of interment which are bestowed upon the dead. But the loss experienced when another dies is different from that which the dying person suffers (*BT* 239, p. 282). We can never live his possibility of not being. Although we can often substitute for one another, no one can stand in for another's dying. One can sacrifice oneself for another but this provides only a reprieve for the other, who still must die in the end: "*No one can take the other's dying away from him.* . . . By its very essence death is in every case mine, insofar as it is at all" (*BT* 240, p. 284). This death which is mine is something I await not as that which brings my life to fruition or as something added to it which makes it whole—for then death would be a kind of fulfillment rather than a disintegration (*BT* 244, p. 288). Nor does Dasein simply stop, like a road which is unfinished. Instead, "The 'ending' which we have in view when we speak of death, does not signify Dasein's Being-at-an-end but a Being-towards the end of this entity. Death is a way to be which Dasein takes over as soon as it is. 'As soon as man comes to life, he is old enough to die'" (*BT* 245, p. 289). Death is always impending as the possibility of not being that Dasein must be ready to assume. Death is an issue for Dasein because what is at stake is Dasein itself, its possibility of no longer being there. *"When it stands before itself in this way, all its relations to any other Dasein have been undone"* (*BT* 250, p. 294; emphasis mine).

It would be absurd to claim that the death of the other and my death are interchangeable, that one could substitute for the other. I can sacrifice my life for another and thus stave off his death for a time, but in the end he must also die. But is this understanding of my relation to the other's death a primordial or existential understanding? Or is there another way of grasping the relation to the other's death? If we ground Dasein's mineness (*Jemeinigkeit*) in its death, if what confers its own being on Dasein, individuates it, is death, then all Dasein's comportments, even Being-in and Being-with, are derivative. In that case, Dasein's being as a whole is bounded and not a genuine Being-in-the-world. If Dasein is not fully relational, if its *transactions* are not what come to an end when it dies, then Dasein does not exist as a rich network of relations to the world and other people but lives as a solitary monad. Either Dasein is closed off through its death, or it is a system of relations whose boundaries are fluid. If, for Heidegger, the answer to the question "Who dies?" is not Dasein's relations to the world of persons and things, then what is left over is the organic ensemble that is the body of Dasein. This is similar to Aristotle's position that matter individuates, a view of death which Heidegger calls "mere perishing."

A self which looks toward its own death is always already a social existent. Of course the psychological and physical pain involved in coming to an end is deeper when I die than when another dies; but, as Heidegger often claims, psychological intensity is not a guarantee of ontological primordiality. If the self is genuinely its social relations then what comes to an end is a system of relations.

The social self which dies is not, however, an ideal entity. It is also a body: self and other are corporeal existents. This is especially important in the context of the death event, in which corporeality carries complex symbolic meaning in the absence of a rich equipmental nexus. The dead are not only human existents whose lives have come to an end; they are also symbols of contemporary violence and of the possible death of the entire human world. On the one hand, corporeality insures that one is not engulfed by the other in an undifferentiated field of symbolic ideality; on the other, the body is also primordially social. This claim is meaningful once we acknowledge that it is not mere mortality which is most deeply threatening to human existence. But, as Hobbes has shown, what human beings fear most is death by violence. Thus corporeality itself is dense with social meaning: the being that dies is an I who is also a we.

For Hegel, finite things are those which are consumed by time, but temporality is ultimately subordinated to the standpoint of the Absolute, that of eternity. Heidegger sees Hegel's analysis as the consummation of the tradition of Western philosophy which subordinates time to eternity. Heidegger, by holding fast to human finitude, shows that time is unsurpassable and constitutes the perspective or horizon from which to think through the meaning of Being. By thinking of Being in terms of time, rather than the converse, Heidegger hopes to stand this tradition on end. But the change he proposes demands radical revision of the starting point of thought. Now we must begin by considering human being. Heidegger calls this kind of being Dasein. Its distinctive characteristic is its concern with the meaning of Being. Dasein expresses its ontological concerns ontically, not in philosophizing about Being but in its everyday relationships to its own existence. We therefore must turn to these comportments as they are expressed in Dasein's average everydayness, the way in which Dasein usually behaves. This is determined by the They, which is not any specific group but "what most people do." This public self has its own distinctive way of showing itself: in language through idle talk, in seeing through curiosity, and in interpretation through ambiguity.

From the perspective of the death event, Heidegger's analyses are (properly) concrete. Nevertheless they begin with historically determined situations and extract from them characteristics which presume to open out into structural features of Dasein. Because these ontic clues are quasi-empirically derived from observations of Western societies of a given period, they do not extend to the death event. If one begins with the necropolis of the twentieth century, the ontic clues are different from those Heidegger chooses. The structure of human existence to which these clues lead is not eternal but historically conditioned. For example, language becomes not idle talk but the cynical doublespeak of the death-world.

Heidegger stresses the character of Dasein's spatial existence as a definitive comportment of Dasein. Thus Dasein's primary relation is to a referential totality interpreted in terms of the being of equipment, of things ready-to-hand, towards which Dasein behaves circumspectively. Heidegger analyzes interpretation, a function of language, in terms of such readiness-to-hand. But in the spaces of the death event equipment cannot determine the primordial structure of human existence. In this context the nonbeing of persons—the positive presence of the extinction of vast numbers of human beings— is fundamental. These meanings are borne by corporeal existence. Space is constituted intersubjectively and, insofar as people are moral beings, this space has a moral dimension. Heidegger's view of Being-with describes social existence in terms of solicitude, but solicitude expresses itself on the ground of a shared world and thus never bypasses the circuit of things organized into a nexus. Love, sexuality, and friendship are absent from Heidegger's account.

In explicating Dasein's authentic comportments, Heidegger turns to the phenomenon of the call of conscience, in which Dasein calls itself to its own potentiality for Being. But this call is essentially a monologue. More, the call reminds Dasein of its primordial guilt, not for something it has done, but as "being defined by a not—its possibility of not being, its impending death. Thus guilt is not tied to social existence but to Dasein's finitude. From the perspective of the death event, if primordial guilt belongs to every Dasein, the guilt of victim and agent are equalized.

Heidegger elaborates the meaning of the nullity that lies at the basis of Dasein's being by describing Dasein's orientation to it in the structure of care and anxiety. Dasein relates to the world through mood rather than through cognition. Anxiety is Dasein's fear for itself in the face of the world as world. Fear derives from anxiety but is directed toward a specific object. In the event of nuclear war annihilation, fear and anxiety as Heidegger describes them would coalesce, because the real object feared is the nonbeing of the totality, a nonbeing which is also the object of anxiety as a disposition.

In his analysis of death, Heidegger claims that death is what confers individuality upon Dasein. Death is what is truly mine: no one can stand in for me in my dying. But the primacy of one's death sublates the social character of Dasein. From the standpoint of the death event what comes to an end is a being constituted by its social relations. More, this being is equiprimordially a body. But the body too carries social significance since (as Hobbes suggests) the primordial fear of death is directed to death by violence, something socially inflicted, the doing of another. The existent who dies is both an I and a we.

VI / Technology and Poetry: The Later Heidegger

. . . He truly is alone,
He of the multitude whose eyes are
doomed
To hold a vacant commerce day by day
With objects wanting life—repelling love;
He by the vast Metropolis immured,
Where pity shrinks from unremitting calls
Where numbers overwhelm humanity,
And neighborhood serves rather to divide
Than to unite.
                                        —William Wordsworth

*I*N CONSIDERING HEIDEGGER'S analysis of Dasein in *Being and Time* it is all too easy to forget the book's aim, which is to "work out the question of the meaning of Being" (*BT* 1, p. 19). Heidegger never loses sight of this question, which is for him the sole theme of philosophy. Since human beings alone inquire into the meaning of Being, *Being and Time* focuses on Dasein as the access route to Being. Only after making Dasein transparent to itself does Heidegger turn in his later work to interrogate the essence of Being, beginning with Being as it has been conceived in the Western metaphysical tradition. Heidegger follows here something like the back-and-forth movement of his inquiry into the essential structure of Dasein. Just as Dasein anticipates what it will find when it questions its own past in order to place what it retrieves—the meaning of its individual and communal parts—ahead of itself, so too the philosopher must know how to question the seminal thinkers of preceding ages in order to retrieve what remains unthought by them. But this philosophical activity does not lack creativity; Heidegger's later work is not sterile and academic. If anything it is more puzzling and original than the analysis of Dasein. The meaning of Being in Heidegger's later thought requires a new type of attentiveness which had previously been lacking in philosophical interpretation. For Heidegger, philosophy bears a special relationship to its history. This history reveals, in its unfolding, a destiny determined by the manner in which Being is thought from the start. Thus by examining philosophy's earliest fragmentary remains, the work of pre-Socratic thinkers, and by attending to its critical turning points, especially to Cartesian philosophy in the modern period, we can bring to light the force of the meaning of Being as it is thought primordially, as well as the historical deflections which continue to cloud the original power of Being. Heidegger's thinking sets before itself what it has retrieved: the meaning of Being. This thinking with, but also against, the tradition is not simply a return: it is also a beginning.[1]

But if the meaning of Being is Heidegger's single ongoing project, his shift in emphasis is significant. In *Being and Time* Dasein projected itself upon possibilities into which it had already been thrown. In starting off with Being, however, human being is appropriated by the history of Being. Being is appropriation (*Ereignis*) and takes possession of man.[2] This process is beyond the control of human beings, for Being can never be anchored down by man. It is not a ground but an abyss which claims man, who derives the meaning of what is most essential for him from the way Being shows itself in a given age. The philosopher's task is to reclaim the meaning of Being through thinking, to purify this history by peeling away its accretions and bringing Being into unconcealment. To put it otherwise, Heidegger undertakes a greening of metaphysics. Although "greening" may suggest a fraudulent Romanticism, I believe it aptly describes Heidegger's project since, for Heidegger, the history of metaphysics concretely impacts upon the earth. The last fruit of this history marks our own era of nihilism and is expressed in atomic power and ecological decline. Heidegger believes that the essence of technology is the final stage of Western metaphysics—that is, technology is not a means: its essence is to exist as the characteristic thought of our time.

Much of Heidegger's rethinking of this history does not bear directly upon the theme of man-made mass death, but two features of Heidegger's later thought are pertinent to this problem. The first is Heidegger's description of technique, not as a sociology of the technical, but as a meditation upon its essence; the second is his reflection on the role of poetry in an age of technique. Although these themes are related to Heidegger's larger problematic, they can be pried loose from this context and considered independently. My own analysis, which takes an altogether different starting point—the destruction of persons—will be placed in conversation with Heidegger's, which locates the peril of the present age in its spiritual decline, as well as in our inability to perceive this degeneration in an essential way.

The Essence of Technique   CITING   NIETZSCHE'S   PHRASE "The wasteland grows," Heidegger describes the meaning of technique as the widening of the devastation that characterizes our time. For Heidegger, devastation is a form of negation more profound than destruction. Destruction only levels the physical and cultural works of Western man. Devastation, however, blocks all future growth by spreading what prevents growth: "The African Sahara is only one kind of wasteland. The devastation of the earth can easily go hand in hand with a guaranteed supreme living standard for man, and just as easily with a guaranteed uniform state of happiness for all men. . . . Devastation does not just mean a slow sinking into the sands. Devastation is the high velocity expulsion of Mnemosyne."[3]

What is blocked and prevented by devastation? Clearly not the proliferation of industrial and consumer goods or the dissemination of information, because these are the signs of devastation. Rather, devastation is the expulsion of memory, the historically weighted spiritual and useful objects which make up the traditions and material culture of Western man. Yet this very tradition, so far as it reflects its ontological base, has destined the present to grasp the real through the metaphysics of technique. For Heidegger not technology *simpliciter* but the essence of technology is reflected in devastation. How does the essence differ from the instruments of technology? How does it bring about the devastation which Nietzsche describes as the wasteland that grows? For Heidegger the essence of technique lays hold of the real through calculative thinking which, in turn, serves the will to produce.

To expose the progress of this decline, Heidegger traces the manner in which the term *techne* is first grasped in Greek thought. For the Greeks, techne is a bringing-forth, allowing "what is not yet present [to] arrive in presencing."[4] This bringing-forth includes the work of the artisan (*techne*) and the poet (*poesis*), as well as the work of nature (*physis*). For Heidegger, through this bringing-forth "something concealed comes into unconcealment" (*QCT* p. 11). Techne is the sphere in which beings are revealed. Plato links techne to knowledge (*episteme*) by using both words to signify knowing something as being at home in some realm of Being (*QCT* p. 13).

It is Aristotle's analysis of causality, however, which dominates the subsequent Western understanding of techne and its manner of revealing Being. For Aristotle, *aition* means "that to which something else is indebted" (*QCT* p. 7). All of the four causes belong together and all share responsibility for the object's coming into being. In this interpretation, the efficient cause, the agent, does not dominate causal explanation. Instead, causality is understood as analogous to the natural process of bursting open. Being is not subjected to domination but coaxed, as it were, into presence. Essential to techne as making is not use or manipulation, but revealing, which it shares with physis. In contrast to this view, medieval interpretations of causality stress the efficient cause, thus bringing the agent into a position of prominence, so that the one who functionally coordinates the process by bringing the other causes together dominates it as producer or maker. Technology, as the manner in which truth comes to pass in the present age, is a mode of revealing Being and is the final phase of this history of causality.

If modern technology too is a way of revealing truth, what is unique in its manner of bringing Being to presence? How does it differ from the ancient understanding of techne? Modern technology, or *technique*, forces nature to supply energy in order to store it. Older technologies take advantage of the energy nature releases but do not try to hold on to this energy for future use, do not lay claim to it: "A tract of land is [now] challenged into the putting out of coal and ore. The earth now reveals itself as a coal mining district, the soil as a mineral deposit. . . . The work of the peasant does not challenge the soil of the field. In the sowing of the grain it places the seed in the keeping of the forces of growth and watches over its increase" (*QCT* pp. 14–15). In technology nature is set upon and becomes the instrument toward a single goal: the highest yield at the lowest cost. What nature yields is stockpiled to become what Heidegger calls a "standing reserve" (*Bestand*) of energy destined for future use. "Unlocking, storing, distributing and switching about" are the new ways of revealing unleashed by technology (*QCT* pp. 15–16).

If this process corrodes human existence, why not put a stop to it? Is man after all not the master of technology? Heidegger argues that although man plans and runs the instruments of technology, he does not control the manner in which Being comes into unconcealment. Just as the thinkers of the past could only respond to the way in which Being addressed them, so man is now claimed by the challenge of technique, which is Being's way of showing itself in the present age.[5] Man is "gathered" by the challenge into an attitude of ordering things as standing reserve. Heidegger calls this challenging attitude enframing (*Gestell*). But what does it mean for man to be gathered into enframing? Heidegger, like Nietzsche, turns to etymological analysis to account for his novel use of language and explicates the idiosyncratic use of Gestell in terms of the force of the prefix *Ge*: *Gebirg* is a manner of gathering mountains into a chain and *Ge-müt* an original gathering from which our particular feelings unfold. *Ge-stell* belongs to this constellation of meanings: Ge-stell is "the challenging claim which gathers man thither to order the self-revealing as standing-reserve" (*QCT* p. 19). In ordinary usage Gestell means "a piece of apparatus" or "a skeleton," so that the term is already connected with gear and equipment. But, for Heidegger, enframing as a way of revealing is not itself something technological; instead, it signifies the essence of technology (*QCT* p. 20).

Heidegger explicates two marks of technique, the will to produce, which he describes in terms of enframing, and calculative thinking, which is in the service of this will. Calculative thinking is the manner of grasping nature in terms of physical forces which can be measured and represented by standard units. But modern physics, not technology, represents nature in this fashion. Physics came into being earlier than technology, and it arose first as a theoretical rather than an experimental science. How could physical science be dominated by a development which arises later than itself, especially when the early stages of physical science appear to be quite different from this development? Modern physics, Heidegger claims, is dominated by the essence of technology—by technology's will to interpret Being as standing reserve—even though this domination is recognized only later. The harbinger of technology, modern physics is already under its sway, even if it fails to recognize this. Science follows from the essence of technology; technology is not applied science.

Although technology and science are thus related Heidegger does not confuse them with one another.[6] The essence of scientific thinking is to represent Being, to make a picture of it. In the present context "the word 'picture' means the structured image that is the creature of man's producing which represents and sets before."[7] In contrast to the Greek techne as a bringing-forth into presence, modern physics stipulates that nature is to be grasped mathematically as "a self-contained system of motion of units of mass related spatio-temporally" (QCT p. 119). The phenomenological character of time and motion are subverted by the effort to measure change in terms of underlying constancies in order to formulate the laws of change: "To set up an experiment means to represent or conceive the conditions under which a specific series of motions can be made susceptible of being followed in its necessary progression, i.e., of being controlled in advance by calculation." (QCT p. 121). Scientific research also intrinsically perpetuates its operations since it must continually adjust its activities to its own results (QCT p. 124).

Heidegger traces this manner of apprehending what-is to a key turning point in the history of Western thought: the Cartesian formulation of the problem of knowledge. For Descartes, the knower becomes the foundation of knowledge and the ground of certainty: man is present to himself through his own thinking. Thought is setting something over and against oneself as an object rather than permitting it to come into presence. Not only is certainty set up as the ideal of knowing but, since subjectivity is the ground of certainty, its attainment is assured in advance. Consciousness is the tribunal before which the truth of what-is is determined: it represents Being to itself. The meaning of Being is now interpreted as the truth of representation. It is inevitable, Heidegger claims, that representation articulate itself in the form of picturing, as world-view, and inevitable that world-views clash since pictures of the world necessarily differ. Each world-view then will organize the power of planning and calculation in its own interest. According to Heidegger, we can trace today's ideological confrontations such as that of communism and capitalism to the philosophy of representation which interprets truth as picturing and terminates in antagonistic world-views.

Is there any aspect of the world in which calculative thinking is the dominant mode of interpretation and which also suggests the transcendence of purely calculative thought? Heidegger points to a reemergence of the qualitative at the heart of quantification itself, to number that can no longer accommodate quantity because the magnitude of the quantity cannot be grasped quantitatively. For example, the speed of air travel is grasped qualitatively rather than in terms of the number of miles covered. Heidegger calls the becoming qualitative of an unthinkable quantity "the gigantic." We have not yet, he claims, begun to ponder the significance of this phenomenon (QCT p. 153).

Heidegger's analysis is of fundamental importance from the perspective of the death event. He opens up for reflection the relationship between "the planetary imperialism of technologically organized man" and the metaphysical foundations of technique. Calculative thinking originates in representation which enables us to link science to its ontological ground rather than to regard its emergence as an epistemic leap depending exclusively on social and economic factors. By differentiating calculative thinking from the will to produce, Heidegger's account of technique offers a new ground for distinguishing science from technology. The complexity and sophistication of modern physics can be appreciated despite its origin in the perspective of technique.[8] This distinction in turn helps to clarify an aspect of the death event which manifests itself as an inner struggle within technique itself. The will to produce may express itself as a revolt against calculative thinking (and not only as an ally of calculation), as in the anti-urban repristinating revolutions in

Cambodia and Peru, even if the need for sophisticated medical and military technologies may reintroduce calculation later.

Equally important from the standpoint of the death event is the question of whether man can ever be considered as standing reserve if he belongs to a reservoir of interchangeable units. Earlier I suggested that Zeno's paradox is the model which governs the interpretation of man in the sorting myths on the part of the myths' manipulators. The paradox presupposes a conception of homogeneous units. But even if Zeno's analysis is a type of calculative thinking, it is in the service of an altogether different ontology from that of modern science: for Zeno Being is one. Zeno's paradox—the denial of motion because of the infinite divisibility of space—results from denying the unity of Being and does not follow from conceiving nature as standing over and against us, as something objective. Thus Zeno's view is infracalculative and without phenomenal application. This is why it accommodates sorting myths so well: they predicate an infinite supply of persons, in contrast to laws of nature which account for concrete phenomena. The paradox, having no field of application, remains emptily formal and abstract. This is attested in the fact that the reservoir of persons selected for death in the death-world never enter the process of producing useful goods: the dead themselves are the end product of the process. Just as the paradox is a radical negation of motion and an eating away of space, so the death world sorts and sorts but produces nothing. Death, not punishment or reeducation, is often the aim of slave labor as well, although slaves are also a source of cheap labor. But slave labor has generally been shown to be less productive than paid labor combined with heavy equipment. In short, man belongs to a reserve but is not the raw material for some further process except in the most stretched and distorted metaphorical sense, since the dead themselves are the telos of the death-world. Heidegger too denies that man can become standing reserve, but on other grounds: "Precisely because man is challenged more originally than are the energies of nature, i.e., into the process of ordering, he never is transformed into mere standing reserve" (*QCT* p. 18). For Heidegger, even if technique as a way of revealing is not man's creation, he cannot become mere raw material since he drives technology forward and thus participates in the process of ordering.

Transcending Technique WE HAVE SEEN THAT FOR HEI-
degger the power of technique is
all-encompassing, touching upon our relations both to nature and to
culture. But what keeps the debasing reign of technique in place?
What power shackles man to this mode of Being's self-revealing?

> The need to secure the supreme and unconditioned self-
> development of all the powers of mankind towards the uncon-
> ditioned domination of the whole earth is the hidden spur that
> goads modern man on to ever new convulsive changes, and
> forces him into binds which guarantee for him that his proce-
> dures are secure and his goals safe. These scientifically estab-
> lished binds appear in many forms and guises. . . . The bind can
> be the unfolding of the power of a nation dependent only on
> itself, or it can be the "proletariat of all lands" or it can be in-
> dividual peoples and races. The bind can be the development of
> mankind in the sense of world-wide community.[9]

According to Heidegger, domination of the earth means the ability
to hold on to it, to secure and fasten it down.

Is it possible to transcend technique, "the setting in order of everything that presences as standing reserve?"[10] We have already seen that
Heidegger rejects pessimism and nihilism. At the same time, the
present age is summoned to enframing as its peculiar mode of revealing. If there is a hope of going beyond the essence of technology,
the solution must lie in the way technology itself is encountered.

In his essay "The Turning," Heidegger shows that enframing conceals its essence from itself, so disguises itself that it comes to presence as a forgetting of the danger represented by technology. One
aspect of the disguise is man's belief that he rules technology when
actually he assists in the process. But even if man is not in charge,
neither is he helplessly delivered over to technology. Being comes to
presence as a destining (*Geschick*) but this destining also changes:
"for what gives destining its character as destining is that it takes
place so as suitably to adapt itself to the ordaining that is ever one
(*QCT* p. 37). Man cannot destroy technology, "whose essence iis
Being itself [and which] will never allow itself to be overcome by
men. That would mean, after all, that man was the master of Being"
(*QCT* p. 38). At the same time Being needs the coming to presence

of man, who is the safekeeper of Being. Thus any change in the destining of Being requires man's cooperation. Heidegger is deliberately vague about how this overcoming is to take place: it is "similar to what happens when in the human realm, one gets over grief or pain" but, since the overcoming is itself a destining, we cannot predict its character (*QCT* p. 39).

If we cannot get hold of technology then we cannot actively do anything: either affirming or attacking technique would be beside the point. Man can, however, open himself to the essence of technology. He can "establish himself in the space proper to his essence and there take up his dwelling" (*QCT* p. 39). Heidegger offers two pathways—thinking and poetry, since both belong essentially to language—through which man's essence encounters Being. For Heidegger (who conforms to Aristotle's view), thinking is "genuine activity." It "lend[s] a hand to the essence, the coming to presence of Being" (*QCT* p. 40). But thinking for Heidegger has nothing whatever to do with knowing facts or concepts. The type of thinking he describes is meditative and contemplative: "[The essence of man] is to be the one who waits, the one who attends upon the coming to presence of Being in that in thinking he guards it. Only when man, as the shepherd of Being, attends upon the truth of Being can he expect an arrival of the destining of Being and not sink to the level of a mere wanting to know" (*QCT* p. 42).

But the danger itself is for Heidegger also salvific. In his later work he often cites the lines of the poet Holderlin: "But where danger is, grows / The saving power also." By "saving" Heidegger means "to lose, to emancipate, to free, to spare and husband, to harbor protectingly, to take under one's care, to keep safe" (*QCT* p. 42). Thus, "when the danger is as the danger," and is no longer forgotten, "the safekeeping of Being comes to pass" (*QCT* p. 43).

But Heidegger also turns to another, more dramatic way of speaking about the turning within the danger, reverting to the metaphor of light and clearing but more violently than before. In *Being and Time* he speaks of Dasein as a clearing, but now he writes: "The clearing belonging to the essence of Being suddenly clears itself and lights up. This sudden self-lighting is the lightning flash. It brings itself into its own brightness, which in itself both brings along and brings in. . . . The truth of Being flashes, the essence of Being lights itself up" (*QCT* p. 44). In so doing Being emits its own light, but also retains the unlighted which keeps safe the darkness of its origin. What comes to pass in this insightful inflashing of Being is the turning about of oblivion. When oblivion is lifted, what comes to light is the "injurious neglect of the thing" (*QCT* p. 45). This sudden flashing is insight into what is, a revealing which lights up both Being and beings. But this mode of disclosure brakes the ferocity of self-will that belongs to the essence of technology as enframing. It is a turning from self-will to the renunciation of self-will: "Only when man in the disclosing coming-to-pass of the insight by which he himself is beheld, renounces human self-will and projects himself towards that insight, away from himself, does he correspond in his essence to the claim of that insight. In this corresponding man is gathered into his own [*ge-eignet*] that he, within the safeguarded element of the world may, as the mortal, look out towards the divine" (*QCT* p. 47).

Heidegger describes the coming into its own of the thing, not as part of a teleologically oriented process, a referential totality, as in *Being and Time*, but as that which brings together the four world neighborhoods, or the fourfold—earth, sky, mortals, and divinities. The world is redefined as reciprocal appropriation of the fourfold, which Heidegger describes as a mirror-play. As world, the fourfold simply "worlds." This is not for Heidegger an empty tautology. It means that there is no causal force behind the world through which it comes into presence. Causal explanation misses the point and tries to contract the meaning of the world to fit the dimensions of human knowing.[11] In this context man's death does not remain the same either. Because of the reciprocal relationship of the fourfold, when we think of mortals we also think of the other three. The term "mortal" is general and seems to encompass everything that perishes, but Heidegger reserves it for human beings alone, for those who, unlike the animals, foresee death. But now, beginning with the perspective of Being rather than *Dasein*, Heidegger speaks of death as the "shrine of Nothing." Through death, Being presences so that death is also "the shelter of Being" (*PLT* p. 179). Man is not different from animals by way of reason; instead the purely human task of man is to *become* mortal. This analysis is similar to Hegel's view of death in the *Philosophy of Nature*, in which man transcends animal existence by foredisclosing his own death.

In his analysis of the turning in an age of technique Heidegger resorts to a variety of images, some of them incompatible: thinking as a craft-like activity, the sudden flash of lightning, the serene mirroring of the fourfold. Heidegger's images are marked by a kind of loftiness: they stand above the historical, that which merely occurs. In fact, Heidegger frequently defends Thales, the pre-Socratic Milesian philosopher who falls into a well while looking at the sky; he reproaches the housemaid who laughs at Thales. This story is perhaps a trope defending his own frequent lack of concern with the concrete even though, as we have already seen, he often leans heavily on empirical reference both in his analysis of Dasein and in describing devastation. But the images Heidegger uses in his later work to describe the turning (thinking as craft, lightning and the mirror-play of the fourfold) only partly reflect this dissatisfaction with the empirical. Nor are they an effort to reach beyond traditional philosophical discourse. The reason he turns to these diverse images bears directly upon our problem. All three images try to answer different questions concerning the character of man's fundamental relation to the thing. Each question calls forth a new generative metaphor.

A. What must thinking be like if it can encounter the thing? Thinking must be in some way like what it apprehends. Since Heidegger has ruled out any straightforward view of thought as representing the thing in an act which conforms to it, he turns instead to making. Thinking is a kind of making, thought a type of craft: "Perhaps thinking, too, is just something like building a cabinet. At any rate it is a craft, a 'handicraft.' 'Craft' literally means the strength and skill in our hands. . . . Only a being . . . who can speak, that is, think, can have hands and can be handy in achieving works of handicraft. . . . Thinking itself is man's simplest and for that reason hardest, handiwork, if it would be accomplished at its proper time" (*WCT* pp. 16–17).

B. How can thinking ever change the way it grasps the thing if it is destined by the original sending-forth of Being to apprehend the thing by representation? To think through this question we must penetrate the working of representational thought. Representation holds things at a distance, leaving them poorly illuminated, and thus etiolates the force of man's contact with things. Only a truer lighting offers a more vital contact. The light of the sun might seem an appropriate metaphor to express this illumination. Yet apart from the historical freight the sun metaphor bears in Platonic thought, the kind of revealing Heidegger seeks not only lights up (like the sun) but also conceals. The lightning flash not only places in bold relief but also conceals as an inflashing.

C. Once we presuppose the turning as inflashing how do we think the thing *now* in this new context? By seizing what we have retrieved from our thoughtful pondering of the Greek tradition and holding it in front of us, we are ready to connect the thing to a new view of the world as a mirroring relation of the fourfold: "Thinking, the thing stays the united four, earth, and sky, divinities and mortals, in the simple onefold of their self-unified fourfold" (*PLT* p. 178). Each of the tropes Heidegger devises is an effort to bring to light the "decline and loss" characteristic of thinking in the age of technique. To be sure, man cannot take hold of technique, for to do so is only to will more aggressively; but he can let Being come into presence, let the thing become what it is: a nodal point to stay the fourfold in their reciprocal mirroring.

Heidegger has been criticized for the obscurity of his language, for his use of tautologies and for his uneasy transitions from one theme to the next to convey his vision of genuine thinking. But the effort to start thinking on its way demands that Heidegger reach for startling metaphors whose meanings do not emerge at once. But if what is genuinely new in the age of technique, what defines it, is the death event, as I claim, then "what is living and what is dead" in the thought of Heidegger cannot be pulled apart by restructuring it or tightening its argument in order to validate or refute its claims. Instead, one must begin elsewhere and think otherwise than Heidegger in order for the significance of his thought on the one hand and its wrong starting point on the other to begin to emerge.

Once again, Heidegger focuses on the coming-into-being of truth and meaning in the context of man's relation to things rather than to persons. Thus, in a particularly telling passage on the manner in which Kant construes the thing, Heidegger writes: "'What is a thing?' is the question 'Who is man?' That does not mean that things become a human product but, on the contrary, it means that man is to be understood as he who already leaps beyond things in such a way that this leaping-beyond is possible only while things encounter and so precisely remain themselves—while they send us back behind ourselves and our surface" (*WT* p. 244). Heidegger points out the difficulties inherent in Kant's approach to the meaning of the thing through the structures of experience. But Heidegger does not challenge what is fundamental for us—the primacy of the relation of man to things rather than to other persons so that, through defining the thing, we also define man. "What is a thing?" is the question "Who is man?"

A striking and fundamental inconsistency in Heidegger's thought now arises. Heidegger sharply attacks as nihilists those who describe the present age in terms of decline and loss, and describes nihilism itself as a technological behavior, a blindness to the destining of Being which shows itself as technique. At the same time he appears to exempt his own phenomenological account of devastation from this charge even when the meaning of devastation is brought to light through its concrete destructive effects. One reason for this discrepancy is that, for Heidegger, the present age is defined by the decline of the humanly significant thing. Using the thing as an ontological clue, he ponders the coming-to-presence of Being and thus restores not the thing alone but, by way of it, also human being. Thus Heidegger does not hesitate to use as starting points for his own reflections what he criticizes in others—a resorting to the mere occurrences of history which supposedly can never provide guiding insights. The priorities thus established remain nothing short of astounding. For Heidegger, such facts as the damming of the Rhine are important data attesting devastation, but the unnumbered dead of the two world wars and the creation of death and slave labor camps as institutional forms are never so much as mentioned in his major essays.

Although Heidegger often claims that technology will not simply disappear, he just as often resorts uncritically to pretechnolocial Romantic models: the life of the peasant becomes paradigmatic for thinking. Like Tolstoy, Hamsun, and others, Heidegger believes the peasant's roots in the soil are exemplary for the thinker.[12] Speaking of his hut in the Black Forest, he writes, "Let us learn to take seriously that simple and rough existence up there. Only then will it speak to us once more."[13] If, *per hypothesi*, the life of the Swabian-Alemannian peasant he extols is a model life, how deeply does the thinker who remains a spectator participate in this life? The philosopher who exults in peasant existence does not actually lead a solitary life (as Socrates already noticed). Even on Heidegger's premises, the philosophical life demands hearers, a thinking-with (*Mitdenkun*), and is not, in its essence, a life comparable to that of the peasant. Taking up residence among peasants thus seems closer to vacationing (a style Heidegger excoriates) than to peasant life itself. Although Heidegger is willing to borrow the agrarian model from Romantic thought, he nevertheless rejects Romantic pessimism. But while decrying pessimism for its bathos, he does not hesitate to valorize "Nietzsche's scream" or to excoriate "the monstrousness that reigns in damming up the Rhine." Although extensive commentaries properly record and interpret changes in Heidegger's thought which result from the shift to Being and appropriation in his later work, it is all too often forgotten that there is an extraordinary unity in Heidegger's thinking as well, a unity deriving from his single-minded concern with world and thing. Heidegger has not written an ontological *Bildungsroman* first of Dasein and then of Being; to the contrary, he has written a legend of the grail, a quest for the thing by way of different paths. It is not man but the thing which enframing leaves "unsafeguarded, truthless" and which, Heidegger believes, philosophy must leap in to rescue.

Poetry and Language   ALTHOUGH MAN CANNOT AC-tively overcome technology, he can open himself to its essence through genuine thinking. But it is also possible to encounter the meaning of Being by way of poetry. For Heidegger there is an inner connection between technology and poetry: Techne, to the Greeks, designated not only making useful objects but also "bring[ing] forth truth into the splendor of radiant appearing" as the "*poesis* of the fine arts" (*QCT* p. 34). In the Greek world, art was not a cultural activity but a revealing-permitting of the true to shine forth. Since the essence of art is akin to the essence of technology but also different from it, art may be the power that will reveal the essence of technology in the age of technology. Since man encounters Being through language we must look to poetry as the quintessential art in which the meaning of Being is revealed.

But a poet who addresses the destitution of our time must speak not only of the visible devastation but of what is lacking, in order to highlight nonbeing. For Heidegger, the present age is characterized by the absence of the holy: the united three, Herakles, Dionysos, and Christ, are gone from the world. "The default of God means that no god any longer gathers men and things unto himself, visibly and unequivocally, and by such gatherings, disposes the world's history and man's sojourn in it."[14]

Even the divine radiance has disappeared so that the age lacks the light by which to see its own privation. The absence of God or the gods leaves the age without ground: now there is only an abyss (*Abgrund*). The poet who can address such an age must reach into the abyss and follow the tracks of the gods who have fled (*PLT* p. 93). But why can the gods not choose to come back of their own accord? Why should we need the words of the poet? Unless man prepares an abode for the gods, the gods will not return. In this context, Heidegger asks whether Rilke is a poet for a destitute time. This question brings the present analysis to its starting point. In reconsidering Rilke's poetry as refracted through Heidegger's commentary and in examining Heidegger's encounter with Hölderlin, the difference between Heidegger's view of language and the one I shall propose should become clear.

Heidegger's interpretation of Rilke's poetry in his major essay "What Are Poets For?" proceeds by way of a gloss on a verse by Rilke.[15] For Heidegger, Rilke's historical relation to poetry is parallel to Nietzsche's historical place in the Western philosophical tradition. Rilke is the premier poet of the will just as Nietzsche is the last great philosopher of will. Rilke reaches into the abyss but this reaching is shackled by the metaphysics of will. Heidegger's account of willing in Rilke also has affinities with Schopenhauer's view of the intellect as an appendage of the will and of nature itself as a willing force. For

Heidegger, Rilke sees man and other living beings as they are related to an identical ground, nature. Each being is not only willed by nature but is also itself a will. Thus will is the ground both of nature as *physis* and of life (*zoé*): it looses or ventures the beings, each one to the being that it is. Beings are flung out, dared. Humans too are centrifugally hurled and suspended over an abyss like the acrobats in Rilke's *Duino Elegies* or the tightrope walker in Nietzsche's *Zarathustra*. All living beings including man are unshielded in being thus ventured. Yet these beings are not altogether abandoned either: they find a ground of security in Being as will. Being both draws and hurls and as such is a center, a point of gravity, which holds the beings in tensive balance. Rilke calls this holding in balance of what is ventured the *Bezug*. The term generally means relation, but Heidegger interprets Bezug as draft and ascribes to it the connotations of the original English sense of draft: drawing or pulling as a load. The draft mediates the opposing forces but also, as the whole draft, names what-is as a whole. How are beings related to the draft? Their being is determined by the way in which they are pulled within the whole draft which Heidegger thinks of as "the gravity of the pure forces, the unheard of center, the pure draft, the whole draft, full Nature, Life, the venture" (*PLT* p. 105). The ontic gradations of beings are determined by their relation to the center as pure gravity. Rilke calls this whole draft "the Open."

We now begin to recross the terrain of our first chapter in a new way. There I spoke of the Open as the "nowhere without no." Now I am prepared to inquire into the relation between the "nowhere without no" and Heidegger's significant but quite different use of the Open. Since the Open is a term which belongs to the most fundamental stratum of Heidegger's thought it is important to distinguish his treatment from Rilke's. For Heidegger the Open is the clearing (as in a forest) where beings come into presence.[16] But the Open for Rilke (on Heidegger's reading) is that which does not block off or "set bounds." It is the great whole of all that is unbounded allowing the ventured beings to be drawn to one another and together, merging with the boundless (*PLT* p. 106). Heidegger seems to identify Rilke's boundless with the boundless (*apeiron*) of the pre-Socratic philosopher Anaximander, but he also endows it with Schopenhauerean will. Heidegger's Open is, by contrast, "lightened" like the forest clearing, whereas Rilke's Open can never harbor the Being of beings. If boundlessness characterizes the Open, then anything encountered within it becomes a barrier: beings experienced over and against man become "objects" while man retreats into himself to become "subject." Man represents the world and thus has a mediated relation to it, whereas flowers and especially animals, for Rilke, are more purely within the Open. Because Rilke has experienced the Open as will, he is at least able to stand in horror before the products called forth by the metaphysics of will, "sham things, dummy life," in contrast to authentic things. The danger to which Rilke's poetry points is, according to Heidegger, that man will lose himself in unconditioned production. In this context, Heidegger expresses his worry that "purposeful self-assertion," rather than the "much discussed atomic bomb as this particular death-dealing machine," is what is truly deadly (*PLT* p. 116).

In a particularly dense analysis Heidegger develops a bipolar conception of Rilke's view of will: willing *with* the venturing or setting personal will *against* it, personal will as pitted against metaphysical will. If we go with the venturing we are ventured sooner and come sooner into the danger, but at least the force of Being cannot go against us. As in hang gliding when we abandon ourselves to the extreme danger of a powerful force, Heidegger seems to mean that there is also a certain safety within the unshieldedness that comes from the force itself. But let us look more closely at the Open into which we are ventured. In the first chapter we saw that for Rilke the Open as boundless is called "the widest orbit." Even that side of life which is averted from us, death, belongs within it. This has important implications for Heidegger's and my analsyis. Life takes death up into itself so that death lies inside the sphere of beings. Thus Rilke's poetry, for all its stress upon death, is death-denying. Heidegger writes: "The self-assertion of technological objectification is the constant negation of death. By this negation death itself becomes something negative; it becomes the altogether inconstant and null" (*PLT* p. 125). This conforms to Heidegger's view that Being as willing blocks off death.

But how are we to grasp the totality in which death is now included? Rilke urges us to become "bees of the invisible," placing the inner objects safely within the heart. Only the angel has fully achieved this conversion. For Heidegger, Rilke's angel is metaphysically the same as Nietzsche's Zarathustra, "beyond the danger, beyond the corporeal, stilled" (*PLT* pp. 134–35). And how does the poet himself figure in this collocation of will, venturing and the Open? The poet ventures himself as language: "Song is existence (Dasein)" (*PLT* p. 138). "More daring by a breath," the poet wills differently from the willing of technique but in harmony with the way Being wills:

> Earth, isn't this what you want: an invisible
> re-arising in us? Is it not your dream
> to be one day invisible? Earth: Invisible!
> What is your urgent command, if not transfiguration?
> Earth, you darling, I will.[17]

Love and Other Persons   HEIDEGGER'S REFLECTIONS ON the meaning of venturing death and the Open ingeniously link Rilke's work to the metaphysics of will. But does this interpretation reach the root of Rilke's poetry? Or does Rilke's relation to the poetic word open out of an altogether different ground? I spoke of Rilke as belonging to the tradition of poets and thinkers who interpret death as the coming-to-an-end of the solitary individual. I also interpreted Rilke's view of death as bringing even nonbeing into the "wider orbit," the totality of beings in conformity with Heidegger's analyses. Yet some clues in Rilke's work point in a different direction. These clues point away from a stress upon will and, even more radically, from Heidegger's own ontological thrust are rich with possibilities for the examination of man-made mass death. In a letter of 1924 from Muzot, cited by Heidegger, Rilke writes:

> However vast the "outer space" may be, yet with all its sidereal distances it hardly bears comparison with the dimensions, *with the depth dimensions of our inner being*, which does not even need

the spaciousness of the universe to be within itself almost un-fathomable. Thus, if the dead, if those who are to come, need an abode, what refuge could be more agreeable and appointed for them than this imaginary space? [18]

On the face of it this letter seems to support Heidegger's reading that for Rilke, beings achieve their ultimate significance through in-finite inwardization. To be sure, there is an aspect of Rilke's work which belongs squarely within the Augustinian tradition of intro-spective consciousness and which culminates in the modern stress on the subject. But another side of Rilke's thought also comes to frui-tion here. Just as Heidegger believes mortals must prepare an abode for the god, Rilke thinks we must prepare an abode for the dead: Rilke's world is one in which not only things but also the beloved pass away. Thus we must hollow out a place for persons in the re-cesses of interior space. But were the dead not, as Heidegger pointed out, always "torn from those who have 'remained behind'" and hon-ored by funeral rites (BT 238, p. 282)? Why is the inward movement necessary? In the death event persons, like Rilke's things, stand in need of an abode since vast numbers of the nameless are extinguished and the rites themselves are obliterated. To be sure, whole groups have perished in the past. Why does interiorization now acquire the extreme urgency Rilke expresses? For Heidegger, Mnemosyne is the name for the retrieval of the history of Being, an ontological quest which floats above the cataclysms of the present as they manifest themselves in the great destructions of peoples. But for Rilke only *individual* memory has the requisite stretch to accommodate the nec-ropolis of the present age. For him the task is to reach into the abyss and to find there a counterlogos able to encompass the scale of what is moving toward extinction as well as the speed of this passing.

Although Heidegger's interpretation of the metaphysics of will in Rilke's poetry illuminates Rilke's view of the Open, in his reading there is a particularly striking omission of a key theme in Rilke's work—thwarted love, the theme of the lover whose beloved dies or rejects the lover or the lover who renounces the beloved but contin-ues to cling to love.[19] Such love exists in an altogether different space from that of sensible experience, from the possibility of active fulfill-ment.[20] In a letter of 1912 from Schloss Duino, Rilke describes such a renunciation on the part of the Portuguese nun whose letters had a considerable impact on his work:

> "My love is no longer dependent on the way you ˙treat me" [cited by Rilke from the nun's letter to her former lover]—the man, as a beloved, was shed, discharged, *loved through*—if one may express it so considerately, loved through as a glove is worn through.
>
> . . . She does not fling the currents of her emotion forward into the imaginary but rather . . . leads this emotion of highest order back into herself: enduring it, nothing else.[21]

The paradigm of resoluteness in Rilke's poetry is not one's own death but the relation to another from whom nothing is to be expected. The self does not call itself and, against the insistent clamor of everydayness, heed the voice of conscience. Instead, the test of authentic existence lies in whether love can exist in the absence of the beloved. Just as life encompasses death, so love engulfs the pain of loss. Rilke's view of love is not that of the intellectual eros of Plato's *Symposium* but that of Christian renunciation. Had the Portuguese nun turned her love to God, Rilke writes, "she would have plunged into God like a stone into the sea."[22]

Heidegger does not address the theme of eros in his essay on Rilke, nor does love form a significant part of Heidegger's thinking in any of his major published works. This is especially conspicuous in his analysis of Dasein, who may be anguished, guilty, resolute, fearful, domineering, or solicitous—but never in love. Even where it is most anguished, Dasein seems to encounter beings in robot-like fashion: neither sensuality nor love transfigures its life. Although in the end Rilke also rejects dialogical existence as the deepest human comportment, the disposition he praises—love renounced but maintained—is founded on it. Rilke's poetry is not just for saying "house, bridge, fountain, jug" and the like but for expressing exemplary suffering:

> . . . Have you so fully remembranced
> Gaspara Stampa, that any girl, whose beloved's
> eluded her, may feel, from that far intenser
> example of loving: "if I could become like her!"?[23]

While Heidegger has recognized Rilke the poet who eulogizes "the intimate broken surfaces of things," he has overlooked Rilke the poet of discourse toward the beloved other.[24] Once Heidegger rejects the idea of an interior stream as belonging to the philosophy of consciousness and thus to the Cartesian view of knowledge as representation, he can only depict Dasein as a chain of pulsations toward world and thing colored by affective tonalities. But the self as an abode for the lost other must remain foreign to Dasein. Thus, apart from traditional rites of remembrance, there is no place for the massacred in Heidegger's work. Memory is not, for Heidegger, a psychological faculty which retains ideas. Instead, the meaning of memory derives from Mnemosyne, the mother of the nine muses: memory is "the gathering of recollection, thinking back." Such thinking gathers and converges upon that which "demands to be thought": that which essentially is. This thinking back is the source of genuine poetry (*WCT* p. 11). Memory has the power to reach behind representation to fetch what-is and then to tell it. But nowhere does this recollecting touch upon the lost beloved or the countless dead of the present age.

In contrasting Rilke and Heidegger I should like to avoid two possible misinterpretations. First is the view that even if poetry opens a discursive space for remembering the lost or dead other, the proper subject of poetry is some aspect of the death event. To the contrary, such poetry may be didactic and trivializing, thus distorting what it tries to sustain. But, poetry is as primordially an invocation of the beloved other or others as it is of things. Since space is intersubjectively constituted within the ambit of the death event, the being of things that dwell in this new space must be differently sung from the things brought to light before these apocalyptic events. How to do so is for poets to discover and not for philosophers to legislate. Second, to contrast Rilke's poetry of love and inwardization with Heidegger's radical concern for things is not an effort to polarize these concerns as if they could be polemically decided. Instead I hope to show that Rilke, poet extraordinary of world and thing, by also addressing the beloved other through renunciation, thinks world and thing by way of another route. I mean to highlight an aspect of Rilke's poetry that has remained unthought by Heidegger (perhaps because Heidegger replaces interiority, in part, by mood or

Stimmung): the possibility of thinking not only my death but also the numberless dead.

"Since we have been a conversation": The World of Hölderlin — FOR HEIDEGGER, HÖLDERLIN IS the premier poet for our time. He addresses our destitution by thinking the essence of man as language, which in turn becomes actual as conversation:

> Much has man learnt
> Many of the heavenly ones has he named
> Since we have been a conversation.[25]

In a gloss on this passage, Heidegger defines *conversation* as speaking with others about something. This act of speaking has two aspects: first, it presupposes a human coming together and hearing of one another and second, it assumes that conversation has an intrinsic unity. A single conversation manifests one thing only, speaks one essential word (*EB* p. 301). For Hölderlin this is what we have always been: the unity of a conversation related to a single word. Yet what persists opens out only in time as what changes but endures through time. Thus if conversation is temporal, it arises simultaneously with and as an expression of our historical existence: "they [historical existence and conversation] belong together and are the same thing" (*EB* p. 302). For Heidegger, the conversation we are names the gods and transmutes "the world into word" (*EB* p. 303). Essential conversation begins in the naming acts of the poet who speaks the essential word. In another context, Heidegger writes: "To name is to call and clothe something with a word. . . . All naming and all being named . . . consists . . . in the calls to come, in a commending and a command" (*WCT* p. 120). Thus naming is a kind of hailing of the being of that which is named. The poet establishes being in acts of naming.

It is clear that even if Heidegger sees langauge as man's possession, he does not interpret language as a tool. Will language then provide a way out of the circuit of world and thing which characterizes Heidegger's fundamental thinking? We can find hints toward an answer in a passage of fundamental significance for grasping Heidegger's view of language: "Language is not a mere tool, one of many which man possesses, on the contrary, it is only language that affords the very possibility of standing in the openness of the existent. Only where there is language, is there world, i.e., the perpetually altering circuit of decision and production, of action and responsibility, but also of commotion and arbitrariness, of decay and confusion" (*EB* pp. 299–300). Perhaps in grasping language as a conversation which founds human historicity, a primordial dimension of language opens up which provides ground for thinking the death event. Yet the use of the term conversation should not mislead us. Heidegger's interpretation of conversation is directed toward preventing a category mistake: "taking language as raw material" (*EB* p. 307). But once the idea of conversation is linked to poetry as uttering the essential word, we must recall that Heidegger's view of poetry throughout his work attests the Ur-unity of poetry and techne in techne itself: techne as poesis rules over language. But for us the language of the death-world can never be primordially spatial, bound to the being of world and thing: space is discursive and intersubjectively constituted. Instead, the language of the death-world must be a language suspended in time and the naming brought into view there must be a naming which relates itself primordially not to space but to time. Thus it cannot be a language which hypostatizes space—therefore in some way an eternalizing language—but one which designates temporal continuity. Only the language which names the near ones—the language of kinship structure—names in the required manner—a point that will be developed in the final chapter. Part of the threat of the death event lies in the possible extinction of this type of naming.

In the age of technique there is still another danger to the structure of human continuity through time, not extinction *tout court* but, through genetic engineering, a loss of the ordering of the generations through time. Here (although he does not treat the theme) Heidegger's analysis of technique and my perspective on the primordiality of kinship converge. Through genetic engineering the identity of the individual human being may disappear. The naming of parent, sibling, and child could become impossible. At present, even when one does not know who one's parents are, the question "Who?" has an answer in terms of specific persons. But the storing of genetic material may place "parents" thousands of years behind "children" while the combining of genetic material and the use of surrogate "maternal environments" may make the identification of an individual's parents impossible. This distortion of corporeal existence must result in a linguistic revolution as well. Genetic engineering does not, of course, alter the threat of the death event but it could create a truly anonymous multitude. Discourse would be compelled to name individuals in some new manner, perhaps functionally, thus restricting existence even more narrowly to the categories of calculative thinking.

Heidegger describes the essence of technology not as something instrumental, a means for producing goods, but as a unique manner of revealing the meaning of Being characteristic of the present age. It manifests itself in devastation, the ravaging of nature, a process which continues to grow with no end in sight. Man is challenged to order things as standing reserve, raw material for the process of production. Heidegger calls this challenging attitude enframing (*Gestell*) and traces it to Descartes' interpretation of knowledge as representation in which subjectivity becomes the standard of certainty while the object of knowledge is set over and against the subject. Two features mark technique: the will to produce and calculative thinking, the manner in which nature is understood by modern physics. To be sure, Heidegger's analysis accounts for the worldwide spread of technology. But the idea of standing reserve is inapplicable to the death event, whose logical shape is determined by Zeno's paradox, an infracalculative formal structure which does not derive from the Cartesian philosophy of representation.

Heidegger's view of technique is not, however, entirely pessimistic. Although technology cannot be destroyed, we can bring technology "into its yet concealed truth" by way of fundamental thinking and through a type of poetry that reaches into the destitution of the age. Heidegger details this restoration in terms of a turning described metaphorically—thinking as craftsmanship, then as the inflashing or lightning flash that brings Being into presence, and finally as the mirroring of the fourfold: earth, sky, mortals, and divinities. But the starting point of Heidegger's analysis precludes an understanding of man-made mass death, since he maintains the primacy of the thing and thus defines man in terms of world and thing. Heideg-

ger's effort to describe genuine thinking looks backward to a time
when things were experienced in their wholeness and he leans on
various Romantic modes of repristinization, for example, the model
of the peasant. From the standpoint of mass death, this is an evasive
effort to backtrack which ignores a fundamental phenomenon.

Heidegger sees not only thinking but also poetry as reaching into
the essence of technique. This theme brings us back to the poetry of
Rilke. Heidegger defines Rilke's view of the whole draft and the
Open in terms of will and thus links Rilke's poetry to the metaphysics
of will and the perspective of technique. Yet because of Rilke's insights into will and into the meaning of the thing, Heidegger finds
in Rilke a powerful vision of the destitution characteristic of the age.

Heidegger criticizes an aspect of Rilke's poetry which bears upon
my view of the death event: Rilke's vision of inwardization as creating an abode for the dead. Heidegger's attack on the philosophy of
consciousness together with his view of memory prevents him from
attributing significance to inwardization. Heidegger never focuses
on thwarted love, a theme of primary concern in Rilke's work: love
renounced, rather than "my death," is the ground of resoluteness in
Rilke's poetry. Thus a language of love as a mode of reaching toward
another person is a primordial facet of poetic discourse in Rilke's
work which remains unnoticed by Heidegger.

In interpreting a verse in which Hölderlin speaks of man as "having been a conversation," Heidegger might be expected to acknowledge here (more than elsewhere) the intersubjective aspect of language. But, by linking poesis to techne, Heidegger establishes their
Ur-unity, and language is once more confirmed as uttering man's
relation to world and thing. Heidegger misses an important type of
naming—the proper name belonging to persons and the naming inherent in kinship structure. This act of naming, an important function of primordial language, remains in the death-world when other
functions of language are precluded.

VII / Self, Language, and Community

Cain.	To give birth to those
	Who can but suffer many years, and die,
	Methinks is merely propagating death,
	And multiplying murder.
Lucifer.	Thou canst not
	All die—there is what must survive.
Cain.	The other
	Spake not of this unto my father, when
	He shut him forth from Paradise, with death
	Written upon his forehead
	—George Gordon, Lord Byron

*T*HE INCONGRUITIES AND PARA-doxes generated by the twentieth-century world of man-made mass death fundamentally and apocalyptically overturn our previous conceptions of finitude. No contemporary thinker has made this phenomenon thematic, much less tried to assess its relevance for developing a conception of the self to which this phenomenon is integral. I only hope to offer some tentative suggestions for developing such a paradigm. The self I describe is not an abstraction based upon empirical observation of survivors of the various segments of the death event. Rather, I appeal to the structures of existence opened up in a world of radically new, efficient technological forms of extinction powered by new social and political means. Most of those alive now are not direct survivors of the vortices of the death event, nuclear war and concentration camps, since its victims are part of the vast necropolis I have described. Yet the scope and character of the event are sufficiently clear so that it can be thought of as a "stable" backdrop for the self's transactions with the world.

Hegel and Heidegger
Revisited
H EGEL BELIEVES THAT THE EN-
lightenment view of reason is re-
ductionistic and fragmenting and that can only issue in abstractions.
The work of the understanding, reflection, can never transcend the
oppositions it generates. Instead, the philosophy of reflection terminates in calculative thinking, a necessary moment in the history of
Spirit but one which is also empty and alienating. Hegel's analysis
illuminates the ethos of scientism by uncovering its logical and ontological foundations in the philosophy of reflection. Although reflection is characterized by subjectivism, since it presumes that
knowledge depends upon the contribution of the understanding, it
also sets the limits of knowledge in the sphere of nature by legislating
that only what is accessible to the understanding can be genuinely
known. Thus the content of knowledge is limited to objects perceptible to the senses, since this is what the understanding can grasp.
Hegel describes the perspective of scientism and calculative thinking
in its modern form and anticipates aspects of the structure of thought
exhibited in the death event. Calculative thinking also characterizes
an aspect of the transactional self I consider.

In contrast to Kant's view of time as a function of the subject,
Hegel interprets time as becoming and destruction. Even if, for Hegel, time is sublated in the Absolute, it is penultimately a destructive
force which sweeps away the detritus of moribund civilizations. Both
aspects of Hegel's view are reflected in the death-world. Victims experience the annihilatory power of time while those who control the
sorting myths try to stop time by creating a simulacrum of end-time
which they hope will eventuate in a static eternity. The effort to create
an eternal present freed from contamination by the impure is, in fact,
the driving force of these myths. The self in its everyday existence,
caught between the accelerated time of technique and the various
efforts to stabilize this process, flounders between these modes of
temporality.

Hegel's description of mastery and servitude also reveals a functional aspect of servile consciousness essential to our analysis of the
death-world. More fully a manifestation of Spirit than the brute force
of physical mastery, servile consciousness remembers, is able to give

an account of itself and to recount the meaning of its struggles. In the death-world, victims may see themselves as bearers of a potentially narrative consciousness, as witnesses of the events of that world. Within the context of the distortions of mastery and servitude in the death-world, the dialectic of warrior and bard is replayed in lurid parody. I hope to show that the struggle to the death at the heart of Hegel's account of mastery and servitude also functions as a generative metaphor for the emergence of a transactional self. This is important for my analysis since the death event impinges not upon a solitary being, a cognition monad, but upon a self already fully social and transactionally constituted.

In the case of Heidegger, I am guided less by his specific conclusions than by the phenomenological protocols he establishes. Thus I remain attentive to the self's everydayness as a transactionally constituted ensemble of behaviors. I prefer to retain the term "self," despite its historical baggage, rather than to devise a neologism or borrow Heidegger's "Dasein," which suggests man's relation to world and things instead of to other persons, thus evincing (as Hegel said of Kant) "too much tenderness to things."

In spite of important reservations concerning its point of departure, I am also guided in my own description of the self by Heidegger's account of technique as a mode of revealing. In Heidegger's view, technique depends on interpreting nature as a reservoir of energy, a standing reserve. The challenge to reveal the real in this manner sets upon man and is expressed by him as the ordering attitude of modern science. Yet since he starts from the point of view of man's relation to the being of things, Heidegger sees the primary distortions resulting from technique as blighted landscapes, urban sprawl, and dreary industrial complexes. The destruction of persons for him becomes a secondary phenomenon. If, to the contrary, the relation to other persons is seen as primordial, the order of priorities is reversed: devastation follows the more primordial phenomenon, mass death. If the self as relation to others exists prior to its enmeshing in the nexus of things, then technique is first and foremost a negation of the relation to persons, rather than simply a consequence of objectification itself. My view of self begins from this premise.

The Foredisclosure   *T*HE FUNCTION OF THE AUTHEN-
Paradigm   ticity paradigm in governing the
way death is seen in the Western philosophical tradition has been
considered. The paradigm is the normative model for interpreting
the process of dying, beginning with Plato's description of Socrates'
comportment in the face of impending death. Dying well means accepting one's ceasing to be with equanimity and maintaining one's
composure until the end. The self is something potential whose actuality is only fully realized after life is exhausted. Detachment is
achieved by shifting perspective away from the ordinary experience
of time to a standpoint outside of time. This shift is meant to deflect
attention from one's daily concerns and from pain and suffering, as
well as to enable one to contemplate what, if anything, lies beyond
death. If life has been well lived—that is, in accordance with creedal
and moral norms, the dying individual need not fear punishment. If
the self is extinguished altogether, then this too should provoke no
fear since there will be no one to punish. But the comforting aspects
of these assumptions could (and frequently did) turn into their opposites. If there is an afterlife, how can one be sure one deserves its
promise of bliss? If there is simply nothing after death, how can this
thought comfort, since extinction is precisely the source of one's
fears?

The authenticity paradigm rests upon a notion of self I have yet
to develop, one which emerges in the history of Western thought in
the context of an ontological problematic. The self is something existing and its relation to death is a relation to nonbeing. Important
differences separate various versions of this view: Platonism, panthe-
ism, and epiphenomenalism offer different interpretations of the self.
But, to the extent that death determines the meaning of self, a common perspective emerges which loosely ties these disparate views
together. Seen from the standpoint of its finitude, the self is, at least
functionally, and often substantively, a bipolar entity. It is on the one
hand a "that" (usually a body) whose coming to an end is grasped in
foredisclosive acts. On the other, it is the foredisclosive acts themselves. The "that" whose end is anticipated, as well as the anticipating
acts which compenetrate it do, in fact, come to an end together,
fulfilling the structure of anticipation. This coming to an end entails

ceasing to interact with inanimate and animate existents, as well as with existents who die in the same fashion as the self. This does not preclude the possibility of a spiritual and mental part of the self living on but, in that case, the foredisclosive acts of this bodiless part stop, since the "that" whose end is foredisclosed has already ceased to be. Thus the functional unity of the parts is severed by death. Historically, the foredisclosure model is an aspect of the deep structure of the substantive self, generally a cognition monad, whose acts are valued to the extent that they are knowing acts. It is not difficult to see that, considerably modified, this view of the relation of death to the meaning of self plays a role in Heidegger's analysis of Dasein's finitude. Some aspects of the foredisclosure paradigm remain important in my view of the self, since the paradigm continues to function in the death event. But the paradigm requires reinterpretation in several important respects since it is grounded on the premise that individual selves are logically and ontologically prior to their social transactions and I take this view of the self to be untenable.

A Transactional Self   *I*N POSITING A SOCIAL SELF I DO NOT deny that there is a stream of experience which is private, open only to the self. But the self to whom this stream is accessible must be constituted first if the stream is related to anything at all, since in the absence of a self there would be nothing to relate the stream to.[1] Such a self can assume the standpoint of another, becoming other not only to the other but also to itself. We must have recourse to social existence from the start, for only then, by taking the viewpoint of another, can something objective be constituted and the individual attain the functional unity of a self.

If social existence constitutes self, then the coming to an end of the existent cannot be understood in the same fashion as the death of the monadic individual. This difference cannot be merely additive, an anticipation of the death of others alongside one's own. Rather, death must be taken up as part of the self-constituting acts of the self which deepen the relation of self to other. Hegel was the first to comprehend completely the intrinsic character of death both in the constitution of human existence simpliciter and in the formation of fully self-conscious existence.

For Hegel, the transition from animal to human being occurs when the relation of need to satiety in the animal is transformed into human desire. In its natural existence the animal has no image of what it requires. Thus it cannot project something recollected ahead of itself through the temporalizing structure of memory and anticipation. In order to break loose from brute lack which seeks only food or union with the other, the animal must recognize "the inborn germ of death" as its own possibility (*PhN* 3, 209). But sheer recognition of mortality is not enough for the emergence of a fully actual self-consciousness. Knowing in advance that he can die, the existent must be willing to risk his life in combat with the other. This is the celebrated struggle to the death, Hegel's figure to describe the origin of self-consciousness and social differentiation through violent encounter with the other. The important point is that a completely realized social existent comes into being not merely by anticipating death but by means of violent confrontation with another.

To grasp the full significance of Hegel's analysis for our problematic we must go beyond it and interrogate the meaning of the structures which come into being when social existence emerges but appear in their full-blown form only later when this existence is stabilized. Self-restraint is the mark of this stability, and language as a system of signs is its most significant characteristic. It is fundamentally important for our analysis to note that language does not arise to supplant an anterior violence or to supplement the remaining residue of violence in society; instead, language *is* the expression of this self-restraint. Even if provocative, language can always be answered with language. The expression "They are still talking" describes linguistic exchange as falling short of actual violence.[2] Thus theories of language which see its primary functions as merely referential or as the communication of information miss an important aspect of its phenomenological context: the silent renunciation of violence. Language and violence are equiprimordial in social existence—for if *homo homini lupus* alone expressed the order of life, reciprocal annihilation would rule out social existence from the start.

Language does not float emptily in social space. Instead, language is always addressed by someone to another person or persons. In addition to the meaning of the discursive elements themselves, the speaker (even when not actually present) is present to the discourse. Thus an utterance includes not only its signification but the act of reaching across towards others. The bearer of language does not, as it were, disappear into the meaning of what is said but remains a silent presence alongside the utterance itself. Language is a non-violent social bonding between speaker and addressee, one which attests language's primordial irenicism.

Language, Naming, and the Structure of the I　*I*N ORDER TO SEE THE RELATION OF language to violence we must pick up the thread of the primordial function of language and show its relevance to the language of the death-worlds. In his later work, Heidegger thinks of primordial language as poetry.[3] Poetry is "the inaugural naming of the gods and of the essence of things. To 'dwell poetically' means to stand in the presence of the gods and to be involved in the proximity of the essence of things" (*EB* p. 306). Poetry thus understood first makes language possible, rather than the converse: language comes to be as poetry, as the naming of gods and things. The naming act of the poet, according to Heidegger, is not merely the application of a name to something already known. Instead, "when the poet speaks the essential word, the existent is by this naming nominated as what it is. So it becomes known *as* existent. Poetry is the establishing of being by means of the word."[4]

If we are attentive to the context of Heidegger's analysis, we encounter an immediate difficulty. Quite apart from the problem inherent in any state-of-nature theory—that we lack access to the founding acts which such a theory hypothesizes—this description of the poet's task already assumes social existence. If "poetry is the primitive language of a historical people," the relation of person to person binding a people as a community must precede the reception of the poetic word. If poetry is calling forth of community there must be an anterior "who" to be called. Against Heidegger's view I argue that language is primordially this calling forth of the other into community. This is attested in the universality of kinship structure.[5] Structural anthropology posits a functional equivalence between kinship structure and language. Lévi-Strauss writes:

> If the incest prohibition and exogamy [the foundation of kinship rules] have an essentially positive function, if the reason for their existence is to establish a tie between men which the latter cannot do without if they are to raise themselves from biological to social organization, it must be recognized that linguists and sociologists do not merely apply the same methods but are studying the same thing. Indeed from this point of view "exogamy and language . . . have fundamentally the same function—communication and integration with others."[6]

In this context language is a calling forth into social relationship.

It is no accident that proper names—the names of persons—are often attacked, together with kinship structures, when the self enters a new community. Thus religious organizations and secret societies often rename their members as part of the process of initiation. Buddhism interprets the name as a kind of category mistake: the personal name seems to be a referring term but, upon analysis, there is nothing the name refers to.[7] An insidious counterpart to this voluntary renunciation of names is the enforced destruction of kinship ties in the Chinese and other cultural revolutions, since these ties symbolize older and more "corrupt" forms of existence.

The function of the personal name takes on special significance in the context of the death world. There a radically new form of language develops, one in which death is attached as a phantasm to every signifier. This language is also cynical since every signifier carries a double meaning, a putative surface meaning and its opposite. The word *work* is used cynically by the myth's manipulators to suggest productive effort even though they, as well as the death-world's victims, know it means unremitting hard labor. Yet the personal name is peculiarly refractory to this cynical doubling. This point was grasped by those who devised the infamous system of tattooing numbers upon the arms of concentration camp inmates and forcing them to use these in referring to themselves in place of personal names. For so long as the personal name does not refer to an institutional role, it retains its power to designate the complex ensemble of corporeal and linguistic behaviors which are invoked in the act of calling. Substantive words which designate social role, unlike personal names, lend themselves easily to cynical doubling. Thus the term "doctor" may designate a healer but may also point (cynically) to one who conducts medical experiments upon human subjects. Although personal names do not permit this type of ironic reference, they may nevertheless embody different and contradictory characteristics. Thus the name Dr. Mengele may join together the affections of the family man and the pursuits of the sadist. Following Heidegger, I believe the self is *as* it is as a whole. The individual may exhibit contradictory characteristics not because some aspect of the self is open to a cynical hermeneutic but because human existence is capable of reversing itself, shifting gear, and thus holding together incompatible traits.

The language of the death-world is attenuated in the sense that it lacks a rich referential structure, but it is dense with psychological reference and metalinguistic irony. Personal names, even if they embody incompatible characteristics, resist the rule of cynical doubling which otherwise governs language in the death-world. This is not because the name has univocal significance or corresponds to an entity which can be pointed out. Rather, the purity of personal names rests upon a quite different ground: the name opens up the possibility of the self's answering for itself. It might be objected that this is because the name, after all, is a referring term. If this were so, what could the name refer to? The body? The ensemble of significations that constitute the stream of its inner experiences? Its past? Its projects? To be sure, in any given situation the name is not other than this ensemble as it presents itself. In fact the name seems to assemble these disparate functions. Yet the personal name is in fact at the *edge* of language. It signifies not a content but its bearer. The name answers for itself by presenting the self that is called forth by it. The one called by name may withhold him- or her self, but this withholding is possible only against the prior ground of self-presentation. From the standpoint of the one addressed by name, the pronominal structure of language thematizes the self's relation to its name. The self answers as an I. In actual discourse the I is always present, even when unuttered, as a nonreferential null point showing that discourse does not float in linguistic space but belongs to a speaker, for whom this null point crystallizes in the pronoun "I."

The I and the Me

*I*N TURNING TO THE PRONOMIAL structure of language we return to the theme of our starting point: the foredisclosure paradigm and its relation to a transactional self. To see this relation we can, as a preliminary try, transpose the paradigm into pronomial form. We can imagine the foredisclosive acts and the *that* which comes to an end as functional differences for which the terms *I* and *me* respectively are the signs. These parallels provide a starting point, but simple transposition to I and me will not do since the foredisclosure paradigm arises in the context of a monadic self and therefore distorts the meaning of self. Earlier the monadic view of self was modified on the grounds that, even if there is a private stream of experience, there must be a self to relate the stream to and this self must be other to itself: I must be able to take the standpoint of another toward the stream. (This functional differentiation is replicated in a social episode of naming. The self that responds is functionally different from the one that is addressed.)

But, if we think of this I as something solid, we risk returning to the substantive self we have criticized. The I which relates itself to the stream and which answers for itself in discourse is a nondiscursive null point forced into discursive presence by the pronomial structure of language. There is actually no subject to grasp the I within the flux of experience since the I is merely phantasmatic. This self is an absence, a lack or emptiness of self.[8] The I becomes other to itself, is made thematic, through the time scheme of existence. The I as temporal movement flashes by, as it were, to become a me as it is integrated into the stream of recollections. The me grows as a tail of retentions of the flash points that were the I. When this occurs the I enters the chain of discourse and is retained as a trace in the me, the self grasped by the other, an ensemble of corporeal linguistic and social behaviors.[9]

Such a self is not purely a linguistic entity, a system of transposable signs, nor is it an aperture through which Being discloses itself. It is also equiprimordially a body. Since the body is given in visual and tactile presentations it might seem that the body falls within the bounds of the me, since it is natural to identify the body as something objective on analogy with the body of another person. But this is by no means self-evident. There is an aspect of corporeal experience which can never become objective, since the body is that by which objects and persons come to be for me. It is the indispensable precondition of self and determines the manner in which objects and persons are for me and in this sense falls on the side of the I.[10] The body through which objects and persons arise for me is experienced as ineradicably mine. The rare pathological conditions in which it is depersonalized only point up this self-sense, since such conditions carry with them a feeling of split personality or an experienced unreality in the dissociation of self from corporeality.[11] This corporeal I is not something substantive or something posited conceptually in order to unify the stream of experience but an original datum of experience altogether different from the experience of the other's body. If I try to think of what cannot be canceled in experience it is just this sense in which the body is given as mine.

Mass Death and Self

THE CONCEPTION OF A LINGUISTIC and corporeal transactional self holds in equipoise the individuating aspect of self, the I pole, and the objectified me. With the advent of man-made mass death this more or less harmonious unity is broken: the I pole is shattered resulting in a negative and apocalyptic subject. Each I experiences the possibility not only of its own coming to an end but also of human extinction in toto as a result of human acts. The poet John Berryman conveys this feeling in the verse:

> —It takes me so long to read the paper,
> Said to me one day a novelist hot as a firecracker,
> because I have to identify myself with everyone in it,
>   including the corpses, pal.[12]

In his analysis of the struggle to the death, Hegel can imagine the possibility of total extinction, but he thinks that if both combatants die, the further development of consciousness also comes to an end. For Hegel, ultimate negation is precluded by the movement of the historical process which, in the end, sublates negation. Now, with the possible annihilation of the totality, negation can, per impossible, become what Hegel calls a "concrete universal," not merely something formally true, an empty abstraction, but something actually existing. What Hegel thinks of as something *zeitweilig*—waiting to be transcended—is attested in actuality by recent events of man-made mass death: nuclear, chemical, and biological warfare, death and slave labor camps which embrace entire nations, events which impact on vast numbers of people and threaten all human existence.

The unprecedented possibility of total annihilation by human agency—unlike the threat of natural calamity—derails the I, first by implicating the transactional self as a possible participant in these acts and second by radically altering the focus of the self's anticipation. The I is overwhelmed by the ubiquity of death and gives itself over to its own foredisclosures of mass death even when these possibilities are put out of mind or only poorly understood. Though this new I deteriorates as a personal center, this state of affairs is not the end of individualism, since the self is already transactional. However, the I of existing individuals is depleted and can, under extreme pressure, so atrophy as to appear functionally dead.

With a decline in the power of the I, the me takes on new importance. Split off from the I, the personal center of language and corporeality, deprived of fresh infusions from the activities of the I, the me loses its distinguishing marks and becomes part of a totality of increasingly similar selves, homogeneous units whose meaning can be expressed in quantitative terms. Such individuals are interpreted either as having negative significance or as lacking significance altogether so that the being of inanimate nature is ascribed to them. This lack of value attributed to human existence suggests that it is possible to permit without hindrance in the world of fact what these negative meanings convey to the imagination: an all-encompassing sphere of death. There are other important sources for depersonalization, as Heidegger's analysis of technique attests. But now individual occurrences of man-made mass death begin to form a pattern not envisaged before, opening up new logical structures which link sporadic episodes of mass death together and reinforce their hold over the dwindling power of the I.

Zeno's paradoxes of motion provide a conceptual structure which underlies these individual segments of the death event, as well as all of its occurrences taken together. But this logic is now transferred without alteration to historical processes within the context of the death event. On analogy with spatial continua it is now possible to imagine a group of people as infinitely divisible and then to try to divide them in accordance with the principles of some political myth such as class membership or race. But since the number of human beings is actually finite this effort is self-defeating, for the ongoing division of persons into some who shall live and some who shall die can only end by exhausting the reservoir of persons. Interpreting a collection of human beings as a spatial continuum is a category mistake with disastrous implications for the historical process.

In the present context, this thought structure has already had important psychological consequences: political myths destabilize the self by shifting the possibility of extinction from one expendable group to another. There is a background awareness that events bearing this logical structure do not simply disappear but may crop up when least expected. This accounts for the combination of terror and surprise that even a symbolic reminder may trigger since it evokes the structure as a whole. Consider the way the Shining Path, the pro-Maoist guerrillas of Peru, first came to be known: "Most Peruvians first heard of Sendero Luminoso [the Shining Path] one morning in 1980, during the last days of the dictatorship, when the people of Lima were confronted by the grisly sight of dogs hanging from the utility poles. The animals wore placards that accused the 'dog' Deng Xiaoping of betraying the Chinese Cultural Revolution. Sendero Luminoso had announced its existence."[13] The newly skewed transactional self of the death event with its logical and psychological structures is related to other selves as *partes extra partes*, but it differs from the monadic individual who is similarly related to others since this new self passes through a social phase in its constitution. Thus the deformation of the transactional self yields not a solitary individual, a cognition monad, but a cipher.

The sublation of the I by omnipresent meaningless death brings to light still another signification of the self. We saw earlier that the I is released into discourse as a phantasm borne by language to attest extradiscursively the meaning of language per se as the restraint of violence. But the unprecedented scale of death that has become possible as the result of technological and bureaucratic sophistication undermines the heretofore psychologically tolerable balance of discourse and violence that for long periods freed the I pole for its relations with the world of natural objects, human artifacts, and other persons. Expressive language itself has now been replaced by the language of calculation. This newly depleted language no longer offers support structures for the I—fantasy, myth, and poetry as these were previously understood—and thus further restricts the sphere of the I.

But, paradoxically, in this very context, the I acquires new extradiscursive meaning. Just as the sheer existence of language points phantasmatically to its nonviolent character, the birth of the death event in our time opens up a new phantasmatic meaning borne by the speaker, one that accompanies all discourse. This is the self's demand that it be permitted to persevere in its existence. This claim differs from Aristotle's belief that living things want to preserve their existence because the telos of the soul is life, as well as Spinoza's view that everything, insofar as it is in itself, tries to persist in its own being. In neither case does the demand carry axiological weight but is, rather, an expression of the living thing's essence.

This is precisely what distinguishes the transactional self's desire to endure in the face of the death event from older self-preservation claims. Because this new self is already transactional, the totality whose extinction is threatened is ingredient to its very being: the demand to persevere must include this newly introjected whole. This demand is not a conscious attempt to make perdurance before death a universal law but is a phenomenologically grounded meaning created by the impact of man-made mass death upon an already social self. Selfhood is an apocalyptic age is in transition from a psychological to an axiological or moral conception of the I pole. This by no means implies that the self will necessarily perform acts of resistance to violence. To the contrary, such resistance becomes increasingly difficult since, in the face of pandemic humanly contrived death, resisting violence requires ever larger quanta of fresh energy from an already depleted self. Yet the dilemmas of the self's existence will from now on be posed within the ambit of this radically altered intersubjective space.

Contemporary existence is characterized by episodes of man-made mass death which, taken together, constitute a death event of unprecedented character and scope whose impact on the formation of self requires a new interpretation of selfhood. Historically, the role of death in the understanding of self has been viewed in terms of the foredisclosure paradigm: the relation of foredisclosive acts to a "that" whose end is foredisclosed. This algorithm functions in the context of a substantitive self generally regarded as a cognition monad. The way this self faces its own death, its character, determines the value ascribed to it. Hegel and Heidegger make significant inroads into this paradigm, but Hegel's philosophy of the Absolute and Heidegger's stress of man's relation to world and things rather than to other persons fall short of grasping the full significance of contemporary man-made mass death. I accept Hegel's view of the struggle but I extend his interpretation to show that the self is not only violent but also equiprimordially linguistic and thus able to restrain violence. This irenic function of language expresses itself as naming by designating the other in terms of kinship and in the use of proper names. The function of naming persists even in the death-world, where language otherwise exhibits a cynical doubling of meaning. I also propose that corporeality belongs essentially to self and is a vehicle of signification beyond biological function, especially in the impoverished environment of the death-world.

The transactional self I favor exists as a bipolar unity: an I which is a nondiscursive spontaneity and a me which is integrated through time into a relational field. But the impact of man-made mass death upon the transactional self destroys the possibility of holding the poles in equipose. By stressing the me and thus collapsing the self's spontaneity—its I pole—the self requires increasing effort to maintain itself. Zeno's paradoxes are the algorithm for this new type of depersonalization in which the me can be objectified and counted and can become a member of a numerically ordered series. Persons become units in an inexhaustible reservoir of similar units. The phenomenon is self-reinforcing and to an extent self-generating. The me is caught in the circuit created by calculative thinking. The I, as a phantasm borne by all discourse and carrying extradiscursive weight, now acquires another signification: the I expresses the self's demand to persevere in life. This new apothegm is not a moral rule but a phenomenological datum. Since the I has become social, its demand must also be read socially. The social I demands that the whole human community, whose possible extinction is part of the formation of the I, persevere in existence. Postmodern selfhood must now be understood as living within the ambit of the tensions created by this demand.

Notes

Preface

1. Robert S. Gottfried, *The Black Death: Natural and Human Disaster in Medieval Europe* (New York: Free Press, 1983), p. 45. I am grateful to Alan Rosenberg of the Philosophy Department of Queens College of the City University of New York for suggesting that the qualifying term *man-made* always precede the term *mass death* wherever the context fails to establish this in order to highlight the factor of human agency and to distinguish present-day phenomena from just such events as the Black Death.

2. Jay Robert Nash in *Darkest Hours* (Chicago: Nelson-Hall, 1976) estimates that twenty-five million people died of Bubonic plague in Europe between 1384 and 1666 (p. 54) and that 15,843 combatants were killed during World War II between 1939 and 1945 (p. 775). (If noncombatants are included the approximate number of persons killed rises to fifty-five million.) These figures are rough and intended to suggest the order of magnitude of the losses suffered in both events.

1. Kingdoms of Death

1. Heidegger cautions against using poetry as a substitute for metaphysics but claims we can learn from poetry what is not spoken in the history of Being. See his "What Are Poets For?" in *Poetry, Language, Thought,* trans. Albert Hofstadter (New York: Harper and Row, 1971), pp. 95f. (Hereafter cited in the text as *PLT*).

2. David's painting shows Plato as present when in fact he should be absent from the death scene.

3. Plato, *Phaedo*, trans. W. H. D. Rouse, 59a.

4. Phillipe Ariès, *Western Attitudes towards Death from the Middle Ages to the Present,* trans. Patricia M. Ranum (Baltimore: Johns Hopkins University Press, 1974), pp. 1–25.

5. For criticisms by Feuerbach, Marx, Kirkegaard, and David Friedrich see Karl Löwith, *From Hegel to Nietzsche: The Revolution in Nineteenth Century Thought,* trans. David E. Green (London: Constable, 1964), esp. chap. 5.

6. For analyses of Kierkegaard's view of the existing individual in relation to Hegel's Absolute see Niels Thulstrup, *Kierkegaard's Relation to Hegel,* trans. George L. Stengren (Princeton: Princeton University Press, 1980), esp. pp. 344–48; Stephen Crites, *In The Twilight of Christendom: Hegel vs. Kierkegaard on Faith and History* (Chartersburg, Penn.: American Academy of Religion monograph no. 4, 1972), esp. pp. 58–95; Mark C.

Taylor, *Journeys to Selfhood: Hegel and Kierkegaard* (Berkeley: University of California Press, 1980), pp. 55ff.

7. *Letters of Rainer Maria Rilke*, trans. Jane Bannard Greene and M. D. Herter Norton (New York: Norton, 1969), 2:112. Page references to this collection will be given in this chapter in the text.

8. In his poem "The Knight," in *Rainer Maria Rilke: Fifty Selected Poems*, trans. C. F. MacIntyre (Berkeley: University of California Press, 1947), p. 21, Rilke writes: "Yet, in the armor of the knight, / behind the sinister rings, / Death squats, brooding and brooding." (Doch in dem Panzer des Ritters drinnen, / hinter den finstersten Ringen, / hockt der Tod und muss sinnen und sinnen.)

9. Rainer Maria Rilke, the eighth of the *Duino Elegies*, trans. J. B. Leishman and Stephen Spender (New York: Norton, 1939), p. 67. (Nur unsere Augen sind / wie umgekehrt und ganz um sie gestellt / als Fallen, rings um ihren freien Ausgang.)

10. Ibid. (Und miemals Nirgends ohne Nicht: / das Reine, Unüberwachte, das man atmet und / unendlich weiss und nicht begehrt.)

11. Ibid., p. 71. And we, spectators always, everywhere, / looking at, never out of, everything! (Und wir: Zuschauer, immer überall, / dem allen zugewandt und nie hinaus!)

12. In *Letters of Rilke* 1:305, Rilke writes of Cezanne: "The convincing quality, the becoming a thing, the reality heightened into the indestructible through his own experience of the object, it was that which seemed to him the aim of his innermost work."

13. According to Erich Heller, *The Artist's Journey into the Interior and Other Essays* (New York: Harcourt Brace Jovanovich, 1976), p. 161, Rilke excluded abstract and cubist art from his praise of the painterly. The Picasso of *Les Saltimbanques* was betrayed by the later Picasso, Matisse, and Braque.

14. Rilke, the ninth of the *Duino Elegies*, p. 77. (Erde, ist es nicht dies, was du willst: unsichtbar / in uns erstehn?—Ist es dein Traum nicht, / einmal unsichtbar zu sein?—Erde! Unsichtbar! / Wass, wenn Verwandlung nicht, ist dein drängender Auftrag?)

15. Erich Heller in *The Disinherited Mind: Essays on Modern German Literature* (New York: Harcourt Brace Jovanovich, 1975), p. 172, offers what is, in effect, a moral critique of this position: "Rilke poetically exploits a marginal position precariously maintained on the brink of catastrophe. The catastrophe, perpetually threatening and only just warded off by the most dazzling acrobatics of soul and mind, is the loss of significant external reality. . . . In Rilke's mature poetry the emotions do the interpreting and respond to their own interpretation."

16. From a lecture on Rodin cited by Leishman and Spender in "Commentary," *Duino Elegies*, p. 100.

17. Rilke, the ninth of the *Duino Elegies*, p. 75. (Sind wir vielleicht hier / um zu zagen: Haus, / Brucke, Brunnen, Tor, Krug, Obstbaum, Fenster,—)

18. "Only a God Can Save Us Now," an interview with Martin Heidegger

in *Der Spiegel* (Spring 1966), trans. David Schendler, *Graduate Faculty Philosophy Journal* 6:2 (1977): 18.

19. Rilke, the ninth of the *Duino Elegies*, p. 73.

20. "The hand of God" is used in "The Angels," from *Das Buch der Bilder*. See *Rainer Maria Rilke: Fifty Selected Poems*, p. 25. "As though with his broad sculptor hands / God was turning the leaves of the dark book of the Beginning." (Als ginge Gott mit seinen weiten / Bildhauerhänden durch die Seiten / im dunklen Buch des Anbeginns.)

21. Rilke, the first of the *Duino Elegies*, p. 24. (Freilich ist es seltsam, die Erde nicht mehr zu bewohnen / kaum erlernte Gebrauche nicht mehr zu üben, / Rosen, und andern eigens versprechenden Dingen / nicht die Bedeutung menschlicher Zukunft zu geben; . . . / und selbst den eigenen Namen / wegzulassen wie ein zerbrochenes Spielzeug. . . . / Aber Lebendige machen / alle den Fehler, dass sie zu stark unterscheiden. / Engel (sagt man) wüssten oft nicht, ob sie unter / Lebenden gehn oder Toten.)

22. Rilke's interpretation of aesthetic ordering is Hegelian. Erich Heller in *Artist's Journey into the Interior*, p. 170, writes: "Between 'the still recognizable form' of things and their being gathered into the Invisible, the Hegelian dialectics come into their own. Rilke meant that the visible world would be '*aufgehoben*'. . . . Rilke has turned it into the apocalyptic poetry of human inwardness that takes over the divine agency of salvation: 'Nowhere will be world but within.'"

23. In *Letters of Rilke* 2:132–33, Rilke comments on the relation of history to the individual: "We, some of us, have long been feeling continuities that have nothing in common with the course of history; . . . but we, constrained between yesterday and tomorrow . . . shall we [remain stamped with] a period on our shoulders, knowers of unforgettable details coresponsible for the big as for the merely fearful; . . . shall we not . . . defer all understanding [and] hold . . . history to be a primeval forest to the soil of which we never reach, because it lies, layer on layer, unendingly, upon tumbled stuff, an apparition on the back of destruction—?"

24. Gil Eliot, *Twentieth Century Book of the Dead* (New York: Ballantine, 1973), p. 28. Although non-technical, Eliot's study is, to my knowledge, the only account which begins with the phenomenon of contemporary man-made mass death and locates the discrete manifestations of this "essence" in terms of numbers of persons destroyed, the manner of their destruction, the breakdown of the distinction between military and civilian personnel, etc. The present study is indebted to Eliot's rough mapping of this terrain.

25. The American pragmatists William James and John Dewey stress the value of such experiences. Thus John Dewey in *Art as Experience* (New York: Paragon, 1979), p. 294, speaks of all experience as having aesthetic quality and of the work of art as "the subject matter of experience heightened and intensified."

26. Micheline Maurel as cited in Terence des Près, *The Survivor* (New York: Oxford University Press, 1977), p. 199.

27. For characteristics of neo-Romanticism see my "Romantic Consciousness and Biblical Faith," in *Auschwitz: Beginning of a New Era*, ed. Eva Fleischner (New York: K'tav, 1974), pp. 331–42.

28. Edmund Husserl, *The Phenomenology of Internal Time Consciousness*, trans. James S. Churchill, ed. Martin Heidegger (Bloomington: Indiana University Press, 1964), pp. 48–49, speaks of "running off" as the mode in which phenomena are temporally constituted.

29. Fernand Braudel, *The Mediterranean and the Mediterranean World in the Age of Philip II*, trans. Sian Reynolds (New York, Harper and Row, 1972) 2:1243.

30. Michel Foucault, *Archeology of Knowledge*, trans. A. M. Sheridan Smith, (New York: Pantheon, 1973), p. 7, shows that history must transform documents into monuments rather than the converse because it "deploys a mass of elements that have to be grouped, made relevant, placed in relation to one another to form totalities."

31. Eliot, *Twentieth Century Book of the Dead*, pt. 1.

32. George Steiner, *In Bluebeard's Castle: Some Notes toward the Redefinition of Culture* (New Haven: Yale University Press, 1971), pp. 53–54, writes: "*L'univers concentrationnaire* has no true counterpart in the secular mode. Its analogue is Hell. The camp embodies, often down to minutiae, the images and chronicles of Hell in European art and thought from the twelfth to the eighteenth centuries. . . . It is in the fantasies of the infernal, as they literally haunt Western sensibility, that we find the technology of pain without meaning, of bestiality without end, of gratuitous terror. For six hundred years the imagination dwelt on the flaying, the racking, the mockery of the damned, in a place of whips and hellhounds, of ovens and stinking air."

33. Nadezhda Mandelstam, *Hope against Hope*, trans. Max Hayward (New York: Atheneum, 1970), p. 45.

34. Maurice Natanson in *Edmund Husserl: Philosopher of Infinite Tasks* (Evanston, Ill.: Northwestern University Press, 1973), p. 37, defines *horizon* as "a line of access in terms of which experience presents itself."

35. Edmund Husserl, *The Crisis of European Sciences and Transcendental Phenomenology*, trans. David Carr (Evanston, Ill.: Northwestern University Press, 1970), pp. 142–43.

36. Ibid.

37. Braudel, *Mediterranean World* 2:1243.

38. Fernand Braudel, *Afterthoughts of Material Civilization and Capitalism*, trans. Patricia Ranum (Baltimore: Johns Hopkins University Press, 1977), p. 7.

39. Maurice Merleau-Ponty, *The Phenomenology of Perception*, trans. Colin Smith (London: Routledge and Kegan Paul, 1962), esp. pp. 67–72.

40. See Terence Penulham's account in *Encyclopedia of Philosophy*, vol. 6 (New York: Macmillan, 1967), s.v. "Personal Identity," pp. 95–107.

41. Pragmatists and process philosophers as well as phenomenologists concede this point. Thus John Dewey in *Experience and Nature* (New York: Dover, 1958), p. 67 writes: "The means of converting the dubious into the assured, and the incomplete into the determinate, is use of and established things, which are just as . . . indicative of the nature of experienced things as is the uncertain."

42. Hannah Arendt, *The Origins of Totalitarianism* (New York: Harcourt Brace Jovanovich, 1973), pp. 411–12.

43. Ibid., p. 438.

44. Ibid., pp. 276ff. Arendt relates the problem of statelessness to deracination: "More often than one would imagine, people took refuge in statelessness after the first World War in order to remain where they were and avoid being deported to a 'homeland' where they would be strangers" (p. 278).

45. Henry Morgenthau, *Ambassador Morgenthau's Story* (New York: Doubleday, Page, 1918), p. 365.

46. Arendt, *Origins of Totalitarianism*, p. 453.

47. Primo Levi, *Survival in Auschwitz*, trans. Stuart Woolf (New York: Collier, 1959), p. 31.

48. Alexander Solzhenitsyn, *The Gulag Archipelago, Two, 1918–1956: An Experiment in Literary Imagination*, vols. 3–4, trans. Thomas P. Whitney (New York: Harper and Row, 1975), p. 179.

49. Emmanuel Levinas, *Total and Infinity*, trans. Alphonso Lingis (Pittsburgh: Duquesne University Press, 1969), esp. pp. 194–216, argues that other persons are given as ethical data. Thus value is phenomenologically grounded not in axioms or rules but in existential referents: persons.

50. Erving Goffman in *Asylums* (New York: Doubleday, Anchor, 1961), p. 7, claims that in every total institution "there is a basic split between a large managed group . . . inmates . . . and a staff . . . integrated into the outside world."

51. Leon Weliczker Wells, *The Death Brigade* (New York: Holocaust Library, 1963), p. 244.

52. Mandelstam, *Hope against Hope*, p. 43.

53. Alexander Donat, *The Holocaust Kingdom* (New York: Holocaust Library, 1963), p. 237. This confirms the hypothesis of Terence des Près that limited altruism is generally the attitude of survivors.

54. Quoted in Gitta Sereny, *Into That Darkness: From Mercy Killing to Mass Murder* (New York: McGraw-Hill, 1974), p. 186.

55. Levi, *Survival in Auschwitz*, p. 103.

56. Donat, *Holocaust Kingdom*, p. 169.

57. Solzhenitsyn, *Gulag Archipelago, Two*, p. 606.

58. Jacques Ellul, *The Technological Society*, trans. John Wilkenson (New York: Random House, 1964), p. xxv. In *Technology and Culture*, ed. Melvin

Kranzberg and William H. Davenport (New York: New American Library, 1975), Robert R. Heilbroner holds a less extreme form of technological determinism. In "Do Machines Make History?" (pp. 28–40), Heilbroner claims that in societies maximizing production and minimizing cost, technical advance and its diffusion "assume the attributes of autonomous processes mysteriously generated by society," though technological determinism is limited in an era where control over technology is still rudimentary. In "Authoritarian and Democratic Technics" (pp. 50–59), Lewis Mumford locates polar forms of social organization in their relation to technology: small-scale production allowing for autonomous "democratic technics" and "authoritarian technics" involving the use of force to compel the performance of technical tasks.

59. See chapter 3 for Hegel's critique of the Enlightenment.

60. See note 35.

61. Husserl, *Crisis of the European Sciences*, esp. pp. 21–59.

62. Ibid., pp. 25–26.

63. Ibid., pp. 60–61.

64. Ibid.

65. My view in this regard is opposed to Ellul's. In *The Technological Society*, pp. 131–32, in accordance with his technological determinism, Ellul sees concentration camps as on a gradient with technological society and therefore requiring no separate account.

66. William Barrett, *The Illusion of Technique: A Search for Meaning in a Technological Civilization* (New York: Doubleday, Anchor, 1979), pp. xi–xii.

67. Arendt, *Origins of Totalitarianism*, pp. 464ff.

68. Donat, *Holocaust Kingdom*, p. 167.

69. Dewey, *Experience and Nature*, p. 185.

70. Ibid., pp. 186ff.

71. Ibid., p. 142.

72. Richard Rubenstein, *The Cunning of History: Mass Death and the American Future* (New York: Harper and Row, 1975), p. 28.

73. Ellul, *The Technological Society*, pp. 6ff.

74. Friedrich Nietzsche. *The Case of Wagner* in *The Birth of Tragedy and The Case of Wagner*, trans. Walter Kaufman (New York: Random House, 1967), p. 170.

75. Claude Lévi-Strauss, *Myth and Meaning* (New York: Schocken, 1979), p. 17.

76. Some have argued that the structure of science as a whole can be mythologized. But while the aim of scientific theory is inclusivity, each theory is limited to a specific range of phenomena. By contrast, a metaphysics studies the most general characteristics of events but does not function as a predictive paradigm dependent for confirmation upon phenomena. See Ian Barbour, *Issues in Science and Religion* (New York: Harper and Row, 1966), pp. 261ff.

77. Claude Lévi-Strauss, *The Savage Mind* (Chicago: University of Chi-

cago Press, 1960), pp. 19–20, refers to an ensemble of means which are not defined in terms of a project as *bricolage*.

78. For an extended account of sacred time and space see Mircea Eliade, *The Sacred and the Profane*, trans. Willard R. Trask (New York: Harcourt, Brace, Jovanovich, 1959).

79. Rubenstein, *Cunning of History*, pp. 27–28.

80. The character of this stability is of historical as well as phenomenological interest. Braudel says in *Mediterranean World* 1:16: "Is it possible somehow to convey simultaneously both that conspicuous history which holds our attention by its continuous and dramatic changes—and that other, submerged, history, almost silent and always discreet, virtually unsuspected either by its observers or its participants, which is little touched by the obstinate erosion of time?" Braudel calls the first *conjoncture* or short-term events, the latter *structure* or long-term realities.

81. Friedrich Nietzsche, *The Will to Power*, trans. Walter Kaufmann and R. J. Hollingdale (New York: Random House, 1968), p. 371.

82. Des Près, *The Survivor*, esp. chap. 7.

83. Levi, *Survival in Auschwitz*, p. 22.

84. Ibid., p. 113.

85. Solzhenitsyn, *Gulag Archipelago, Two*, pp. 529–33.

86. Gregory Bateson in *Toward a Theory of Schizophrenia*," in *Steps to an Ecology of Mind* (New York: Ballantine, 1972), pp. 206–12, describes the repeated traumatic experience of receiving a negative injunction, then a second and conflicting injunction, while the victim is prevented from escaping this double bind. This explains the etiology of schizophrenia.

87. Maurice Merleau-Ponty, "On the Phenomenology of Language," in *Signs*, trans. Richard C. McCleary, (Evanston, Ill.: Northwestern University Press, 1964), pp. 89ff.

88. Ibid.

89. Tadeusz Borowski, *This Way for the Gas, Ladies and Gentlemen*, trans. Barbara Vedder (Harmondsworth, Middlesex: Penguin, 1977), p. 31.

90. Levi, *Survival in Auschwitz*, p. 25.

91. Quoted in Sereny, *Into That Darkness*, p. 148.

92. Levi, *Survival in Auschwitz*, p. 82.

93. Donat, *Holocaust Kingdom*, p. 168.

94. Solzhenitsyn, *Gulag Archipelago, Two*, p. 242.

95. Arendt, *Origins of Totalitarianism*, p. 371.

96. Merleau-Ponty, *Phenomenology of Perception*, p. 393, writes: "To say than an event *takes place* is to say that it will always be true that it has taken place." He also claims, "The non-temporal is the acquired."

2. The Logic of Mass Death

1. Plato, *Parmenides*, 128c.

2. Hermann Fränkel, "Studies in Parmenides" in *Studies in Presocratic*

Philosophy, ed. R. E. Allen and David J. Furley (Atlantic Highlands, N.J.: Humanities Press, 1975) 2:102–03.

3. Zeno, frag. 3 in Milton Nahm, *Selections from Early Greek Philosophy* (New York: Crofts, 1945), p. 122.

4. Fränkel, "Studies in Parmenides," p. 105. Zeno's paradoxes remain tenacious because, as Rudolf Carnap and Herbert Feigl point out, they must be solved by using a new mathematical language. See Grover Maxwell and Herbert Feigl, "Why Ordinary Language Needs Reforming," in Richard Rorty, *The Linguistic Turn: Recent Essays in Philosophical Method* (Chicago: University of Chicago Press, 1967), p. 795.

5. Fränkel, "Studies in Parmenides," p. 103.

6. Arendt, *Origins of Totalitarianism*, p. 469.

7. Lévi-Strauss, *Myth and Meaning*, p. 17.

8. On the relation of myth in general to experience see *Lévi-Strauss, Savage Mind*, pp. 16–22; on totalitarian myths to experience see Jean-Paul Sartre, *Search for a Method*, trans. Hazel E. Barnes (New York: Alfred A. Knopf, 1963), pp. 24–31, and Arendt, *Origins of Totalitarianism*, p. 469.

9. A. R. Luria, *The Making of Mind*, ed. Michael Cole and Sheila Cole (Cambridge: Harvard University Press, 1979), pp. 78ff, argues that practical reasoning dominates the experience of his nonliterate subjects.

10. Eliot, *Twentieth Century Book of the Dead*, pp. 236–37, concludes that total death is the aim of the twentieth century "death machine."

11. Walter Schmittals, *The Apocalyptic Movement: Introduction and Interpretation*, trans. John E. Steely (Nashville, Tenn.: Abingdon Press, 1975), p. 39.

12. *Pseudo-Clementine Homilies* 20:2, cited in Ibid., p. 21.

13. Ibid.

14. Ibid., p. 23.

15. Ibid., p. 41.

16. Ray L. Hart, *Unfinished Man and the Imagination: Toward an Ontology and a Rhetoric of Revelation* (New York: Herder and Herder, 1968), pp. 372–73, discusses the theological significance of this effort.

17. Ibid.

18. Schmittals, *The Apocalyptic Movement*, p. 89. See also Hans Jonas, *The Gnostic Religion* (Boston: Beacon Press, 1963), pp. 55ff. Elaine Pagels, in her introduction to *The Gnostic Gospels* (New York: Random House, 1981), esp. pp. xxxi–xxxix, provides a brief overview of perspectives taken on this and related questions by R. M. Grant, E. R. Dodds, and others. She argues that Christian orthodox polemics against gnosticism are politically motivated.

19. Schmittals, *The Apocalyptic Movement*, pp. 90–91.

20. Ibid.

21. For a description of the conflation of apocalyptic and gnostic myth see ibid., pp. 107–08.

22. Norman Cohen, *The Pursuit of the Millennium* (New York: Oxford University Press, 1970), p. 19.

23. Ibid., p. 29.

24. Ibid., p. 108. See also Eric Vögelin, *From Enlightenment to Revolution*, ed. John H. Hallowell (Durham, N.C.: Duke University Press, 1975), esp. pp. 1, 11–12.

25. On the basis of an elaborate numerology, Joachim expects forty-two generations to intervene between each period. This places the anticipated millennium between 1200 and 1260. See Cohen, *Pursuit of the Millennium*, p. 110.

26. Ibid.

27. Ernest Nolte in *Three Faces of Fascism*, trans. Leila Janowitz (New York: New American Library, 1965), pp. 542ff, contrasts theoretical transcendence toward a whole with practical transcendence, "the social process . . . which continually widens human relationships, thereby rendering them more abstract [disengaging] the individual from traditional ties and [increasing] the power of the group until it finally assails even the primordial forces of nature and history." J. P. Stern in *Hitler: The Führer and the People* (Berkeley: University of California Press, 1975), p. 97, criticizes Nolte on the grounds that Hitler's attack on transcendence is itself undertaken "in the language of transcendence, as the answer to a religious longing."

28. Mary Douglas in *Purity and Danger: An Analysis of Concepts of Pollution and Taboo* (Harmondsworth, Middlesex: Penguin, 1970), esp. pp. 47–53, analyzes the fears provoked by anomalies (natural kinds that resist classification) in nonliterate societies.

29. Hitler, *Mein Kampf*, trans. Ralph Mannheim (Boston: Houghton Mifflin, 1943), p. 178.

30. Ibid.

31. For an analysis of the controversy between mechanists and vitalists in nineteenth-century biology see Ernest Cassirer, *The Problem of Knowledge: Philosophy Science and History since Hegel*, trans. William H. Woglom and Charles W. Hendel (New Haven: Yale University Press, 1974), chap. 11.

32. George L. Mosse, *Germans and Jews* (New York: Grosset and Dunlap, 1970), p. 85. See also Fritz Stern, *The Politics of Cultural Despair: A Study in the Rise of German Ideology* (Berkeley: University of California Press, 1974), p. 92.

33. Stern, *The Politics of Cultural Despair*, p. 41.

34. Ibid., p. 49.

35. Ibid., p. 59.

36. Ibid.

37. Arendt, *Origins of Totalitarianism*, pp. 322ff.

38. Cited in ibid., p. xxxiii.

39. Ibid., p. 321.

40. *Quotations from Chairman Mao Tse-tung*, n.t. (New York: Bantam, 1967), p. 166.

41. Fox Butterfield, "Hundreds of Thousands Toil in Chinese Labor Camps," *New York Times*, January 3, 1981.

42. This idea may be historically rooted in the Confucian doctrine of the rectification of names, which holds that the names of social roles express social ideals which individuals should strive to actualize, e.g., "Let the minister be minister." See Robert Lifton, *Revolutionary Immortality: Mao Tsetung and the Chinese Cultural Revolution* (New York: Random House, 1968), p. 64.

43. *Quotations from Chairman Mao*, p. 43.

44. Arendt, *Origins of Totalitarianism*, p. 322.

45. Solzhenitsyn, *Gulag Archipelago, Two*, p. 101.

46. Levi, *Survival in Auschwitz*, p. 66.

47. Solzhenitsyn, *Gulag Archipelago, Two*, p. 91.

48. Butterfield, "Hundreds of Thousands Toil in Chinese Labor Camps."

49. *Iliad* 20:48–49.

50. See Plato, *Republic*, 2:372–73.

51. *Apology* 26a–27d; *Crito* 41a–53a.

52. John Ferguson, *War and Peace in the World's Religions* (New York: Oxford University Press, 1978), p. 80.

53. Ibid., p. 84.

54. Ibid., p. 104. Paul Valliere in "The Spirituality of War," *Union Theological Seminary Quarterly*, 25 (1983): 5–14, distinguishes types of war in terms of their value structure: holy (biblical), heroic (Greek), and political wars. Only the last opens the issue of just and unjust wars. Michal Waltzer in *Just and Unjust Wars: A Moral Argument with Historical Illustrations* (New York: Basic Books, 1977), chap. 7, examines the consequences of this religious tradition.

55. Ferguson, *War and Peace in the World's Religions*, p. 104.

56. Ibid., p. 105.

57. Augustine, *The City of God*, trans. Gerald G. Walsh, Demetrius B. Zema, Daniel J. Honan (New York: Image Books), 19:7, p. 446.

58. Ibid., 19:12, p. 452.

59. Ibid., 19:13, p. 457.

60. Thomas Aquinas, *Summa Theologica*, 2a–2ae, ques. 40, follows Augustine in holding that "the use of the sword is licit for those in public authority." See F. H. Russell, *The Just War in the Middle Ages* (Cambridge: Cambridge University Press, 1975), chap. 7.

61. Thomas Hobbes, *Leviathan, Parts One and Two* (Indianapolis: Library of Liberal Arts, 1958), 1:14, p. 110.

62. John Locke, *Two Treatises of Government* (New York: New American Library, 1963), 1:11, p. 257.

63. Immanuel Kant, *On History*, trans. Lewis White Beck, Robert E. Anchor, and Emil Fackenheim (Indianapolis: Bobbs-Merrill, 1963), p. 105.

64. Ibid., p. 106.

65. Arendt, *Origins of Totalitarianism*, pp. 326ff. Michael Waltzer's *Just*

and Unjust Wars tries to "recapture the just war for political and moral theory." Thus his cases, even if historical, are tied to principles of casuistry rather than to actual historical differences and thus do not highlight the uniqueness of the present. Much earlier, John Dewey in *Human Nature and Conduct* (New York: Random House, 1957), pp. 107–08, notices a historical shift: "So many new transformations entered into [World War I], . . . that the psychological forces traditionally associated with it have undergone profound changes. We may take the *Iliad* as a classic expression of war's traditional psychology. . . . But where are Helen, Hector and Achilles in modern warfare? The activities that evoke and incorporate a war are no longer personal love, love of glory or the soldier's love of his own privately amassed booty, but are of a collective prosaic political and economic nature."

66. Eliot, *Twentieth Century Book of the Dead*, pp. 26ff.

67. Augustine, *City of God*, 19:7.

68. Arendt, *Origins of Totalitarianism*, p. 45.

69. Eliot, *Twentieth Century Book of the Dead*, p. 50.

70. Immanuel Kant, *Critique of Pure Reason*, trans. Norman Kemp Smith (London: Macmillan, 1958), B19–20, pp. 55–58.

71. Ibid., B5, p. 44.

72. In his *Opus Posthumous*, Kant leans toward the view that certain principles of physics can be known a priori. But most neo-Kantians deny this. Thus Kurd Lasswitz writes: "Never may critical philosophy presume to define the conditions of experience and the principles of physics a priori; it can do so only through the historical process; and just as physical knowledge changes so too will the conditions of experience change in the course of history"; cited in Ernst Cassirer, *The Philosophy of Symbolic Forms, vol. 3: The Phenomenology of Knowledge*, trans. Ralph Mannheim (New Haven: Yale University Press, 1977), pp. 470–71.

73. Paul Natorp and Hermann Cohen express a preference for mathematical physics, whereas Rickert and Windelband turn to historical models. See Cassirer, *Problem of Knowledge*, p. 11.

74. Cassirer, *The Phenomenology of Knowledge*, pp. xiii–xiii, writes: "In my book *Substanzbegriff und Funktionsbegriff* (1910) I started from the assumption that the basic and constitutive law of knowledge can most clearly be demonstrated where knowledge has reached its highest level of necessity and universality. This law was therefore sought in the field of mathematics and the exact sciences, in the foundations of mathematical-physical objectivity. Accordingly the form of knowledge as there defined coincided essentially with the form of exact *science*." By contrast, in the *Philosophy of Symbolic Forms* he shows that "there are formative factors of a truly theoretical kind which govern the shaping not only of the scientific world view but also of the natural world view implicit in perception and intuition." Thus conceptual, discursive knowledge is grounded in language and myth. Although Cassirer is guided by Hegel's view of truth as the whole, (3:xiv), neverthe-

less mathematical and scientific thought are "at the top of the ladder" which climbs from "the primary configurations" to "the world of pure knowledge" (3:xv). Similarly, Husserl in *The Crisis of European Sciences*, p. 121, writes: "Science is a human spiritual accomplishment which presupposes the intuitive surrounding world of life, pregiven and existing for all in common. . . . For the physicist it is the world in which he sees his measuring instruments, hears time-beats, estimates visible magnitudes etc.,—the world in which . . . he knows himself to be included with all his activity and all his theoretical ideas." In spite of this discovery of the life-world, Husserl considers science and mathematics as achievements "we can never cease to admire." But now we must bring the pregiven life-world in which they are rooted into view. In "A Discussion between Ernst Cassirer and Martin Heidegger" (the well-known conversation at Davos, Switzerland, in March 1929), trans. Frank Slade in *The Existentialist Tradition*, ed. Nino Langiulli (New York: Doubleday, 1971), pp. 192–203, Heidegger takes issue with neo-Kantians, such as Cassirer, who see Kant as the theoretician of the natural sciences. For Heidegger, Kant's concern is ontology. Heidegger's relation to Husserl is more complex. Thus in *Being and Time* he writes: "Edmund Husserl has not only enabled us to understand once more the meaning of any genuine philosophical empiricism; he has also given us the necessary tools. 'A-priorism' is the method of every scientific philosophy which understands itself. There is nothing constructivistic about it. But for this very reason *a priori* research requires that the phenomenal basis must be properly prepared" (40 n. x, p. 490). Heidegger chooses as the proper horizon of this effort the average everydayness of Dasein, or human being.

75. Ernest Cassirer, *The Philosophy of Symbolic Forms*, vol. 2: *Mythical Thought*, trans. Ralph Mannheim (New Haven: Yale University Press, 1955), pp. 37–38.

76. Mikel Dufrenne, *The Notion of the A Priori*, trans. Edmund S. Casey (Evanston, Ill.: Northwestern University Press, 1966), p. 45.

77. H. Standish Thayer, *Meaning and Action: A Study of American Pragmatism* (Indianapolis: Bobbs-Merrill, 1973), pp. 244–49.

78. "A Pragmatic Conception of the A Priori," in *Collected Papers of C. I. Lewis*, ed. John D. Goheen and John L. Mothershead Jr. (Stanford: Stanford University Press, 1970), pp. 231–46. For an extended account of C. I. Lewis' view see Sandra B. Rosenthal, *The Pragmatic A Priori: A Study in the Pragmatic Epistemology of C. I. Lewis* (St. Louis, Mo: Warren H. Green, 1976), esp. pp. 1–44. For a comparative critique of the a priori in transcendental idealism by pragmatists and phenomenologists see Sandra B. Rosenthal and Patrick C. Bourgeois, *Pragmatism and Phenomenology: A Philosophic Encounter* (Amsterdam: B. R. Gruner, 1980), esp. pp. 53–72, 141–59.

79. Ludwig Wittgenstein, *On Certainty*, trans. Denis Paul and G. E. M. Anscombe, ed. G. E. M. Anscombe and G. H. von Wright (New York: Harper and Row, 1972), nn. 231–36, pp. 30–31.

80. A contemporary attack on rationalistic apriorism is found in Willard

van Orman Quine's "Two Dogmas of Empiricism," in his *From a Logical Point of View* (New York: Harper and Row, 1961). He argues that the pragmatism of Rudolf Carnap and C. I. Lewis "leaves off at the imagined boundary between the analytic and synthetic. In repudiating such a boundary [he] espouse[s] a more thorough pragmatism" (p. 146).

3. Hegel and the Crises of Cognition

1. H. S. Harris, in *Hegel's Development towards the Sunlight, 1770–1901* (Oxford: Clarendon Press, 1972), p. 96, writes: "The tension between eternal reason and historical development, between the abstract and the concrete universal was present in Hegel's mind from the beginning."

2. I choose the term *theater* deliberately since it was an early and ongoing interest of Hegel's. See ibid., pp. 262ff.

3. William James, "A Pluralistic Mystic," in *Memories and Studies* (London: Longmans, Green, 1917), p. 406.

4. G. W. F. Hegel, *Phenomenology of Spirit*, trans. A. V. Miller (Oxford: Oxford University Press, 1979), 452, p. 270. (Hereafter cited in the text as *Phen.*)

5. Alexander Kojève in "The Dialectic of the Real and Phenomenological Method in Hegel," in *Introduction to the Reading of Hegel: Lectures on the Phenomenology of Spirit*, comp. Raymond Queneau, ed. Allan Bloom (New York: Basic Books, 1969), p. 207, writes: "The synthesis must describe the being not only as a *product* or a result but also as a *given* that can provoke other negating actions—that is, as a being to be revealed in a (new) Thesis."

6. René Descartes, *Meditation Six*, in *Philosophical Works of Descartes*, trans. E. S. Haldane and G. R. T. Ross (New York: Dover, 1955), 1:190.

7. G. W. F. Hegel, *Lectures on the History of Philosophy*, trans. and ed. E. S. Haldane and Frances H. Simson (1892, reprint New York: Humanities Press, 1955) 3:428. (Hereafter cited in the text as *HPh.*)

8. *HPh.* III 3:455. See also Robert Solomon, "Hegel's Concept of *Geist*," in *Hegel: a Collection of Critical Essays*, ed. Alasdair MacIntyre (Notre Dame: Notre Dame University Press, 1972), pp. 141ff.

9. Taylor, *Journeys to Selfhood*, pp. 84ff.

10. Marcel Proust, *Swann's Way* in *Remembrance of Things Past*, trans. G. K. Scott Moncrieff (New York: Random House, 1934), 1:8. John N. Findlay in *Hegel: A Reexamination* (New York: Oxford University Press, 1958), p. 42, writes: "Hegel is quite free from the neo-realist picture of consciousness as a system of 'searchlights,' of which certain primary ones are trained upon objects, while other secondary beams are trained on these primary beams, and can perhaps succeed in lighting up their source as well." The lantern metaphor is instructive so long as Spirit is not identified with the lantern's beam alone.

11. See note 6 in chapter 1. Karl Barth in *Protestant Thought from Rousseau to Ritschl*, trans. Brian Cozens (New York: Harper and Row, 1959), p.

272, writes in connection with rejecting Hegelianism: "It might of course be possible that Hegelianism indeed represented in classic form the concern of the nineteenth century, but precisely as such came to reveal the limited nature of this concern, and the fact that it was impossible to proceed from it to the settlement of every other question of truth. And for that reason it was, curiously, condemned."

12. Emil L. Fackenheim, *The Religious Dimension in Hegel's Thought* (Bloomington: Indiana University Press, 1967), p. 164.

13. Findlay, *Hegel: A Reexamination*, pp. 18, 21, 77, 146, suggests that this is the position of F. H. Bradley and J. M. E. McTaggert but not of Hegel himself, since for the former, contradictions are decisively overcome in the final form of the Absolute.

14. John N. Findlay, "Hegelianism and Platonism," in *Hegel and the History of Philosophy: Proceedings of the 1972 Hegel Society of America Conference*, ed. J. J. O'Malley, K. W. Algozin, and F. G. Weiss (The Hague: Martinus Nijhoff, 1974), pp. 74–75, stresses the necessity of both logical specification and existential instantiation in Plato in order to press the similarity between Plato and Hegel. But this brings the neo-Platonic elements latent in Plato into prominence. H. G. Gadamer in "Dialectic of the Ancient Philosophers," in *Hegel's Dialectic: Five Hermeneutical Studies*, trans. P. Christopher Smith (New Haven: Yale University Press, 1976), p. 32, writes: "Now at the end of the two thousand year tradition of Neoplatonism, being captivated by the *logos*, something which the Greeks of the classical period experienced as delirium, and out of which Plato, in Socrates' name, sees the truth of the Idea emerging, can be seen to be close to the speculative self-movement of thought as it is explained in Hegel's dialectic."

15. G. W. F. Hegel, *Lectures on the Philosophy of Religion*, trans. E. B. Speirs and J. B. Sanderson (1895, reprint New York: Humanities Press, 1974), 1:71ff. (Hereafter cited in the text as *PhRel*.)

16. Ibid., 2:73. Hegel discusses the independence of good and evil in Persian religion.

17. This is C. G. Jung's interpretation of Yahweh in *Answer to Job*, trans. R. F. C. Hull (Cleveland: World, 1960), pp. 101–02. For a phenomenological account see Paul Ricoeur, *The Symbolism of Evil*, trans. Emerson Buchanan (New York: Harper and Row, 1967), pp. 232ff. The "Adamic myth," Ricoeur claims, belongs to anthropocentric consciousness. Man is the beginning of evil even if cosmic evil may appear as an earlier factor. *Man* has the power to "unmake" (*défaire*) himself. Paul Tillich in *Systematic Theology* (Chicago: University of Chicago Press, 1951), 1:259–60 offers an unreconstructed Hegelian interpretation of evil.

18. For a brief account of Feuerbach's view of this idea in his analysis of religion as projection, see Löwith, *From Hegel to Nietzsche*, pp. 71–82.

19. *PhRel* 3:303. Hegel writes: "Man knows God only insofar as God Himself knows Himself in Man."

20. G. W. F. Hegel, *The Philosophy of Nature*, pt. 2 of the *Encyclopedia of*

the Philosophical Sciences, trans. Michael J. Petrie (London: George Allen and Unwin, 1970), 1:Introduction, add., 191–92. (Hereafter cited in the text as *PhN.*)

21. Friedrich Nietzsche, *Thus Spake Zarathustra,* trans. R. J. Hollingdale (Harmondsworth, Middlesex: Penguin, 1969), p. 61.

22. G. W. F. Hegel, *The Philosophy of History,* trans. J. Sibree (1899, reprint New York: Dover, 1956), p. 321. (Hereafter cited in the text as PhH.)

23. A Marxist interpretation of these contradictions is found in George Lukacs, *The Young Hegel: Studies in the Relation between Dialectics and Economics,* trans. Rodney Livingstone (Cambridge: Cambridge University Press, 1976), p. 417.

24. Löwith, *From Hegel to Nietzsche,* pp. 4–7.

25. For an account of taint and defilement see Ricoeur, *Symbolism of Evil,* pp. 33–40. René Girard, *Violence and the Sacred,* trans. Patrick Gregory (Baltimore: John Hopkins University Press, 1972), p. 8, describes the demonization of the other: "The sacrifice serves to protect the entire community from *its own* violence; it prompts the entire community to choose victims outside itself."

26. Hannah Arendt, *Eichmann in Jerusalem: A Report on the Banality of Evil* (New York: Viking, 1964), p. 276.

27. Jean Amery, *At the Mind's Limits,* trans. Sidney Rosenfeld and Stella P. Rosenfeld (Bloomington: Indiana University Press, 1980), pp. 25–26, 35–36.

28. Ibid.

29. G. W. F. Hegel, *The Philosophy of Right,* trans. T. M. Knox (1894, reprint Oxford: Oxford University Press, 1979), 67, p. 95. (Hereafter cited in the text as *PhR.*)

30. Findlay, *Hegel: A Reexamination,* p. 312.

31. William K. Frankena, *Ethics* (Englewood Cliffs, N.J.: Prentice-Hall, 1963), p. 14.

32. Ibid., p. 16.

33. For an analysis of *Sittlichkeit* (morality in accordance with custom) as overcoming economic alienation see Charles Taylor, *Hegel and Modern Society* (Cambridge: Cambridge University Press, 1979), pp. 125–34. An Aristotelian reading of sittlichkeit as rootedness is found in Alasdair MacIntyre's *After Virtue: A Study in Moral Theory* (Notre Dame: Notre Dame University Press, 1981). He does not, however, stress Hegel's importance in giving a modern interpretation to customary morality.

34. Löwith, *From Hegel to Nietzsche,* pt. 2, chap. 1.

35. According to Solzhenitsyn, *Gulag Archipelago, Two,* pp. 637ff., this leads to betrayal as a form of existence.

36. Arendt, *Eichmann in Jerusalem,* p. 273.

37. Aristotle, *Nichomachean Ethics,* 1177 a 12–13, stresses the contemplative life; a synthetic view appears at 1101 a 14ff.

38. G. W. F. Hegel, *The Philosophy of Mind,* pt. 3 of *The Encyclopedia of the*

Philosophical Sciences, trans. William Wallace (1894 ed)., with the *Zusatze* from Boumann's 1845 edition, trans. A. V. Miller (reprint Oxford: Clarendon Press, 1971), 552, p. 291. (Hereafter cited in the text as *PhM*.)

39. Hegel discusses each of these philosophers at length in *HPh*.

40. Marcel Proust, *Within a Budding Grove*, in *Remembrance of Things Past* 1:405.

41. G. W. F. Hegel, *Logic*, pt. 1 of *The Encyclopedia of the Philosophical Sciences*, trans. William Wallace (1894, reprint Oxford: Clarendon Press, 1975) (hereafter cited in the text as *L*), 96, p. 91: "Nature is far from being so fixed and complete as to subsist even without Mind (*Geist*): in Mind it first ... attains its goal and its truth ... Mind is not merely a world beyond Nature and nothing more: it is really ... seen to be Mind, only when it involves Nature as absorbed in itself."

42. G. W. F. Hegel, *The Science of Logic*, trans. W. H. Johnston and L. G. Struthers (New York: Macmillan, 1929), 1:69. (Hereafter cited in the text as *SL*.)

43. G. W. F. Hegel, *On Christianity, The Early Theological Writings*, trans. Richard Kroner (New York: Harper and Row, 1961), p. 304. (Hereafter cited in the text as *ETW*.)

44. In his introduction to ibid., pp. 1–66, Kroner argues that Hegel turns from the Kantianism of the first two parts of "The Positivity of the Christian Religion" to Romanticism in the last part (later also overcome). The earlier attitude is identified with Judaism; Kantianism and Judaism are then both rejected. Walter Kaufman, in "The Young Hegel and Religion," in MacIntyre, *Hegel: Critical Essays*, p. 74, insists that Hegel remains in strong sympathy with the Enlightenment, and that his classicism should not be confused with a quest for roots in Germanic feudal models. He believes that the later Hegel should be read through the prism of these early antitheological writings. Emil Fackenheim in *Religious Dimension in Hegel's Thought*, p. 7, denies that the early works are critical for understanding the mature Hegel. In his "Hegel and Judaism: A Flaw in the Hegelian Mediation," in *The Legacy of Hegel: Proceedings of the Marquette Hegel Symposium, 1970* ed. J. J. O'Malley, H. P. Kainz, and L. C. Rice, (The Hague: Martinus Nijhoff, 1973), p. 164, he claims that Hegel draws Judaism into the sphere of religious truth as divine-human separation, an important moment in the history of religions but one which will be surpassed in the "union and non-union of Christianity."

45. See Walter Cerf's introductory essay in G. W. F. Hegel, *Faith and Knowledge*, trans. Walter Cerf (Albany: State University of New York Press, 1977), esp. pp. xvi–xxiv. (Hereafter cited in the text as *FK*.)

46. Kant, *Critique of Pure Reason*, B95–96.

47. Ibid.

48. Hegel's criticism is strikingly modern. J. L. Austin in *Sense and Sensibilia*, reconstructed by G. J. Warnock (Oxford: Oxford University Press, 1975), esp. p. 61, criticizes Berkeley's and Kant's ontology of the sensible

manifold by showing that sense data are not the primitive source of meaning which verifies our statements about material objects, but that linguistic context determines meaning (p. 140). Like Austin, Hegel argues that dependence on sense data locks in the dichotomy of material things and sensation and, for Kant at least, dependence upon the subject pole of experience.

49. Although Hegel treats both aesthetic and teleological judgments, the purposiveness of Nature is, for him, more important, since it is the field for the realization of freedom. See *PhN* remark, p. 145.

50. Richard Rorty, *Philosophy and the Mirror of Nature* (Princeton: Princeton University Press, 1979), p. 104, assesses Wilfred Sellar's view of the myth of the given in the context of the contemporary break with philosophies of representation. Hegel's importance as a critic of the epistemology of reflection has gone almost unnoticed.

51. The criticism of the analytic-synthetic distinction has become a hallmark of contemporary philosophy. J. L. Austin in "Are There A Priori Concepts?" in *Philosophical Papers*, ed. J. O. Urmson and G. J. Warnock (Oxford: Oxford University Press, 1979), pp. 46–47, shows that the question of the existence of universals reflects difficulties in the use of language, whereas Kant's question about the origin of our concepts can be dissolved into different sorts of conditions preceding our possession of them. Similarly W. V. Quine in his classic essay, "Two Dogmas of Empiricism," in *From a Logical Point of View, Logico-Philosophical Essays* (New York: Harper and Row, 1961), pp. 42–43 denies that a boundary between synthetic and analytic propositions can be drawn, since the field of empirical significance does not have the statement as its basic unit but the "totality of our so-called knowledge or beliefs," with experience as its boundary condition. Thus no particular experience impacts directly on any particular statement at the center of the field. From a different point of view, Jacques Derrida in *Speech and Phenomenon*, trans. David N. Allison (Evanston, Ill.: Northwestern University Press, 1973), pp. 85–86, deconstructs the problem of the origin of our concepts in terms of time rather than linguistic use. A priori concepts reflect a timeless present and ignore the structure of delay in the actual temporalization of language. It would be misleading to suggest that Hegel's critique corresponds to any one recent dissolution of the problem of the a priori, but his claim that we require total context (which is itself socially constructed) for breaching the distinction is in agreement with the thrust of many powerful contemporary treatments of a priorism.

52. *Phen* 39 p. 23. Cf. *L* 215, 279–80.

53. See M. S. Harris' introduction to *FK*, p. 10.

54. This is particularly true of the immediacy of feeling and faith over and against the "truth" of reflection. See *Phen* 796, p. 484.

55. Descartes, *Two in Philosophical Works of Descartes* 1:155.

56. *SL*, vol. 1, chap. 2, remark 2, p. 216. The passage is cited by Jacques Derrida in "Le puits et la pyramide," in *Hegel et la pensée moderne: Seminaire dirigé par Jean Hippolyte au Collège de France* (1967–68), ed. Jacques

D'Hondt (Paris: Presses Universitaires de France, 1970), p. 83. It is the climax of his analysis of signs and writing.

57. George Santayana, "Goethe and Faust," in *Goethe: A Symposium*, ed. Dagobert D. Runes (New York: Roerich Museum Press, 1932), p. 62, writes: "The Romanticist . . . should be a civilized man, so that his primitivism and egoism have something conscious about them . . . At the same time, in his inmost genius, he should be a barbarian, a child, a transcendentalist, so that his life may seem to him absolutely fresh, self-determined, unforeseen and unforeseeable. It is part of his inspiration to believe that he creates a new heaven and a new earth with each revolution in his moods. . . . Like Faust, he flouts science . . . disowns all authority, save that mysteriously exercised over him by his deep faith in himself. He . . . absolves himself from his past as soon as he has outgrown or forgotten it . . .[and] justifies himself on the ground that all experience is interesting."

58. Jacques Derrida, *Speech and Phenomenon*, pp. 134ff.

59. Ibid., p. 54.

60. Ibid.

61. Ibid., pp. 129–60.

62. Ibid., pp. 145–46.

63. Derrida, "Le puits et la pyramide," p. 81.

64. Aristotle, *Metaphysics*, 1014b 17–1015a 20.

65. Kojève in "A Note on Eternity, Time and the Concept," in *Introduction to the Reading of Hegel*, pp. 31–32, writes: "Only with Aristotle does time make its way into Absolute Knowledge. The Eternity to which the (eternal) Concept is related is now situated in Time. But Time enters into Absolute Knowledge only to the extent that Time itself is eternal ('eternal return')." But for Hegel, "Time is the Concept itself which is *there* in empirical existence."

66. See Klaus Hedwig, "Hegel, Time and Eternity," *Dialogue* 9 (1970): 139–53; Michael Murray, "Time in Hegel's *Phenomenology of Spirit*," *Review of Metaphysics* 33 (June 1981): 682–706.

67. Hedwig, "Hegel, Time and Eternity," 145.

68. Ibid.

69. Against Kojève, Nathan Rotenstreich in "The Essential and Epochal Aspects of Hegel's Philosophy," *Review of Metaphysics* 23 (June 1970): 699–716, insists on the primacy of the eternal as the timeless present which, in Hegel, is the true annulment of time. Michael Murray in "Time in Hegel's *Phenomonology*," 704, argues that the conclusion of the *Phenomenology* points to the dimension of future time as breaking into existence, "the end that constitutes a new beginning."

70. Nathan Rotenstreich, "Essential and Epochal Aspects of Hegel's Philosophy," 707.

71. *Phen* 808, 492; cf. *PhH* p. 73.

72. Theodore de Bary, *The Buddhist Tradition* (New York: Random House, 1972), p. 25.

73. William James, *Principles of Psychology* (1890, reprint New York: Dover, 1950), 1:340.

74. The archeological character of memory does not undermine the triple dimensions of time by stressing the past. See *PhN* 257 add., p. 232, on the restlessness of time.

75. The Apocalyptic dimension of contemporary history is conspicuous in the recent work of Thomas J. J. Altizer. In *The Self-Embodiment of God* (New York: Harper and Row, 1977), silence, negation, and finality supersede speech, affirmation, and history.

76. T. S. Eliot, "The Waste Land," *Collected Poems* (New York: Harcourt Brace, 1936), p. 72.

77. Kojève, "A Note on Eternity, Time, and the Concept," *Introduction to the Reading of Hegel*, p. 148. But within time, Hegel comments, "mediocrity endures and finally governs the world" (*PhN* 257 add., p. 232).

78. Kojève, "Note on Eternity, Time, and the Concept," p. 148.

79. T. S. Eliot, *Four Quartets* (New York: Harcourt Brace, 1943), p. 5.

4. Hegel and the Aporias of Existence

1. *PhN* 1:247, p. 205; 248 remark, p. 209.

2. Arthur O. Lovejoy, *The Great Chain of Being* (Cambridge: Cambridge University Press, 1936), p. 49.

3. *PhN* 3:351 add., p. 105; 365, add., see also p. 169.

4. Kojève, "Death in the Philosophy of Hegel," pp. 136.

5. For an analysis of tragedy from this standpoint see Judith N. Shklar, "Hegel's Phenomenology: An Elegy for Hellas," in *Hegel's Political Philosophy: Problems and Perspectives*, ed. Z. A. Pelczynski (Cambridge: Cambridge University Press, 1971), pp. 83ff.

6. Des Près, *The Survivor*, p. 214.

7. Cited by Anthony Barnett in "Cambodian Terminal," *New York Times*, May 14, 1980, from documents from the Pol Pot regime archives at the interrogation center of Pnom Penh.

8. The effort to regain the experience of wholeness may be at the root of shamanistic impersonation. See Mircea Eliade, *Myths, Dreams and Mysteries* (New York: Harper and Row, 1960), chap. 3.

9. Des Près, *The Survivor*, p. 219, cites psychoanalyst Viktor Frankl's account of this experience.

10. For a brief account relating Hegel's thought to the science of his time see M. J. Petry's introduction in *PhN* 1:11–123.

11. Werner Heisenberg, *Physics and Beyond: Encounters and Conversations*, trans. Arnold J. Pomerans (New York: Harper and Row, 1972), p. 33, cites Wolfgang Pauli to this effect.

12. Gadamer, *Hegel's Dialectic*, p. 41.

13. Ibid., p. 48.

14. *Bhagavad Gita* 11:32. The Nazis regarded the *Bhagavad Gita* as an

Aryan document and tried to interpret its teachings as applying (prophetically) to their own situation. Thus Heinrich Himmler is cited as claiming that the *Bhagavad Gita*'s promise that Krishna will be born anew whenever men lose respect for justice applies to Hitler and the German people. See Felix Kersten, *The Kersten Memoirs, 1940–1945*, trans. Constantine Fitzgibbon and James Oliver (New York: Macmillan, 1957), p. 152. Although this source is not always reliable, there is no reason to mistrust it in the present case.

15. Kojève, "Death in the Philosophy of Hegel," pp. 127–28.

16. Strauss, *The Political Philosophy of Hobbes: Its Basis and Its Genesis*, trans. Elsa M. Sinclair (Chicago: University of Chicago Press, 1966), p. 10.

17. Kojève, "Idea of Death in Hegel," 149.

18. Strauss, *The Political Philosphy of Hobbes*, pp. 15–16.

19. Ibid., p. 20n.

20. Ibid., pp. 21–22.

21. Ibid.

22. Kojève, "Idea of Death in Hegel," 143–44.

23. Ibid., 143.

24. Ibid., 145.

25. *PhM* 432 *Zusatz*, p. 173. Hegel distinguishes dueling from the fight for recognition. See ibid.

26. Kojève, "Idea of Death in Hegel," 153.

27. Donat, *Holocaust Kingdom*, p. 169.

28. *PhR* 258 *Zusatz*, p. 279. Shlomo Avineri, in *Hegel's Theory of the Modern State* (Cambridge: Cambridge University Press, 1972), pp. 176–77, points out that the authoritarianism attributed to Hegel is mitigated when Hegel's sentence "Es ist der Gang Gottes in der Welt dass der Staat ist" is rendered "It is the way of God in the world that there should be [literally, is] the state." Avineri claims that Hegel did not mean to say that the state is "the march of God on earth . . . but that the very existence of the state is part of a divine strategy, not a merely human arbitrary fact." (*PhR* 258 add., p. 279) In any case the text is derived from notes by Hegel's students and not included in Hegel's own edition of the *Rechtsphilosophie*.

29. G. W. F. Hegel, *Political Writings*, trans. T. M. Knox (Oxford: Oxford University Press, 1964), p. 210.

30. K. H. Ilting, in "The Structure of Hegel's Philosphy of Right," in *Hegel's Political Philosophy: Problems and Perspectives*, pp. 105–06, points to difficulties in Hegel's view of authority due to Hegel's emphasis of historical and political continuity as its source, rather than the transition from a state of nature to civil society by way of a social contract.

31. Some recent criticism derives from Karl R. Popper, *The Open Society and Its Enemies* (Princeton: Princeton University Press, 1950). Popper links Hegel's theory of war to totalitarian views of the state.

32. The motto is borrowed from Machiavelli's *The Prince* by Edward Black in "Hegel on War," *The Monist* 57 (October 1973): 470, as pertinent

to Hegel's view of violence. But Avineri, in *Hegel's Theory of the Modern State*, pp. 53ff., argues that Hegel confines Machiavelli's importance to Florentine politics.

33. Nietzsche, *Will to Power*, esp. secs. 556, 560. For an analysis of the difference of forces see Giles Deleuze, "Active and Reactive," in *The New Nietzsche*, ed. David Allison (New York: Dell, 1977), esp. pp. 83ff.

34. Barth, *From Rousseau to Ritschl*, p. 271.

35. Alexander Solzhenitsyn, *One Day in the Life of Ivan Denisovitch*, trans. Max Hayward and Ronald Hingley (New York: Praeger, 1963), pp. 2–4.

36. G. W. F. Hegel, *Lectures on the Philosophy of World History: Introduction*, trans. H. B. Nisbet and Duncan Forbes (Cambridge: Cambridge University Press, 1975), p. 145.

37. Ibid., p. 21.

38. Barth, *From Rousseau to Ritschl*, p. 286.

39. Jean-Jacques Rousseau, *The Social Contract*, trans. Willmoore Kendall (Chicago: Henry Regnery, 1954), p. 20.

40. Ibid., pp. 38–41.

41. See J. F. Suter, "Burke, Hegel and the French Revolution," in *Hegel's Political Philosophy: Problems and Perspectives*, p. 55. Cf. Manfred Riedel, "Nature and Freedom in Hegel's Philosophy of Right," in ibid., pp. 319–20. For an account of the transition from the political philosophies of Hobbes and Rousseau to Hegel, see Taylor, *Hegel and Modern Society*, pp. 72–84.

42. Rousseau, *Social Contract*, p. 43.

43. Ibid., pp. 42–43.

44. Ibid., p. 44.

45. Cited in Avineri, *Hegel's Theory of the Modern State*, pp. 83–84, from Hegel's *Gasammelte Werke*, vol. 4 (Hamburg, 1966), p. 445.

46. For Heidegger's analysis of this tendency see chapters 5 and 6.

47. Lifton, *Revolutionary Immortality*, p. 33.

48. Edward Rothstein, "Musical Freedom and Why Dictators Fear It," *New York Times*, August 23, 1981.

49. Avineri, *Hegel's Theory of the Modern State*, pp. 7ff.

50. Findlay, "Hegelianism and Platonism," p. 62.

51. Barth, *From Rousseau to Ritschl*, pp. 272–73.

52. See Kenneth L. Schmitz, "The Conceptualization of Religious Mystery: An Essay in Hegel's Philosophy of Religion," pp. 108–36; and Emil L. Fackenheim, "Hegel and Judaism: A Flaw in the Hegelian Mediation," pp. 161–95, both in *The Legacy of Hegel: Proceedings of the Marquette Hegel Symposium, 1970*.

53. Schmitz, in "The Conceptualization of Religious Mystery," esp. pp. 112–19, develops this point. The kenosis of the Father is the subject of Thomas J. J. Altizer's *The Self-Embodiment of God* (New York: Harper and Row, 1972).

54. See Altizer, *Self-Embodiment of God*, chap. 1.

55. For an analysis of this and related aporias in Hegel's philosophy of religion see Fackenheim, *Religious Dimension in Hegel's Thought*, esp. chaps. 4 and 15.

56. Blaise Pascal, *Pascal's Pensées*, n.t. (New York: Dutton, 1958), 206, p. 61.

57. Arthur Cohen, "The Holocaust as Tremendum," Cross Currents 30, 4: (Winter 1980): 422, 430.

58. Friedrich Nietzsche, *Ecce Homo*, trans. Walter Kaufmann (New York: Random House, 1967), p. 35.

59. Nietzsche, *Will to Power*, p. 35.

60. Ibid., p. 40.

5. Finitude and the Structures of Existence: The Early Heidegger

1. *SL* 1:117, p. 129. This passage is central for understanding Hegel's view of finitude. See Werner Marx, *Heidegger and the Tradition*, trans. Murray Greene and Theodore Kisiel (Evanston, Ill.: Northwestern University Press, 1971), esp. pp. 59–71.

2. *PhN* 258 in translation cited by Marx in ibid., p. 64.

3. Martin Heidegger, *Being and Time*, trans. John Macquartie and Edward Robinson (New York: Harper and Row, 1962), 45, p. 71. (Hereafter cited in the text as *BT*.)

4. *BT* 1, p. 19; 16–17, pp. 36ff; 365, p. 416.

5. Members of the Frankfurt school notice the abstract character of this concreteness. See Martin Jay, *The Dialectical Imagination: A History of the Frankfurt School and the Institute of Social Research* (Boston: Little, Brown, 1973), p. 72.

6. By now "1984," as used in George Orwell's novel, is a trope for this type of language. In his less well known "Politics and the English Language," in *A Collection of Essays by George Orwell* (Garden City, N.Y.: Doubleday, Anchor, 1954), pp. 162–76, he argues that thinking clearly is a first step toward political regeneration and depends upon getting rid of bad linguistic habits.

7. Andrei Platonov, *The Foundation Pit*, trans. Thomas P. Whitney (Ann Arbor, Mich: Ardis, 1973), p. 108, catches the spirit of irony that unmasks the duplicity of ideological language more strikingly than the work of many better known writers.

8. This is the thrust of much recent French phenomenology. See Jean Paul Sartre, *Being and Nothingness*, trans. Hazel Barnes (New York: Philosophical Library, 1956), pp. 303–61 and Merleau-Ponty, *Phenomenology of Perception*, pp. 67–203.

9. Merleau-Ponty's later work subordinates Being to body. See Maurice Merleau-Ponty, *The Visible and the Invisible*, trans. Alphonso Lingis, ed. Claude LeFort (Evanston, Ill.: Northwestern University Press, 1968), p. 265.

10. *The New York Times*, August 18, 1983, p. 27.
11. Plato considers the logical structure of this argument in *Phaedo* 92a–95c. He rejects the view that souls are harmonies and thus, by nature, all equally good (because harmony admits of no degree). This argument cannot account for bad souls.
12. Heidegger, in his "Der Gespruch des Anaximander," in *Holzwege* (Frankfurt: Klosterman, 1951), pp. 296–343, interprets the term *dike* not as "justice" but as "arrangement." He then reads "for they give *dike* and make reparation to one another for their injustice" in terms of "the revealing and concealing coming-to-presence of beings." See William J. Richardson, *Through Phenomenology to Thought* (The Hague: Martinus Nijhoff, 1963), pp. 514–26. W. K. Guthrie in *The Greek Philosophers from Thales to Aristotle* (New York: Harper and Row, 1960), pp. 23–31, interprets the fragment as naturalistic cosmology. Hermann Fränkel in "Studies in Parmenides," pp. 27ff, treats becoming as a sphere of injustice and the *apeiron* as the unlimited undifferentiated first cause of the world. Heidegger's approach is close to John Burnett's view that, in the authoritative text, the idea of punishment is not implied. Instead, "as *dike* is regularly used of the observance of an equal balance between the opposites hot and cold, dry and wet, the *adikia* here referred to must be the undue encroachment of one opposite on another as . . . in the alternation of day and night." See Burnett's *Early Greek Philosophy* (London: Adam and Charles Black, 1952), p. 54 n. 1.

6. Technology and Poetry: The Later Heidegger

1. Marx, *Heidegger and the Tradition*, p. 117.
2. See Otto Poggeler, "Metaphysics and the Topology of Being," in *Heidegger: The Man and the Thinker*, ed. Thomas Sheehan (Chicago: Precedent, 1981), p. 178.
3. Martin Heidegger, *What Is Called Thinking*, trans. Glenn Gray (New York: Harper and Row, 1968), p. 30. (Hereafter cited in the text as *WCT*.)
4. Martin Heidegger, "The Question concerning Technology," trans. William Lovitt, in *The Question concerning Thechnology* (New York: Harper and Row, 1977), p. 10. (Hereafter this volume is cited in the text as *QCT*.)
5. Ellul, *The Technological Society*, p. 128, writes: "*Technical civilization* means that our civilization is constructed *by* technique (makes a part of civilization only what belongs to technique), *for* technique (in that everything in this civilization must serve a technical end) and *is* exclusively technique (in that it excludes whatever is not technique or reduces it to technical form)."
6. For an analysis of the difference between technology and science in Heidegger's thinking see Harold Alderman, "Heidegger's Critique of Science and Technology," in *Heidegger and Modern Philosophy: Critical Essays*, ed. Michael Murray (New Haven: Yale University Press, 1978), pp. 35–51.
7. Heidegger, "The Age of the World Picture," in *QCT*, p. 134.

8. Heidegger goes so far as to admire the philosophical grounding of contemporary physics: "The present leaders of atomic physics, Niels Bohr and Heisenberg, think in a thoroughly philosphical way and only therefore create new ways of posing questions and above all, hold out in the questionable." See Heidegger's *What Is a Thing*, trans. W. B. Barton Jr. and Vera Deutsch (Chicago: Henry Regnery, 1967), p. 67. (Hereafter cited in the text as *WT*.) But we must view such statements with caution. Beginning with his early reflections on the nature of science, Heidegger criticizes its ontological presuppositions. In a lecture delivered in 1915, "The Concept of Time in the Science of History," he attacks the way the meaning of time in the theory of relativity distorts our notions of time when applied, mutatis mutandis, to the science of history. He warns: "The recognition of the fundamental significance of the historical concept of time and its total otherness as it exists in physics will make it possible to penetrate the peculiar nature of the science of history and to establish it theoreticallly as an original attitude of the mind irreducible to any other science." The text of this lecture, translated by Harry S. Taylor and Hans W. Uffelman, appears in *The Journal of the British Society for Phenomenology* 9, (January 1978): 3–10. In the same vein Heidegger claims: "Science's knowledge which is compelling within its own sphere, the sphere of objects, had annihilated things as things long before the atom bomb exploded." See "The Thing," in *PLT*, p. 179.

9. I cite Walter Biemel's translation. See his "Heidegger and Metaphysics," in Sheehan, *Heidegger: The Man and Thinker*, p. 167. The reference is to Heidegger's *Nietzsche*, vol. 2 (Pfullingen: Neske, 1961), p. 145.

10. Heidegger, "The Turning," in *QCT*, p. 37.

11. Heidegger, "The Thing," in *PLT*, p. 180.

12. Martin Heidegger, "Why Do I Stay in the Provinces?" in Sheehan, *Heidegger: The Man and the Thinker*, p. 29.

13. David Krell in his analysis of Heidegger's *Nietzsche: Nihilism*, trans. David Krell (New York: Harper and Row, 1982) vol. 4, esp. pp. 276–94, attests the persistence of a single theme, in this case the nothing, both in the analysis of the Dasein and in the meta-ontological works.

14. Heidegger, "What Are Poets For?" in *PLT*, p. 91.

15. Rilke's verse, published posthumously, is in *Gesammelte Gedichte*, vol. 4 (Leipzig: Pöschel und Trepete, 1934), p. 118. The poem is untitled. I cite the version from *PLT*, p. 99.

> As Nature gives the other creatures over
> to the venture of their dim delight
> and in soil and branchwork grants none special cover
> so too our being's pristine ground settles our plight
> we are no dearer to it; it ventures us
> except that we, more eager than plant or beast,
> go with this venture, will it, adventurous
> more sometimes than Life itself is, more daring

by a breath (and not in the least
from selfishness). . . . There, outside all caring,
this creates for us a safety—just there,
where the pure forces' gravity rules; in the end,
it is our unshieldedness on which we depend,
and that, when we saw it threaten, we turned it
so into the Open that, in widest orbit somewhere,
where the Law touches us, we may affirm it.

16. Heidegger, "The Origin of the Work of Art," in *PLT*, pp. 45ff.
17. Heidegger cites the ninth of Rilke's *Duino Elegies*, *PLT* p. 141. I cite MacIntyre's translation.
18. Heidegger cites Rilke's let*t*er of August 11, 1924 from Muzot, *PLT* pp. 128–29.
19. The theme is central in the first of the *Duino Elegies*.
20. Love foresworn is also a leitmotif of Kierkegaard's life and work. His tormented relinquishing of his fiancée, Regina, is transfigured in the Abraham story in *Fear and Trembling*, as well as in *Stages on Life's Way* but for him faith transcends renunciation of the beloved. Thus his well-known exclamation: "If I had had faith I would have stayed with Regina."
21. Rilke, *Letters* 2:47.
22. Ibid., p. 48.
23. Rilke, first of the *Duino Elegies*, p. 23. (. . . Hast du der Gaspara Stampa / denn genügend gedacht, dass irgend ein Mädchen, / dem der Geliebte entging, am gesteigerten Beispiel / dieser Liebenden fühlt: dass ich würde wie sie?)
24. Rilke, *Letters* 2:228.
25. Cited by Heidegger in "Holderlin and the Essence of Poetry," *Existence and Being*, trans. Werner Brock (London: Vision Press, 1949), p. 300. (Hereafter cited in the text as *EB*.)

7. *Self, Language and Community: Some Conclusions*

1. George Herbert Mead, *On Social Psychology: Selected Papers*, ed. Anselm Strauss (Chicago: University of Chicago Press, 1964), pp. 242ff.
2. Emmanuel Levinas, in *Totality and Infinity*, trans. Alphonso Lingis (Pittsburgh: Duquesne University Press, 1969), although breaking with a communication theory of language, is the first contemporary thinker I know who stresses the importance of the bearer of language as an ethical signifier. While the bearer has ethical significance, he or she interprets language itself as belonging to the realm of phenomenality and by that fact implicated in violence. I suggest that language is (per contra) a break with a more primordial violence.
J. L. Austin, in *How to Do Things with Words* (Oxford: Clarendon Press, 1962), speaks of the performative character of certain utterances. Levinas,

in *Totality and Infinity*, thinks of the linguistic situation itself as having per-locutionary force (in Austin's sense) from the start, but he interprets language as a "fall."

3. Heidegger, "Hölderlin and the Essence of Poetry," in *EB*, p. 307.

4. Ibid., p. 304; cf. *WCT*, p. 120.

5. Heidegger acknowledges the legitimacy of anthropological studies of kinship. See *BT* 51 n. 11, p. 90.

6. Claude Lévi-Strauss, *The Elementary Structures of Kinship*, trans. Richard Harle Bell, ed. John Richard von Sturmer and Rodney Needham (Boston: Beacon Press, 1969), p. 493. The internal quotation cited by Lévi-Strauss is from W. I. Thomas, *Primitive Behavior* (New York, 1937).

7. For a Buddhist account of the self as a functional unity see *The Questions of King Milinda*, vol. 1, trans. T. W. Rhys Davies (New York: Dover, 1963), esp. pp. 40–44.

8. The idea of the self as lack is Jean-Paul Sartre's focus in *Being and Nothingness*, as well as Jacques Lacan's thesis in his lecture on psychoanalysis at the École Pratique des Hautes Études. In *The Four Fundamental Concepts of Psychoanalysis*, trans. Alan Sheridan, ed. Jacques-Alain Miller (New York: W. W. Norton, 1977), p. 235, interpreting analytic transference as a relation of two desires, Lacan says: "Desire is the axis, the pivot, the handle, the hammer by which is applied the fore-element, the inertia, that lies behind what is formulated at first, in the discourse of the patient, as demand." Both Sartre and Lacan are indebted to the lectures of Alexander Kojève, given from 1933 to 1939 at the École Pratique des Hautes Études. In his *Introduction to Hegel*, p. 40, Kojève claims: "To be anthropogenetic, then, Desire must be directed toward a nonbeing—that is toward another *Desire*, another greedy emptiness, another I. . . . I is a nothingness that *nihilates* in Being, and not a Being that *is*."

9. The shifting of self-concepts depending on how the other is seen is developed in Martin Buber, *I and Thou*, trans. Ronald Gregor Smith (New York: Charles Scribner and Sons, 1958), pt. 1; in Gabriel Marcel, *Being and Having: An Existentialist Diary*, trans. Katherine Farrer (New York: Harper and Row, 1965), pt. 1; and by Levinas throughout *Totality and Infinity*.

10. Merleau-Ponty, *Phenomenology of Perception*, p. 303.

11. See Merleau-Ponty's treatment of numerous case studies in *Phenomenology of Perception*.

12. John Berryman, "Dream Song, 53," in *Dream Songs* (New York: Farrar, Straus and Giroux, 1969), p. 60. The *Norton Anthology of Poetry*, ed. Alexander W. Allison, Herbert Barrows, Cesar R. Blake et al. (New York: W. W. Norton, 1975), p. 1153n, claims these lines refer to novelist Saul Bellow.

13. Mario Vargas, "Inquest in the Andes," *New York Times Magazine*, July 31, 1983, p. 22.

Index